TWO
MEETING
IN
MID-AIR

TWO ARROWS
MEETING
IN
MID-AIR

The Zen Koan

John Daido Loori

Edited by
Bonnie Myotai Treace
and
Konrad Ryushin Marchaj

CHARLES E. TUTTLE CO., INC.
Boston • Rutland, Vermont • Tokyo

Published in the United States in 1994 by
Charles E. Tuttle Company, Inc. of Rutland, Vermont and
Tokyo, Japan, with editorial offices at
153 Milk Street, Boston, Massachusetts, 02109.

Copyright © 1994 The Mountains and Rivers Order

Excerpts from *Alice in Wonderland* by Lewis Carroll are taken from the
Everyman's Library edition published in 1993 by J. M. Dent, Ltd.

Excerpts from Walt Whitman's "Leaves of Grass" are taken from the
Everyman's Library edition published in 1993 by J. M. Dent, Ltd.

Library of Congress Cataloging-in-Publication Data

Loori, John Daido.
  Two arrows meeting in mid-air : the Zen koan / by John Daido Loori ;
edited by Bonnie Myotai Treace and Konrad Ryushin Marchaj.
    p. cm. —(Tuttle library of enlightenment)
  1. Koan. I. Treace, Bonnie Myotai. II. Marchaj. Konrad Ryushin. III.
Title. IV. Series.
BQ9289.5.L66 1994
294.3'444—dc20   94–7737
                                                      CIP

ISBN 0-8048-3012-6

Cover design by Fahrenheit

3 5 7 9 10 8 6 4 2
Printed in the United States of America

Dedicated to the Zen practitioners who are making real
the transmission of the Dharma from East to West.

CONTENTS

FOREWORD

This book, *Two Arrows Meeting in Mid-Air*, is the second collection of talks presented at Zen Mountain Monastery by John Daido Loori, Sensei. While the basic format is similar to his first book, *Mountain Record of Zen Talks*, there are significant differences. The structure is more refined, and materials included are from a broader range of resources, such as Dogen Zenji's collection of 301 koans. In a refreshing expression of the teachings, the author has also included materials relating to the "eight gates," which he has developed as a scheme for practice and appreciation of Dharma.

The title of this book, *Two Arrows Meeting in Mid-Air*, is from the *Ts'an-t'ung-ch'i* (Jap. *Sandokai*) or *Identity of Relative and Absolute*, which is chanted daily in Zen temples. Composed by Zen Master Shih-t'ou Hsi-ch'ien, this poem expresses "being one," or unity as the true nature or intimacy of our existence. When Shih-t'ou was 15 years old, his Dharma grandfather, the Sixth Patriarch Hui-neng, passed away. He continued to practice with his elder Dharma brother, Ch'ing-yuan Hsing-ssu. Ch'ing-yuan asked him, "Where have you come from?" "From Hui-neng," replied Shih-t'ou. "What have you brought with you?" Ch'ing-yuan asked. Shih-t'ou said, "I had it before I became Hui-neng's student, and it has never been lost." This "it" is the essence of two arrows meeting in mid-air.

The *Ts'an-t'ung-ch'i* consists of only 220 Chinese characters. However, it is said that the heart of all the voluminous sutras and discourses of the *Tripitaka* is concisely expressed in this poem on the identity of relative and absolute. This "identity" is the intimate unity in our very lives of these seemingly opposite aspects—oneself and others, subject and object, relative and absolute, Buddha and sentient beings, delusion and enlightenment, nothing and everything, ordinary and holy, and so on.

"Two arrows meeting in mid-air" is just this intimacy. It is also the intimacy of a teacher and student. You may wonder how two arrows could actually meet in mid-air. It is virtually impossible. Yet this analogy, derived from writings of Lieh-tzu, is very practical and real. A teacher, Fei-wei, and a student, Chi-ch'ang, were two adepts of archery. Chi-ch'ang became more and more skillful and eventually believed that no one was better than himself. He went so far as to believe that if his teacher were dead, he, Chi-ch'ang, would be the best in the world. One day, he tried to kill his teacher. They happened to meet in a field, and Chi-ch'ang shot an arrow at Fei-wei. Responding, Fei-wei shot back. The arrows met in the air and fell to the ground. Chi-ch'ang shot a second and a third arrow and the same thing happened each time. But Fei-wei had only three arrows, and Chi-ch'ang had four. He shot the fourth arrow. Fei-wei picked up a branch and stopped the arrow with a thorn on the branch. After this encounter, they mutually vowed to be as father and son.

The symbolic and yet very real implication of these two arrows meeting in mid-air is precisely this taking of the teacher's life as one's own. This is true Dharma transmission—the student confirming this intimacy as his or her very own life.

Four generations after Shih-t'ou, Master Tung-shan Liang-chieh, the founder of Chinese Soto Zen, took up this intimacy and wrote *San-mei-k'o* or *Jeweled-Mirror Samadhi*. The jewel is one's true entity; the mirror, the objective spheres reflecting the parts of one's own life. The *samadhi* is the unity, the Buddha's wisdom that Guatama himself proclaimed at the moment of his enlightenment: "How miraculously wondrous! All beings have the Tathagata's wisdom and virtue." The intimacy is simply realizing that your true nature and the phenomenal world are meeting right here, now, as your life. In the compelling talks that comprise this collection you are invited to realize that intimacy yourself, to make it your own.

Thirteen generations after Master Tung-shan, Dogen Zenji, the 51st successor from Shakyamuni and founder of Japanese Soto Zen, captured the heartbeat of this teaching once again in the fascicle "Udumbara Flower" in his collection of writings, *Shobogenzo:*

> ...Shakyamuni was once preaching to a large assembly gathered on Vulture Peak. He held up an udumbara flower without speaking, and blinked. Then Mahakashyapa smiled. Shakyamuni said, "I possess the Eye and Treasury of the True Law and the Serene Mind of Nirvana. I now bestow it to Mahakashyapa."
>
> All of the seven Buddhas of the past including Shakyamuni and all the Patriarchs who came after him held up a flower and transmitted the True Law in this manner. Holding up the flower is holding up the Buddha-mind; it is the actualization of their enlightenment. All aspects of the flower—ideal and real, subjective and objective, external and internal—are contained in the act of holding up the flower. The entire flower is the original Buddha-mind and Buddha-body.
>
> ...At the very moment of holding up the flower, all of Shakyamuni, all of Mahakashyapa, all of beings, all of us are stretching the single hand

together, and holding the flower in the same way. It has never ceased right up to the present. (Based on Dogen Zenji's *Shobogenzo*, translated by Kosen Nishiyama and John Stevens, Daihokkaikaku, pp. 116–20.)

This udumbara flower is the *Saddharma Pundarika*, the lotus flower—the core of the *Saddharmapundarika Sutra (Lotus Sutra)*, in which it is taught that all phenomena are no other than the true entity. The very state of holding up the udumbara flower is that of the two arrows meeting in mid-air—of true intimacy, of Dharma transmission. How do we open our life as the udumbara flower, as the Eye and Treasury of the True Law and Serene Mind of Nirvana? As Daido Sensei comments, our practice is not just studying koans, but how we truly appreciate all of our lives as the holding of the udumbara flower itself. Daido Sensei's commentaries can help you reveal your own life as the blossoming of this flower. We take this up as *genjo-koan*, as the practice of our everyday life.

Hakuyu Taizan Maezumi
Zen Center of Los Angeles
Los Angeles, California
Autumn 1993

PREFACE

This excellent compendium of Dharma talks on the Zen koan is entirely appropriate and timely, and will likely serve as a reference book, a kind of "Zen workbook," since its discourses are tightly interwoven with the vivid history of Zen and its great teachers. *Two Arrows Meeting in Mid-Air* forms a tapestry of wonderful Zen stories, all of them complemented by the kind and insightful commentary of John Daido Loori, Sensei, the abbot of Zen Mountain Monastery.

Though our paths wander, Daido Sensei and I have traveled the same trail across the American Zen landscape. We both started our studies with Rinzai Master Nakagawa Soen and his disciple Shimano Eido. In later years, we turned to Sōtō Zen practice with Taizan Maezumi Roshi who received transmission in both Rinzai and Soto lineages, and with Tetsugen Sensei, now a Dharma brother of Daido Sensei. In studying with teachers of both sects, we continued a significant tradition, for Soen Roshi, already a Rinzai abbot, had caused a great clicking of fans in the Rinzai hierarchy by traveling to the northern sea coast of Japan to study with the great Sōtō Master Sogaku Harada (who had studied earlier with great Rinzai masters and detested all hierarchies and sectarian disputes). There Soen formed a lifelong friendship and association with Harada Roshi's disciple Hakuun Yasutani, who would later join him in pioneer visits to the United States (and whose teachings in *The Three Pillars of Zen* have been so influential in American Zen).

Thus all of our teachers, and their teachers, were well-steeped in both of the great Zen traditions that today are well-established in America, with the karmic consequence that in our lineage, American Sōtō Zen contains a vital element of Rinzai practice with its strong emphasis on koan study, while maintaining the traditional Sōtō focus on "just-sitting," or *shikantaza*.

Since Zen was brought to America by Japanese teachers, the great figures in these accounts are known to most American students by the Japanese transliterations of their Chinese names. Daido Sensei, following Robert Aitken Roshi, Thomas Cleary, and other recent commentators, uses the true names for the great patriarchs of the T'ang Dynasty. I shall miss Master Rinzai, Master Ummon, Master Joshu, but this more appropriate usage is inevitable, and long overdue. To "that terrible dog," as Soen Roshi used to call the animal whose Buddha-nature is illuminated in the primordial koan, it matters little whether it is Master Joshu or Master Chao-chou who responds so forcefully to the earnest monk, since the universal teaching is still MU!

The sincere practitioner of zazen will absorb much atmosphere and insight from this fine collection of astonishing observations and exchanges, which will water the ground where a true perception of reality may flourish.

Peter Muryo Matthiessen

ACKNOWLEDGMENTS

This book on koan practice would not be possible without the existence of excellent English translations of traditional Chinese and Japanese koan collections. In preparing the talks, I used Zenkei Shibayama's *Zen Comments on the Mumonkan*, Thomas Cleary's *The Blue Cliff Record* and *The Book of Serenity*, the two translations of *The Record of Transmitting the Light* by Francis Dojun Cook and Thomas Cleary, and the recently available *Master Dogen's Three-Hundred Koan Shobogenzo*. In many cases these were used in conjunction with "in-house" translations of the Zen Center of Los Angeles where it was appropriate. The availability of these works attests to the growing interest in the Dharma in the West, and the value of koan study in one's spiritual practice.

The task of transcribing these talks was meticulously attended to by Pat Jikyo George, Janice Senju Baker, and Ann Hoshin Ritter. The editorial work was done by Bonnie Myotai Treace and Konrad Ryushin Marchaj. I am grateful for their persistence in gathering and organizing these chapters. My special thanks are extended to Francis Dojun Cook who read through the manuscript and checked it for historical and editorial consistency.

This book emerges from the active training matrix at Zen Mountain Monastery. Without the committed participation of students in koan study—their openness, questioning, and determination—it would have been impossible to write. I appreciate the opportunity to work with people who are engaged in true personal search, and to share this path with them.

Finally, a deep bow of gratitude to my teacher, Hakuyu Taizan Maezumi, and all the teachers before him who have tirelessly dedicated their lives to the transmission of the genuine Dharma.

INTRODUCTION

KOANS: DIRECT INSIGHT INTO ZEN TEACHING

Talking and writing about koans is not the usual practice of Zen teachers. Zen scholars or university professors may take up the subject of koans in their discussions and courses, but Zen teachers don't routinely analyze koans in terms of their psychology, philosophy, structure, or dynamics. We *do* koans. We don't talk about them. The closest we come to talking about a koan is in the context of a Dharma discourse. This is not an intellectual presentation but rather a direct pointing to the heart of the Buddha-Dharma truth that comes from the teacher's realization of the koan. The twenty-one chapters making up the core of this book are Dharma discourses.

Koans can't be explained. Always the danger is that any explanation offered will be misunderstood, that people will be misguided, heading off in the wrong direction in their search for the truth. Soon after the compilation of *The Blue Cliff Record* by Master Hsüeh-tou in eleventh–century China, Master Ta-hui, who was a passionate champion of genuine koan training, burned all available copies of the collection, including the plates and the woodblocks used to print the book. He saw his students clinging to the content of the text rather than trusting and concerning themselves with the immediate experience of the teachings. He did what seemed appropriate at that time and place.

In the twentieth century, Western students who find their way to Zen Buddhism are well informed. With education and communication being what they are these days, the average beginning Zen student arrives with a wealth of data that no monastic had in the past. One of the factors motivating most modern practitioners is their intellect. So, in order to do good "Zen fishing" and guide a student into serious practice, which is one of the vows of a Zen teacher, it is sometimes useful these days to bait the hook with some beautiful, juicy, intellectual worms.

All that notwithstanding, what you will read in this book are words and ideas that describe the reality and not the reality itself. After you've assimilated everything there is to assimilate about koans, throw it all away and keep going. And when you've reached that goal and emptied yourself, throw that away and keep going. Ultimately, you will come to the place of enlightenment. When you get there, throw that away and keep on going. The Dharma is boundless. There are no edges to it, and the minute we try to contain it, all its aliveness, vibrancy, and relevance is lost.

The answers to all the questions any of us have and will have lie within each one of us. There is no attempt made in Zen training to introduce anything from the outside. Indeed, there's a saying in Zen that in the whole world there are no Zen teachers, nor is there anything to teach. The reason for such a statement arises with the very beginnings of Buddhism and is contained within the enlightenment experience of Shākyamuni Buddha.

When Shākyamuni first began his spiritual quest, his search for answers to the questions of life, death, and human suffering, he began by following a path that was common in those days. It was the path of renunciation. He left his family and household, stripped himself of all his possessions, shaved his head, put on the robe of a mendicant, and went into the forest to engage the ascetic practices perfected during that time in India. For seven years, he practiced long periods of meditation, fasting, and sleeplessness. Finally, he reached a stage of such emaciation and weakness that he fell unconscious. When he revived, he reconsidered what he was doing and realized that through self-abnegation he had not gotten any clearer.

Resolved to find the answers more directly, he took nourishment and healed his body, much to the dismay of his fellow monastics, who actually ran away from him. One commentator, referring to this stage of Shakyamuni's life, said that he was probably the loneliest man on the face of the earth. He had nothing to hold onto. He had nobody to guide him. There was no Buddhism; he wasn't a Buddhist. He was totally on his own. When we completely delve into our practice today we recreate the same state of being, the same condition of total trust in ourselves.

After making himself strong, the Buddha sat in solitary zazen and one morning, upon seeing the morning star, he realized *anuttara-samyaksambodhi*, which we translate as supreme enlightenment. Upon that realization, the very first statement he made was, "Isn't it marvelous! Isn't it wonderful! I and all sentient beings on earth together attain enlightenment at the same time." What he was saying is that in his enlightenment he realized that, at this very moment, all sentient beings are perfect and complete, lacking nothing. What he had searched for he already was.

The same perfection is the basic nature of all sentient beings. Given that premise, teaching becomes a very difficult task. Consequently, Shakyamuni was very reluctant to start. It took a lot of convincing by the old friends who gathered around him before he began the first turning of the Dharma wheel. His teachings took the form of a myriad of *upaya*, or skillful means; all of it simply to get us to realize that which is already present.

The process of Buddhist training involves seeing very

deeply into oneself and realizing the inherent perfection that is there. It takes us beyond the constrictions of our conditioning—the conditioning of our parents, education, culture, and peers. It gets us to the ground of being beneath all that.

It is that realization that was transmitted on Mt. Gridhrakuta, years later, from Shakyamuni to his first successor Mahakashyapa. Two thousand students had gathered on Vulture Peak to hear Buddha give a discourse. When Buddha appeared, he held up a flower and, without saying a word, twirled it in his fingers. In the audience, Mahakashyapa smiled and blinked his eyes. The Buddha said, "I have the all-pervading true Dharma, incomparable Nirvana, the exquisite teaching of formless form. It does not rely on letters and is transmitted outside scriptures. I now pass it on to Mahakashyapa." That was the first transmission. The Buddha somehow recognized that Mahakashyapa had realized what he himself had realized. Mahakashyapa communicated that to the Buddha, and the Buddha accepted it. This episode forms one of the koans in the *Mumonkan: The Gateless Gate*.

A similar thing happened a generation later. Ananda, the Buddha's attendant, had been present in the assembly at Vulture Peak when Mahakashyapa received the transmission. Ananda was not only the attendant of the Buddha but also the Buddha's cousin. He had an incredible memory and remembered, to the letter, all the talks that the Buddha ever gave. He retained everything down to the smallest details. It is said that all the sutras came from Ananda's memory, that they were put down in writing as Ananda recited each of the Buddha's discourses. For twenty years Ananda was at the Buddha's side, hearing every word, yet it was Mahakashyapa in the great assembly that received the transmission. The transmission had nothing to do with the knowledge, or the information that Ananda had.

After the Buddha died, Ananda became a student and attendant of Mahakashyapa, who was now the teacher. One day, after reflecting on the incident that took place on Mt. Gridhrakuta, Ananda said to Mahakashyapa, "At that time on Vulture Peak, when the Buddha gave you the robe and the bowl, what else did he give you? What else did you get? What do you have that I don't have?" He was full of doubt. Mahakashyapa answered, "Ananda!" Ananda said, "Yes, Master!" Mahakashyapa said, "Take down the flagpole." At that, Ananda was greatly enlightened. "Take down the flagpole" was another way of saying that the lecture was over. In those days, whenever a discourse was being given by a teacher, a banner would fly on the flagpole. To take down the flagpole meant that the talk had ended. "Ananda!" "Yes, Master!" "Take down the flagpole." The discourse was over. Ananda was enlightened. That was the incident of the mind-to-mind transmission from the second to the third generation.

The very same thread continued on for generation after generation for 2,500 years. Not through lectures, sutras, philosophical treatises, or belief systems but mind-to-mind. A direct insight into the teaching was carried for twenty-eight generations in India. Then it was brought to China by Bodhidharma. It flowered there during the T'ang Dynasty and continued for twenty-eight more generations. Masters Eisai and Dogen carried the lineage from China to Japan. From there it crossed over to this continent at the turn of the 20th century. It was always transmitted the same way—directly, intimately, mind-to-mind.

It is reputed that Master Bodhidharma said that Zen is "a special transmission outside the scriptures, with no reliance on words and letters, a direct pointing to the human mind, and the realization of Buddhahood." That has pretty much remained the definition of Zen down through the centuries to the present day. What Bodhidharma was reiterating is that the transmission of Buddhist realization is not dependent on religious writings. Usually, the scriptures or core texts represent a critical aspect of religious training. Buddhism probably has more scriptures than any other religion, simply because the Buddha taught for forty-seven years, an extraordinary amount of time for a spiritual leader to be around. The literature of Buddhism is vast. Several monasteries could be filled from cellar to attic with the books on Buddhism.

But these sutras are the descriptions of reality, not the reality itself. They are descriptions of the truth, not the truth itself. What is the reality? Intellectual understanding and beliefs have nothing to do with the truth that's transmitted. The truth is direct. This, it can be argued, makes Zen unique among the world's religions.

Most other schools of Buddhism teach the Buddha-Dharma in ways similar to other religions. There are schools of Buddhism that rely on the sutras. They say that through study of the sutras and deep understanding of them you can ultimately become enlightened. There are schools of Buddhism that intently follow the moral and ethical precepts, the *Vinaya*. When you follow those moral and ethical precepts you manifest the life of a Buddha and realize yourself as a Buddha.

In Zen, what's emphasized is introspection, going very deep into yourself to find the foundations of your life, realizing yourself through the process of studying your self. Master Dogen said, "To study Buddhism is to study the self. To study the self is to forget the self. To forget the self is to be enlightened by the ten thousand things." Once the illusion of self is out of the way, all that remains are the ten thousand things. "And to realize the ten thousand things is to cast off body and mind of self and other. No trace of enlightenment remains, and this traceless enlightenment continues endlessly." In a sense, this short paragraph from Dogen encapsulates the totality of the Buddha-Dharma.

What remains once the self has been forgotten? What is left when there is no longer a self? Everything! The whole universe remains. But now there is no longer an idea of self that separates us from it. I say "idea of self" because from a Buddhist perspective, the self is an idea. It doesn't exist. It's something we create from moment to moment. Ask yourself, what is the self? See what you come up with. For most people, the response is a list of aggregates: my self is this body, these thoughts, feelings, ideas, concepts, memories, and dreams. The list doesn't directly address the question, "What is the self?" Similarly, walls, ceiling, floor, windows, and doors don't address the inquiry, "What is a room?" They are aggregates. They are not "roomness" itself. From a Western philosophical point of view, what remains when you remove the aggregates is an essence. The essence of the self is a soul. This assumption of the essence of the self is central to much of religion, East and West.

In Buddhism, the *experience* of thousands of men and women throughout the ages, starting with Shakyamuni Buddha, is that when you go very deep into the self, when you go beyond the aggregates, beyond conditioning, what remains is nothing. The self is a mental construct. It's that mental construct that separates us from the rest of the universe and from each other. That basic illusory premise, according to the Buddha-Dharma, creates greed, anger, ignorance, pain, and suffering. When the self is forgotten, the barrier between the self and the ten thousand things, the whole phenomenal universe, is dissolved. Then the intimacy with the ten thousand things is realized as one's own personal body and mind. When that is realized, an entirely different way of perceiving ourselves and the universe is available to us, a way that expresses basic wisdom and compassion.

Koans are about bringing us to that realization. They are specifically designed to cut through the layers of conditioning we have accumulated since birth, to cut through the programs out of which we absentmindedly live our lives. Conditioning starts at birth and continues throughout our entire life. It goes on day after day, constantly reinforced by the social norms, by our relationships and interactions, and by media and advertising. Koans focus on these layers of conditioning, examining them, peeling them back, layer by layer. Koans take us deep into the fabric of the thing we call the self, ultimately showing us the ground of being. Underneath those layers of conditioning is a complete and perfect enlightened being, a Buddha. Koans get us not only to realize that inherent nature, but teach us to live our lives out of that which has been realized. Not out of what we've been told, not out of the inherited list of what we should or shouldn't do, but out of what we've realized from our own direct experience. Koans are about manifesting that and actualizing that in everything we do.

ZAZEN AND THE KOAN

We can say that koans date back to the beginning of Zen, to the very beginning of Buddhism itself. Probably the first koan that one encounters in Buddhism is the story of the legendary birth of Shakyamuni Buddha. According to the legend, upon his birth, Shakyamuni took three steps forward, pointed upward to heaven with one hand and downward to the earth with the other, and said, "Between heaven and earth, I alone am the honored one." A more familiar koan among the general public is "The Sound of One Hand"—*You know the sound of two hands clapping. What's the sound of one hand clapping? Don't tell me. Show me!* "The Sound of One Hand" is a typical first koan in the Hakuin system of koan study. Another beginning koan is "The Original Face"—*What is your original face, the face you had before your parents were born? Don't tell me. Show me!*

In order to appreciate the vitality of koan study, one must understand that the question, "What is the sound of one hand clapping?" is not a riddle or a paradox. It's a question that has to do with the most basic truth. It's no different from the questions, "What is reality? What is life? What is death? What is God? Who am I?"

Koans are pivotal inquiries that by their very nature frustrate our usual way of dealing with questions. A koan can't be resolved through linear sequential thought. In fact, a koan is specifically designed to short-circuit the intellectual process. Another aspect of consciousness needs to be engaged in order to reach any depth of insight into a koan. Koans open up the intuitive, "direct knowing" aspect of our consciousness.

Koans appear on the surface to be paradoxical. But the fact is that there are no paradoxes. Paradox exists in language. Paradox exists in the words and ideas that describe reality. In reality itself, there are no paradoxes. The use of the koan is an attempt to go beyond the words and ideas that describe reality, and to directly and intimately experience that reality itself. The answer to a koan is not some parcel of information, or some new way of seeing something. Rather, it's one's own intimate and direct experience of the universe and its infinite facets. It's a state of consciousness.

The answer to a koan is not in any script. It is not a formula of words, although it can be contained in words. It can be anything. It can be a shout, a nod, the blinking of an eye, the holding up of a flower. And it can be words, but there are live words and there are dead words. Dead words are, "The universe and I are the same thing." That's an explanation. Any book on Buddhism will tell you that "the universe and I are the same thing." How could that be expressed in a way that's not so stultified? You might say that, "When we play the fiddle in Mt. Tremper, they dance in Great Britain." That's a way of showing the unity. Or, "When I itch, my teacher scratches." There are ways to express it with words, but the words need to be alive. They need to be your words. They have to be broad and expansive enough not to kill the spirit of what's being expressed and, most importantly, they must express the truth of the koan.

Koan study is not something that happens in a vacuum, yet you work on a koan yourself. Ultimately the solution to the koan must come from the student. You go very deep into your own states of consciousness, through your own layers of conditioning, in order to arrive at the ground of being. All this is assisted by various skillful means, the most critical and vital of which is zazen. Zazen is the heartbeat and the core of Zen and koan study. In the beginning stages of practice it allows the mind to become quiet and to focus, bringing attention to this very moment. Most of us are preoccupied with our concerns. We are preoccupied with the past or with the future. And while we're so involved with the past and the future, we miss the moment-to-moment awareness of our lives. Our life slips by and we barely notice its passing. When you miss the moment, you miss your life, because life takes place only in this moment.

Little by little, through the process of zazen, we learn to quiet our internal dialogue, that incessant conversation that we have with ourselves. Gradually, we are able to put our attentiveness on the breath. The breath is just one of the many points of focus used in meditation. But zazen is more than just meditation. It's more than just stilling the mind. Zazen is the manifestation of our life. It is everything that we do in a way that's fully present, alert, and aware in the moment. In the process of working with our thoughts—acknowledging them, letting them go, and coming back again to the breath—we begin to develop what's called *joriki*, or self-power. *Joriki* is a direct result of letting go of thoughts and bringing attentiveness back to the breath. Each time you do that, you strengthen your concentration. Through zazen, the whole body and mind are involved in *joriki*.

Joriki is of vital importance in preparing yourself for work on a koan, because it enables you to put your mind where you want it, when you want it there, for as long as you want it there. *Joriki* eventually becomes what we call *samadhi*, or single-pointedness of mind. It's that single-pointedness of mind that needs to be developed before any kind of fruitful work with a koan can begin. Zazen continuously nurtures our *samadhi*, providing the pivotal foundation for engaging the koan. When *samadhi* has developed sufficiently, the student begins to work with the first koan.

In frustrating the intellect, koans dismantle the customary way of solving problems and open up new dimensions of human consciousness. Our usual means of answering a question depends on what has been successful in the past. All through our lives and educations, we've been taught to use our minds in a particular linear and sequential way. That's the way we measure I.Q. That's the way we pass examinations, solve problems and riddles, and work our way to success. If you have a good intellect and analytical talent, chances are good that you've moved very high in whatever field you are working in. When it comes to the creative process and spiritual questions, a whole different kind of consciousness is involved. That consciousness is not linear and sequential. All of us possess it. Somehow our education has minimized or completely excluded it, and that is very limiting in our lives.

The process of zazen is a never-ending, ceaseless activity of self-inquiry. It is sometimes called the "backward step," and it has to do with turning inward. What's critical in the process of studying the self is not holding onto anything. If there are any unresolved aspects of yourself, if there are suppressed issues or tensions, they need to come to the surface before you can handle the realization of who you are and what your life is. You can't push them out of the way. Zen training is specifically designed to make that impossible.

For a student who's in residential training at Zen Mountain Monastery, there's no place to hide. Every morning, every night—and during the intensive training Ango period, every afternoon—you're asked to sit with yourself. All distractions and responsibilities are removed. You're sitting in silence, working with the breath. Thoughts are coming up. Most of these thoughts are white noise, and you can just acknowledge them, let them go, and come back to the breath. Beginning sitters, for the first time in their lives, have an opportunity to really listen to themselves. During our everyday lives we don't realize that we are engaged in a constant internal conversation. We talk to ourselves all the time. I remember when I was a child, my family used to chuckle at my grandmother because she'd walk around all the time mumbling to herself. Some twenty years later I realized that I do that too. I just don't say it out loud. We are preoccupied as we comment, analyze, judge, reflect, evaluate, systematize, categorize, name. All of that is perpetually going on, and there is no space to experience now, to experience the moment. Zazen gives us access to our monologue and the means to see through it. People starting zazen usually come to dokusan stunned at how active their minds are, convinced that they're the only ones in the world who experience this phenomenon. We all do it. We all distract ourselves.

In zazen, that internal dialogue begins to slow down. This happens by persistent work with the thoughts that come up. You acknowledge them, you let them go, and you come back to the breath. Again and again. Once in a while, something very significant comes up and you need to attend to that. Something is happening in your life. It's not just noise, it's not just random thought. It's crucial. It has to do with a relationship, grief, decisions. When you let it go, it comes right back again. That persistence is a signal to process it exhaustively, not to push it aside and ignore it. It's a signal to give it permission to run its course. In the process of letting it run its course, you're going to experience all the emotional stuff that goes with it. Sometimes there's a lot of pain associated with zazen. Everybody's sitting there, looking like wonderful Buddhas, cross-legged, with half-smiles on their faces, but that does not reflect accurately the struggle that may be going on inside.

As you're listening to yourself openly, you're feeling the feelings you were afraid to feel, thinking the thoughts you were afraid to think. There's no real quiet or peace as long as there is suppressed turmoil. The further you go into your zazen, the more confidence you develop in your ability to let go. Every time you let go of a thought, you empower yourself with the ability to let go of thoughts, to let go in general. As your confidence grows, your ability to process suppressed conflicts broadens. Little by little you work out the twists and the kinks. The whole process becomes kind of a gigantic cosmic cleansing, cleaning out the accumulated baggage of a lifetime. Eventually, the mind settles down and begins to get quiet.

Before the teacher introduces the first koan, the student has to cultivate stillness and let it acquire some depth. This is critical, as the first koan usually pushes all our buttons and churns up psychological debris. Everything has become quiet, serene, spacious. The teacher in the dokusan room has been supportive and nourishing. Suddenly, she turns into an adversary, demanding a clear response to the koan. "What is it? Go deeper. Not good enough. Work harder." And there you are, on your own. "What is it? What is it? What is it?" keeps coming up, resonating in your whole being. The answers start coming up and they are all turned down. "What is Mu?" "Mu is this." "Not good enough." "Mu is that." "Go deeper." "Mu is everything." "Not yet." "Mu is nothing." "Doesn't reach it." "Mu is both everything and nothing." "Misses it."

Meticulous effort is necessary for effective koan work. What is meticulous effort? How do you exert it? Meticulous effort means effort with attention to detail as well as with global awareness. It doesn't necessarily mean a lot of grunting and groaning. It depends on a student's personality. You know there's an answer. You have faith that there's an answer. You know hundreds of other people have seen it. So you persevere. You keep trying, and you keep getting rejected. You keep getting thrown back on yourself. Doubt becomes greater. It begins to shake up the solidity that you think you've developed. Finally, the whole intellectual process gets frustrated to the extreme, and you make the quantum leap. You suddenly see it as though out of the blue.

KOAN DYNAMICS

The initial insight is usually only a glimpse of the truth. Yet the consequences of it are far-reaching. Most people who see it have no idea what they are seeing, because the minute they try to grab onto it, it's gone. It's very slippery. The minute you try to intellectualize, it disappears. You end up clutching an intellectual skeleton that's no longer it. What follows the first koan and the initial breakthrough is a sequence of koans whose role is to clarify that original insight. In our lineage there are one hundred of these miscellaneous koans which the student takes up before moving on to the classic collections. The first insight has to do with the absolute basis of reality, what we call the *dharmakaya*. Clarifying and thoroughly understanding the *dharmakaya* is a process that continues throughout the entire training of a student, which may take anywhere from ten to twenty years.

As students move through the koan system, they develop more and more clarity. The progression is usually irregular, with periods of smooth sailing interrupted by moments when great doubt reappears. A person may be moving along, passing koans, when he or she runs into an impassable wall—a killing-sword koan. The teacher will use these koans to "kill" the ego of the student. That is one of the teacher's vows. Throughout the miscellaneous koans there are several opportunities for the teacher to wield this killing sword. Up to that point you have been gaining confidence in yourself, in your ability to see the koans. You've been moving along quite nicely and things are beginning to make sense. And just when they're making the most sense, the rug gets pulled out. Nothing makes sense anymore. The student is again thrown into turmoil.

This pattern returns again and again throughout the training. From one perspective, this is the basis of the teacher-student relationship. The teacher vows to dismantle any attachments that the student clings to. When the student gets nice and comfortable, the teacher pulls the rug out, and the student falls. The teacher rushes over and helps the student to his or her feet again; once the student is brushed off and standing firmly, the teacher pulls the rug out again. Down goes the student. This is repeated again and again until the teacher can pull the rug out without the student falling. They bow to each other and the process is completed. The flower has gone to the next generation.

The matrix of koan study and the grounding of zazen are refined tools that create an opportunity for self-realization. The driving force behind the search is what the student brings to the koan. That personal foundation of self-study has been referred to as the "three pillars of Zen." It is made up of great faith, great doubt, and great determination. Great faith is the sincere trust in the process: not only of Buddhism and Zen, but of koan study itself, and the bottom line is trust in oneself, in one's own ability to break through the koan. If you don't believe you can, you won't. You can't. To break through, you need to have total trust in yourself and in your ability to do it. It's not something that's going to happen by accident, but rather something that you're going to do with your own body and mind. You have the capability to do it, and you will do it. That is the great faith.

The great doubt is the question of life and death. Who am I? What is truth? What is life and death? What is pain, reality, God? These are the questions that drove Shakyamuni out of his comfortable palace and into the forest, that made Dogen travel to China. All of these questions about the ultimate nature of reality can be reduced to the student's koan. The koan becomes the distilled essence, the heart of all these questions. Great doubt and great faith are in dynamic equilibrium. They create a spiritual tension. The great doubt is described by the Chinese Master Wu-men as being like a red-hot fiery ball that's stuck in your throat. You can't swallow it and you can't spit it out. You are just burning with doubt.

Equal to the great faith and great doubt is great determination. The stability and the strength of this tripod is inestimable. Great determination is the kind of determination that Bodhidharma spoke of: "Seven times knocked down, eight times get up." There is nothing that can stop you. It may take time. It may take endless effort. It may take the rest of your life, but you're going to do it.

That determination is vital in koan study, particularly in respect to the evolving and shifting teacher-student relationship. Our upbringing and our educational system place an immense value on approval. Everybody's looking for approval. It starts with Mommy and Daddy. As we go through school, we're rewarded for our successes with stars, A's, smiles, and promotions. Approval continues all the way through our lives. In our jobs we're looking for validation from the boss; in our relationships, from our mates. Approval seems to make the world turn. It also consistently approaches and changes into dependency. It creates a lack of trust in oneself, in one's own self-sufficiency. In Zen training, it is eliminated altogether. This is one of the reasons why Zen gets a reputation for being somber. Zen teachers don't approve. They don't tell students what to do.

This situation is especially difficult for students while they are working with their first koan, usually Mu. Sometimes it takes years to see that first koan. During those years, the student will go to the teacher hundreds of times and present an understanding, and the teacher will reject it. "Go deeper." Ring the bell. The student goes back to his or her seat. This rejection happens over and over again. If students haven't built up some self-esteem prior to that, some stability in zazen, they suddenly find themselves in a quandary because the teacher's support evaporates. The only place you can look for support is very deep inside yourself.

The enduring teacher-student relationship is in a constant state of evolution, from the first meeting to the end. Essentially, there are five different ways that the teacher and student interact. The primary and most pivotal is the face-to-face teaching of dokusan. It takes place during periods of zazen when the most direct work on a koan is being done. The teaching or pointing that occurs in dokusan always comes from the point of view of the realized koan. Sometimes the dialogues may not seem rational. They don't always make sense. As long as you're processing it in a linear, logical fashion, it's not going to make sense. Only when it's seen from the perspective of the absolute does it begin to make any kind of sense. Koans are usually dark to the mind, but radiant to the heart.

Private face-to-face interview tends to be very short, very much to the point. The whole thing takes place in a minute or two. If you're working on a koan, you either see it or you don't. From the teacher's perspective, it's easier to work with koan students, because there are no prolonged discussions. If they haven't seen it, the bell rings and they go back and work with it. If they have seen it, they go on to the next koan. Very simple.

The second kind of interaction is a discourse or *teisho*. This is a commentary on a koan or on some point of the Dharma, based on the teacher's own experience. Like dokusan, the discourse comes from the point of view of the realized koan. The teacher presents the koan as if the audience were an audience of realized beings or Buddhas. In order to hear its truth, you need to shift your way of listening.

Another kind of encounter or teaching is *mondo*, which is basically a question-and-answer session. It's usually informal and intellectual. It doesn't attempt to approach the inquiry from the point of view of the absolute. Rather it guides the student by means of explanation. The question-and-answer chapter at the end of this volume is an example of a *mondo*.

Then there's *shosan*, or Dharma combat. Dharma combat tends to be more confrontational and less intellectual. There's more head-squeezing similar to what happens during dokusan. In a way, *shosan* is public dokusan. The teacher pushes the student, particularly in areas where the student is resisting or holding back. Good teachers will use every kind of device available to get the student to a point of realization.

Finally, casual encounters are another mode of teaching. In everyday meetings and work situations, opportunities arise to present the Dharma. Sometimes these encounters take place intellectually; sometimes they are like a

Dharma combat. The conversation between Nan-ch'üan and his disciple in "Nan-ch'üan's Peony," Chapter 10, hints at the potential of these informal encounters.

EARLY HISTORY OF KOANS

Koans have existed from the beginning of Zen but they weren't necessarily used as koans. There were always questions that would pop up among students and between teachers and students. The responses were appropriate to the moment, immediate and direct. Sometimes they were interactive and dynamic, sometimes explanatory. Students began recording and collecting them. As the centuries went by, some teachers started to use the recorded dialogues of the past as a way of teaching their own students.

There have been other sources of koans. Teachers have showed great ingenuity in using whatever is available and seems relevant. Events in the life of the original Buddha, compilations of the sayings of other masters, and ordinary philosophical statements have served as starting points of koans. The sutras are a gold mine of koans. In *The Blue Cliff Record*, a single line from a poem written by the Third Ancestor, "The great Way is not difficult, it only avoids picking and choosing," is used three times, as is its treatment by Chao-chou.

Koans were apparently used as teaching devices during the golden age of Zen in China but were not collected or systematized until the Sung dynasty. Various teachers included in their compilations koans that they deemed significant for the monastics in their communities. Some of these collections have come down to us in modern times. One of them is *The Blue Cliff Record*, which was put together around 1128 by Hsüeh-tou, who was a master in the Yün-men school of Zen. Once that school died out, *The Blue Cliff Record* was passed down through the Rinzai lineage. Another collection is the *The Book of Equanimity*. Collected by Hung-chih, a master in the Soto lineage, it was patterned after *The Blue Cliff Record*. Both *The Blue Cliff Record* and *The Book of Equanimity* contain a hundred koans, each accompanied by a prologue, verse, footnotes, and commentary.

Around 1229, the *Gateless Gate*, or *Mumonkan*, was arranged. It is regarded by most scholars and teachers as being the most mature of all of the collections of koans. The forty-eight koans that make it up were put together by Master Wu-men. In 1303, Master Keizan compiled *Transmission of the Light*, which is a collection of fifty-three koans culled from the enlightenment experiences of the ancestors, starting with Shakyamuni Buddha and continuing through to Keizan's teacher, Ejo.

The Chinese collections of the Sung dynasty were brought to Japan in the thirteenth century. Master Eisai was responsible for transmitting the Rinzai lineage. A number of Chinese teachers who flocked to Japan during that era continued the tradition of systematized koan study. Still, rigorous koan study did not last long. By the next century it had either turned into lifeless exercises or died out altogether. Possibly the reason for this turn of events was that the koan system had become too rigid and formalized, its spirit lost. The original koans were live exchanges between a teacher and a student. They were vivid events. When they became systematized, turned into topics of endless discussions, they were strangled with analysis. It was as if people had tried to bottle the spring breeze. The koan lost all of its freshness and vitality.

Master Hakuin and the
Revitalized Koan

This state of affairs continued until the time of Master Hakuin in eighteenth–century Japan. Hakuin came from a Rinzai lineage other than the Oryo lineage that had originally arrived in Japan through Eisai. Hakuin revitalized the koan system, modernized it, and incorporated it into the training of his monastics. He introduced his own koan, "The Sound of One Hand Clapping," as the first case for students to work with. Although he organized the koans along a specific sequence, Hakuin used them from memory. They weren't written down anywhere. It was not until subsequent generations that they were collected and again formalized. After Hakuin, Masters Inzan and Takuju kept the koan system alive and relevant, introducing it into the modern era. The Inzan and Takuju Rinzai lineages survive down to this day, and both are part of our training at Zen Mountain Monastery. In addition to being a master in the Soto lineage, my teacher was trained in both Rinzai traditions, and in turn he has trained his successors in both of them. The training in all the three lineages continues at this Monastery.

In systematizing his koan system, Hakuin classified koans according to types. A good book which reviews that classification in some detail is Isshu Miura's and Ruth Sasaki's *The Zen Koan*. Hakuin breaks up the koans into five groups. The first group are cases called the *dharmakaya* koans, or *hosshin* koans. These koans deal with the absolute nature of reality.

After students get a good grounding in the *dharmakaya*, the Hakuin system then begins to use what are called differentiation or *kikan* koans. Once you have seen the absolute basis of reality, you then need to see how that absolute basis functions in the world. To have fully experienced and realized the ground of being is to experience the unity of all phenomenon, the place of no separation. That's what is meant by "forgetting the self and being enlightened by the ten thousand things." You and the ten thousand things are one reality. But, of course, a person who has that experience—the experience of no eye, ear, nose, tongue, body, mind; no color, sound, smell, taste, touch, phenomena; no world of sight, no world of consciousness—is not very functional. You couldn't cross the street without getting hit by a car if you couldn't differentiate between yourself and the car and didn't know enough to get out of the way. To experience the absolute unity is one aspect of reality. The other aspect of it is to see how that manifests in the world of differentiation.

The third group of koans brought together by Hakuin are called *gonsen* koans. They deal with words and phrases. Our use of language tangles us up, and attaches us to positions or ideas. Koans in this group are used to loosen up the areas of verbal constriction, to help clarify the places where we attach to and get misled by words and phrases.

The fourth type of koans are *nanto* koans, cases that are difficult to pass through. They are difficult because the real point of the koan is very subtle. It's not up on the surface. Even the question is not clear until you've penetrated through levels of the koan. The heart of the *nanto* koans is easily missed. A master said, "It's like a buffalo passing through a lattice window. It's head and four legs and its body have passed through, but the tail cannot pass. Why is it that the tail cannot pass through?"

The fifth kind of koans in the Hakuin system are the *goi* koans, or the koans of the Five Ranks of Master Tungshan. The Five Ranks are a series of fifty koans that address the relationship between the absolute and the relative or, more accurately, deal with the relationship between all dualities—good and bad, heaven and earth, male and female, up and down, sacred and secular. All these apparent dualities are seen in terms of a dynamic matrix. The Five Ranks are based on Hua-yen philosophy, or what's called the four-fold Dharmadhatu, the interpenetration of dualities and the mutual causality and co-origination of all phenomenon.

In studying the Five Ranks, we look at the different dualities and how these dualities are interdependent and mutually arising. The final koan that we deal with through the Five Ranks is Mu. Mu is seen within each of the five ranks. In a way, the koan Mu pops up throughout the entirety of the koan system over and over again. You can say that the whole koan system is nothing other than 700 different ways of expressing Mu. When Mu is understood fully and thoroughly, all koans are understood fully and thoroughly.

Still the koan training isn't over. After the Five Ranks we take up the Precepts, the moral and ethical teachings of the Buddha, as koans. The sixteen Precepts are accepted at the beginning of training on the basis of faith, faith that they are the definition of the life of a Buddha, faith that when you practice the Precepts you're practicing and living the life of a Buddha. A student in the beginning stages has not realized that. Experience hasn't revealed that. The student has faith in the Precepts. But in order for the training to be complete, the Precepts must become the manifestation of the practitioner's life. The 120 koans on the Precepts must be thoroughly penetrated and assimilated as one's own body and mind.

Following the Precept koans at Zen Mountain Monastery, we've added what we call the *108 Koans of the*

Way of Reality. These are koans, culled from modern and ancient sources, that specifically deal with questions modern practitioners encounter and are concerned with: questions regarding the environment, relationships, war and peace, gender, and family.

At Zen Mountain Monastery, koan study is embedded in a matrix of training that touches all aspects of our lives and draws on all facets of our personalities. We refer to the matrix as "The Eight Gates." These are zazen, study with the teacher, liturgy, Precepts, art practice, body practice, academic study of Buddhism, and work practice. For students engaged in the practice of the Eight Gates, koans surface all the time in each of the eight areas. For example, in daily liturgy, every time you chant "Form is emptiness, emptiness is form. Form is exactly emptiness, emptiness exactly form," the question may arise, What is that line saying? Aren't those two contradictory declarations? How could form be emptiness and emptiness be form? Or the statement, "No eye, ear, nose, tongue, body, mind." We have eye, ear, nose, tongue, body, mind. What is the sutra talking about? In the Precepts, we hear that the virtue of the Buddha treasure "sometimes appears in vast space, sometimes appears in a speck of dust." What does this mean? In art practice, we often say, "Let the brush paint by itself." That's the way calligraphy happens. Dogen said that his teacher T'ien-t'ung Ju-ching was himself a sharp pointed brush, and that's how he painted spring: "When you paint spring, you can't paint just plum blossoms and flowers. Painting spring can only be done by a sharp pointed brush." In terms of body practice, the great Master Yün-men said, "Medicine and sickness heal each other. All the world is medicine. Where do you find the self?" This is one of the fundamental teachings, at the heart of what we call body practice. Body practice is not just pumping iron, running, or playing tennis. It is body and mind harmony.

In the training matrix, the koan is part of our everyday encounters, our everyday dialogues. It comes up in the sutras. It comes up in the workplace. It comes up in the discourses. It comes up in dokusan. All the questions are constantly pointing to the same place, to the life of each one of us. And all the questions have to be resolved in the very same place—in the life of each one of us. But unless it's *your* question, it can never be *your* answer. It needs to be of vital, undeniable importance to you. It needs to have created the condition conducive for great faith, great doubt, and great determination to arise. Otherwise, practice is imitation, or just another way of staying busy. It needs to be approached with the whole body and mind. The history of koan study has shown us that those people who break through have always undergone the very strenuous, deep work of painstaking introspection.

All in all, in our lineage there are some 700 koans. Different schools do different numbers and treat koan study differently. The traditional Hakuin system consists of about 350 koans. Most of the Rinzai lineages use the Hakuin system. The Korean lineages basically do one koan, the koan Mu, but they treat it in 150 different ways. Aside from a small minority who have completed formal koan study, members of the Soto school take up koan study at the university. Most of the monastics who finish their training at Eihei-ji or Soji-ji monasteries in Japan have at least a Master's degree in Buddhist studies. This includes analysis of the major koan collections. The system of doing koans face-to-face in dokusan and being required to realize the koans is functioning only in the Rinzai school. Only those teachers who have completed koan study themselves, and have been approved by a master who has completed koan study, should be studying koans with their disciples. Koan teachers who weren't themselves trained in koan study misunderstand the koan system and then pass on that misunderstanding to their students. This is regrettable.

There are many reasons other than koan study to be interested in koans. Koans provide a beautiful historical context for understanding Buddhism. They provide an important way of tracking the evolution of the Dharma through the centuries, from India to China to Japan, and now to this country. Koans exemplify the creativity that is inherent in learning. This form of learning in the West is similar to that of a master-apprentice relationship in artistic and craft traditions. Koans tap into a unique dimension of our use of language. Still, the bottom line of koan study is self-realization.

The koan is a sharp lancet. You turn the koan toward yourself, pointing it at the skin bag, the idea of a self that separates us from the ten thousand things. Koans continually cut away all of the extras, stripping away layers of conditioning, getting us to the ground of being. They are the double-edged sword of Manjushri. One edge of the blade kills the ego, the other gives life; one edge is wisdom, the other compassion. Each koan, experienced with the whole body and mind, is an initiation into a new way of being. Each koan presents us with a possibility of experiencing true freedom, the freedom which is our inherent birth right.

ONE

ORIGINAL SOURCE

*Koans of the
Way of Reality,
Case 104*

PROLOGUE

> *From the beginning the truth is clear and free of
> dust. In the valley of the endless spring one sits in silence
> observing the forms of integration and disintegration,
> the impermanent and deceptive images of the world can
> no longer deceive; deluded within enlightenment,
> enlightened within delusion. All things are perfect and
> complete in their suchness. The blue river flows into the
> great ocean, the green mountain fills the sky.*

THE MAIN CASE

> *The old monastic Su-lao of Hung Prefecture asked
> Ma-tsu,[1] "What is the meaning of Bodhidharma coming
> from the West?"[2] Ma-tsu pushed Su-lao so hard that he
> fell down to the ground.[3] With that Su-lao suddenly
> attained realization.[4] Clapping his hands and laughing*

1

loudly he arose and said, "How wonderful it is! How wonderful it is! The original source of hundreds and thousands of samadhis, the boundless and wonderful meaning.⁵ You can come to understand it all of a sudden just from the end of a single hair."⁶ Then he made prostrations and left.⁷

THE CAPPING VERSE

Back to the origin, returning to the source.
Effort is over.
The intimate self is blind and deaf.
Dwelling in one's true abode unconcerned,
*   the river flows, flowers are red.*

Returning to the original source is one of the steps in the ten stages of spiritual practice as delineated at Zen Mountain Monastery. Breaking up such an organic process into ten or fifteen or five segments is somewhat arbitrary. The fact is that we do progress through a series of stages of development, but they're not clear-cut and neatly separated from each other. To one degree or another, in each of the ten stages the other nine are present.

The prologue points out what the original source is about. *From the beginning the truth is clear and free of dust.* There never was any other way. The problem is that we don't usually see it. When a person starts off on the search, everything that's ever attained in the tenth stage is already present right there at the very beginning. But somehow it's obscured, obscured by the conditioning of our parents and teachers, our culture, nation, education, and peers. Conditioning begins at birth and continues throughout our lives. Little by little, layer by layer, our original perfection becomes more and more concealed and forgotten. It doesn't go away, but we're not aware of it. We function out of accumulated programs and habits, rather than out of the inherent nature and clarity we're born with. In a sense, a spiritual journey is a crazy process, because the whole struggle brings us back to where we started from.

Rather than positing an original defect or sin that needs to be transcended, in Buddhism we begin with the assumption of inherent perfection. Our practice is to return to the inherent perfection that's originally there. There's nothing to be transcended. There's just a lot of baggage that we need to unburden ourselves of. *From the beginning the truth is clear and free of dust. In the valley of the endless spring one sits in silence observing the forms of integration and disintegration. . . .* The "valley of the endless spring" is a reference to that state of consciousness that we call enlightenment. The endless spring is the endless spring of enlightenment, where everything is fresh, new, perfect, and complete—moment to moment. That's the way it is, whether we realize it or not.

One sits in silence observing the forms of integration and disintegration. . . . This line refers to the ninth stage of training or the state of consciousness that precedes "coming down off the mountain and going back into the world," to manifest in everyday activity what has been realized. The eighth, ninth, and tenth stages are really an encapsulation of the totality of training. In the first seven stages of development, we experience, to one degree or another, a little bit of each of the last three stages. These last three stages are considered to be the three *kaya*—the three bodies of the Buddha. The three bodies of all sentient beings.

The eighth stage is the *dharmakaya*, the experience of body and mind falling away. It is the experience of no eye, ear, nose, tongue, body, or mind; no color, sound, smell, taste, touch, or phenomena. The negation of all things. The absolute basis of reality. Out of that emerges the *sambhogakaya*, or the body of bliss, the reward body. And that reward body is what we speak of as the "return to the source," the ninth stage. From that source we venture into the marketplace, coming down off the mountain back into the world. This is the tenth stage, *nirmanakaya*, the physical body of the Buddha manifested in the world.

Sambhogakaya is essentially the state of enjoying the truth that one has embodied. It hasn't yet been manifested completely in action. That's why at this point of training we thoroughly study the Precepts. The Precepts function as the incentive for manifesting compassion in the tenth stage. The body of bliss itself is an incentive, as we want all sentient beings to experience that clarity. It is also in the ninth stage that integration and disintegration are clearly present. The impermanence and the interdependence are constantly around us. We see it in nature and among people. And there are times when we are able to do something about it, and times when we are not.

It can be very painful to watch others struggle through the process of self-discovery, just as painful as it is to watch one's children grow up through their experiences, knowing that there is very little one can really do to help them. We can provide some guidance, a bit of direction, but ultimately, the struggle is their own. Sometimes it's very obvious that we can help, and we do it, and sometimes they're not interested in our help, and we can only watch the unfolding.

The same dynamic is present with students in intensive Zen training, the same need to go through experiences oneself. As the hard shells of our egos begin to rub and bang up against one another, we create all kinds of unnecessary pain and misfortune. Here we are, all on the same path, all attempting to accomplish the same thing, yet anger, envy, and greed interfere. Our conditioning surfaces. Sesshins provide the space and time for it to surface. Allowing it to surface is one of the very important aspects and functions of zazen. As you sit there, day after day, lots of aches and pains set in. Your body hurts and you are tired. We react to that hurt in different ways. For some people, it triggers emotional responses that haven't been resolved. Memories and tensions come up into consciousness, and we have a wonderful opportunity to work with them. The pain easily elicits reactions that we've spent our life perfecting. When things get tight and tough and you feel cornered, you can usually withdraw and hide. In sesshin, it's difficult to do that. You notice your withdrawal right away. If you don't notice it, the teacher notices it, or a monitor notices it. Usually there is some assistance provided by the supportive environment of the sesshin. Some people become aggressive amid their pain and turn it into anger. When you're hurting, you want to hurt back. When you sit for long periods of time, your legs are going to hurt. That's the cause of the pain. But somehow that doesn't enter into consideration when you are looking for something concrete to attach the anger to. The sesshin form conveniently provides various targets to focus one's rage on. You can get angry with the monitors who talk too much, with the head server, with the teacher. The temperature in the zendo is too cold, or too warm. Sitting periods are too long, the zendo is too big, there are not enough interviews. The list of justifications for the anger is endless. But even that anger doesn't last very long. Because if the anger finally crystallizes as an outburst or a confrontation, it's usually dealt with appropriately. The responsibility is turned back to the student. This way you can own it, see it, learn and grow from it. The whole process simply and clearly exposes the patterns of conditioning that we continually embrace.

Sitting in silence observing the forms of integration and disintegration is a great teacher, a wonderful teacher of patience. You begin to learn when it's appropriate to move and when it's appropriate to be still. The prologue goes on to say, . . . *the world can no longer deceive; deluded within enlightenment, enlightened within delusion.* All things are perfect in their suchness. The return to the source is a return to the beginning. You end up where you started from. The blue river flows into the great ocean. The green mountain fills the sky. There's an old saying in Zen that in the beginning of practice, mountains are mountains, and rivers are rivers. And then after many years of training and study with a master, you realize that mountains are not mountains, and rivers are not rivers. Then, the practice continues. And ultimately, you see that mountains are mountains, and rivers are rivers. Somehow the first and second appreciations of "mountains are mountains, and rivers are rivers" are really different. It is the profundity of that distinction that makes all the difference in the world in the way we live our lives, in the way we experience ourselves and the universe. Obviously, nothing changes, yet. . . .

A person before realization looks like a person after realization. There is a lot of unmitigated confusion about enlightenment. Supposedly, enlightened people walk on water. If there is something extraordinary about the way they carry themselves, they haven't gotten anywhere yet. If there is anything special about them, there is still leaking. The sage who comes down off the mountain is an ordinary person, covered with worldly dust. He cannot be distinguished from anyone around him. If he stands out, the formal training is not complete.

The main case: *The old monastic Su-lao of Hung prefecture asked Ma-tsu.* The title "old monastic" indicates that Su-lao was a rather mature practitioner, not just a mere beginner. And Ma-tsu was one of the greatest masters in the history of Zen. His monastery had over a thousand monastics. At least eighty-four of them became his successors and countless others came to realization under him but weren't transmitted to. Ma-tsu was a Dharma heir of Nan-yüeh, whose teacher was the Sixth Ancestor, Hui-neng. Hui-neng also transmitted to Ch'ing-yüan who passed the Dharma to Shih-tou, and these two branches formed the heart of the Golden Age of Zen in T'ang Dynasty China.

Su-lao was one of the inheritors of Ma-tsu's Dharma. The experience depicted in this koan was probably one of the key factors in his realization. He came to Ma-tsu and asked, *"What is the meaning of Bodhidharma coming from the West?"* In a sense, what he was asking is, What is the essence of Zen, the truth of the Way? What's the basis of the teachings? This is the question that has been asked a hundred thousand times during the history of Zen. One could probably write several books on its different answers. There are as many answers as there are questioners, each one appropriate to the circumstances. Yet each one does not differ one iota in truth from any other. During his teaching years, Ma-tsu was repeatedly asked this very same question.

Once a monastic came to Ma-tsu and said, "Going beyond the four propositions and hundred negations, what is the meaning of Bodhidharma coming from the West?" In other words, surpassing every possible way of saying, explaining, or demonstrating it, what is the ultimate meaning of Zen truth? Ma-tsu said, "I'm the abbot and I've got a lot of work to do. Why don't you go ask the head monastic, Chih-tsang." The monastic went to Chih-tsang and asked the same question. Chih-tsang said, "Why don't you ask the abbot?" "You see, he told me to come and ask you." The head monastic replied, "I have a headache, go ask brother Pai-chang." The monastic did and Pai-chang said, "Coming this far, after all, I don't know." And so the monastic went back to Ma-tsu, told him what had happened, and added, "I don't understand." Ma-tsu said, "Pai-chang's head is black, the head monastic's head is white." Same question, different answers, same truth.

In the tradition of the classic koan collections, I have added notes to the lines of the main case to help students see the point being made. The notes to this koan are as follows. *The old monastic Su-lao of Hung Prefecture asked Ma-tsu.* The note: "He comes on straight away. He wants to know. Rocky Mountains are high, Catskill Mountains are low." *"What's the meaning of Bodhidharma's coming from the West?"* The note: "It's an old, worn-out question known everywhere. But still, he wants to put it to the test." *Ma-tsu pushed Su-lao so hard that he fell down to the ground.* The note: "He goes right up and takes him out. Why is he being so kind to this monastic?" The shove was a gesture of kindness often used during that time. Ma-tsu used it because he was very successful with it. He'd brought several people to enlightenment by hitting them with his stick. He brought Pai-chang to enlightenment by tweaking his nose, and another monastic with a great shout that left the man deaf for two days. Many of the direct, physical techniques that later became part of Rinzai School probably started with Ma-tsu. They were accepted and appropriate in China back in those days. It is very unlikely that they would work as effectively in the West today.

The direct action and its kindness arise out of Matsu's compassion to help someone to experience this incredible Dharma for themselves, and not to go outside themselves looking for answers about the ultimate truth. The direct action points out that the ultimate truth is one's own body and mind, one's own life, struggles, joy, and pain—all of it. *With that Su-lao suddenly attained realization.* The note: "Mountains are mountains, rivers are rivers." Zen is very difficult to explain. If you say to anybody, "Mountains are mountains, and rivers are rivers," everybody will nod affirmatively. Even a two-year-old knows that. Why did it take this old monastic so long to see that mountains are mountains, and rivers are rivers? There must be something going on. The question is, What is it?

Clapping his hands and laughing loudly he arose and said, "How wonderful it is! How wonderful it is! The original source of hundreds and thousands of samadhis, *the boundless and wonderful meaning."* The note: "Neither of them understands. He's making quite a fuss. He should just shut up." *"You can come to understand it all of a sudden just from the end of a single hair."* The note: "It engulfs the myriad forms. Between heaven and earth, what more is there?" A single dew-drop, a single tip of hair, the whole universe, ten thousand universes. *Then he made prostrations and left.* The note: "Among the dead, a live one. He's treading on the ground of reality. Where do you think he went when he left?"

From the beginning, the source is flawless, free of dust, free of imperfection. In a sense, we can say that complete, crystal clear awakening is like not yet awakening.

Still, there's a fundamental difference. Master Ta-mei once wrote, "Dear students, turn your head around and enter the origin. Do not search for those who have sprung out of it." In other words, don't run around expecting that you're going to get it from somebody who has already experienced it. It needs to be your own experience. "When you have gained the origin, what has sprung out of it will come to you of itself. If you want to know the origin, then penetrate your own original heart. This heart is the source of all beings in the world, and outside it. When the heart stirs, various beings arise. But when the heart itself becomes completely empty, the various beings also become empty." "Heart" in these lines is *hsin*, "heart-mind." When the mind moves, when the emotions move, the ten thousand things go into their differentiation, heaven and earth are separated, self and other are separated. When the mind becomes empty, the ten thousand things are empty. If your heart is driven neither by good nor bad, then all beings are just as they are.

This is sometimes called the great "Yes." To reach the great suchness of all beings, the great Yes-ness, the student must inevitably go through the region of absolute Not-ness, negation. That's *shunyata*—no eye, ear, nose, tongue, body, or mind—where even this utter Not-ness must itself come to nothing. Emptiness is completely empty. And then, just at the point where that great Zen experience of absolute nothingness becomes nothing, there arises the great "Yes!" to all beings. Here each and every thing is absolutely and unequivocally affirmed, and our Zen becomes one of activity and action.

The eighth stage, *dharmakāya*, is the stage of total negation and non-differentiation. Self and other disappear, body and mind fall away. In the ninth stage, *sambhogakaya*, differences are present, and the negation becomes affirmation. It's out of this transformation that the unhindered life of the sage develops. What's seen is that the true nature is originally pure, originally perfect, and that it's present in all beings and things. It doesn't increase, and it doesn't decrease. It can't be gained, and it can't be lost. It can't be given, and can't be received. Our real world—the mountains and the rivers—is nothing other than the original nature, the Buddha-nature.

What's also seen is that all things are constantly changing. Everything is in a perpetual state of transition, of becoming. One thing arises, another thing disappears. Life and death. And it's in the stillness amid all that flux that the forms of integration and disintegration are seen.

Master Lin-chi once said, "Such a person stands in the midst of a throng on a busy road, and in spite of it, never turns away from the original self." Such a person can no longer put a distance between self and home, even when he or she is busily engaged in the business of the world. Smack in the middle of all the relationships, complexities, and distinctions, the accomplished Zen student dwells in the true nature of non-difference. Such a person acts and at the same time does not act. This is called "the action of non-action." There is the recognition of the whole "catastrophe" of existence as a great dance, the dance of samsara. And you dance right along with the whole universe. There's nothing else you can do if you're flesh and blood. But you do not lose sight of what it's all about—the forms of integration and disintegration. As Buddha said in the closing lines of the *Diamond Sutra*:

> *Thus shall ye think of all this fleeting world:*
> *A star at dawn, a bubble in a stream;*
> *A flash of lightning in a summer cloud,*
> *A flickering lamp, a phantom, and a dream.*

This is not just a nihilistic outlook on the nature of things. Many people misunderstand the eighth stage of training as being incontrovertibly nihilistic. That's why the affirmation in the ninth stage, the return to the origin, is so vitally important. And the return to ordinariness. In that return to ordinariness, all sophistication and spirituality have fallen away. My teacher once called it "innocent naiveté."

When you realize the incredible demands that this practice makes on people, and the tremendous determination that is necessary in order just to sit, day after day, and study the self, you appreciate the difficulties and the intricacies of the path. And you see the possibility that this spiritual aggressiveness could end up becoming real boorishness and heavy-handedness, if not properly channeled.

As the training process continues, the rough edges are polished into a very smooth pearl. The naiveté is a true, gullible innocence, the kind of trusting that characterized Master Te-shan in his later years. At the beginning of his teaching career, he was a tyrant. He was the original thirty-blows-of-the-stick teacher. No matter how you answered him, you could not avoid getting hit. Then, toward the end of his life, encountering Hsüeh-feng's challenge, "Where are you going old man, carrying your bowls when the drum hasn't sounded?" he just meekly said, "Oh," and returned to his room. Yet, to an ear that can hear it, this was the roar of a lion, and it filled the universe. Unfortunately at the time, Hsüeh-feng was still deaf and missed it.

Arriving at the ninth stage is a result of an enormous amount of hard training and genuine struggle. And what it all comes down to is returning to the beginning, the origin. That's what Lin-chi meant when he came to realization with the old hermit and said, "So, there's nothing special about the truth that Huang-po embraces!"

Because this practice is about returning to the origin, it is possible to say that my teacher gave me nothing. And it's because of that that I'm deeply grateful. Otherwise I would still be attached to his leash. It's very difficult to work with students for years, to give them nothing and have them realize their own inherent power, their capacity for being gentle, yet strong, compassionate people. Lin-chi called such a state of being "taking away the person, and not taking away the environment." He presented four possibilities: "In one case, I take away the person, and I leave the environment; in the next situation I take away the environment and leave the person; in the third situation, I take away both person and environment; and in the fourth, I take away neither."

Despite its ordinariness, there's no question that one could never reach this origin, this source, even with the highest and clearest of knowledge. This is because it's got nothing to do with knowledge, information, or understanding. It's got nothing to do with believing. It's got to do with using it everyday without knowing it. And that unknowing becomes an innermost aspect of one's unconscious being. In this sense, there's a certain amount of blindness in it, of what we call transcendental blindness. The capping verse refers to it:

> *Back to the origin, returning to the source.*
> *Effort is over.*
> *The intimate self is blind and deaf.*
> *Dwelling in one's true abode unconcerned,*
> *   the river flows, flowers are red.*

The transcendental blindness sees the equality of all things, and yet can function in the world of differentiation, among the ten thousand things. *Dwelling in one's true abode unconcerned....* This is seeing the forms of integration and disintegration, and being able to either deal with them, or just watch them. Sometimes, if you do more than just watch them, you may interfere and take away their power. Sometimes that's what "doing good" does. It steals power. What seems a little bit ruthless is really an act of compassion. It's easy to be a hero and do good, to go rushing around helping people. It's most difficult to just watch them struggle and keep your hands off, letting people feel their own power, letting them fall and get to their feet. The fact is you can't do anything for anybody. Each person must do it alone. We can help, but we can't do it for him or her. It would be a very different kind of training and practice if that were possible.

Dwelling in one's true abode unconcerned, the river flows, the flowers are red. Everything is just as it is—the true "thusness" of things. It is in this state of being that the inexhaustibility of this incredible Dharma is seen. Out of the stillness, the ten thousand things arise. They are simply the everyday worldly self, the *original* everyday worldly self. It dwells simultaneously on the mountain and in the world, having entered the marketplace, without leaving the mountain.

The wonderful discovery of realization is that our perfection is inherent. It has always been there. That's what makes it so powerful. We truly do not attain anything. So why is there such a struggle? Our conditioning runs very deep. We can reach a point where we become aware of the pain and suffering but choose to ignore it. There are many ways to do that, and hundreds of millions of people go from cradle to grave not even being dimly aware that they can do something about it. Others are aware of the possibility but choose not to engage the process. Still others only go through the motions, the surface forms that do not really impart any strength. And a handful of people really do it. But the fact is all of us have precisely the same potential, the same equipment as the Buddha, as the ancestors. Every single one of us. The ones that accomplish it and the ones that don't.

Why some do and others don't beats me. But somehow it's clear that when people come this far on this tough journey, having passed through the obstacles and the gates, to sit themselves on a cushion as a student of the Way, the spiritual fire must be burning. They feel its heat. I don't know why, but when I realize that you've chosen to do this, I am overwhelmed. And I'm grateful for the opportunity to practice with you.

TWO

PERILS, PEARLS, AND THE PATH

Master Dogen's Three-Hundred Koan Shobogenzo, Case 185

PROLOGUE

It includes heaven and encompasses the earth. It is beyond the sacred and the secular. Revealed on the tips of a hundred thousand weeds—the wondrous mind of Nirvana, the exquisite teachings of formless form. From deep within the forest of brambles, the light of the mani pearl is released. This is the adamantine eye of the adept.

THE MAIN CASE

Lu-tsu said to Nan-ch'üan, "Nobody recognizes the mani pearl,[1] but there is one in the storehouse of the Tathagata.[2] What is this storehouse?"[3] Nan-ch'üan replied, "Teacher Wang and yourself,[4] coming and

going—it is nothing other than that.[5] *Lu-tsu asked,
"What about those who don't come and go?"*[6] *Nan-
ch'üan replied, "They are the storehouse too."*[7] *Lu-tsu
asked, "Then what is the pearl?"*[8] *Nan-ch'üan called,
"Master Tsu!"*[9] *Lu-tsu answered, "Yes."*[10] *Nan-ch'üan
said, "Go away. You don't understand what I mean."*[11]
At that moment, Master Lu-tsu had an insight.[12]

THE CAPPING VERSE

*It illuminates itself,
The solitary light of one bright pearl.
No. . . . It illuminates the ten thousand things.
See—there are no shadows.
When looking, who does not see?
Seeing, not seeing—Bah!
Riding backward on the ox
Distant mountains endlessly unfold.*

Perils, pearls, and the path: we tend to think of these
things as separate and distinct entities. We like to see the
spiritual path as something incontrovertibly positive, but
the path can also be quite a peril in itself. Even the idea of
"a spiritual path" immediately creates boundaries and
restrictions. Perils, on the other hand, can be pearls. The
very things that are barriers in our practice can be transformed into gates of realization.

In this koan, Lu-tsu says, *Nobody recognizes the mani
pearl, but there is one in the storehouse of the Tathagata.*
The storehouse of the Tathagata is the source of all things.
Tathagata means "thus come." Sometimes it's used as a
name for the Buddha, and sometimes to refer to "such-

18

ness." All things arise from the storehouse of the Tathagata—good things and evil things, big things and little things, pure things and impure things. The ten thousand things emanate from this great storehouse of suchness.

The Chinese character translated here as "mani pearl," or "one bright pearl," has also been variously translated as the "cosmic gem," "crystal," and "diamond." It actually means "bead," such as the bead on a mala. In Japanese a mala is called *juzu*, and the name of the bright pearl is *ikkamyoju*. The *ju* in both words means something very precious, and *myo* means bright, brilliant, clear, luminous—definitely a very precious thing. Many depictions of Chinese dragons show them protecting a big, beautiful luminous pearl under their chin. You have to deal with the dragon if you're going to take hold of this gem. But what is the dragon? What is the pearl? That's what this koan is about.

The koan comes from a collection of Master Dogen's koans that have become available in English only in recent years. One of the great masters of the thirteenth century, Dogen, after studying for a number of years in China, brought the teachings of the Soto school to Japan. The Soto school emphasizes *shikantaza*, or "zazen only" as the way of Zen. According to the Soto school, Dogen was not interested in koans, which were used primarily in the training of the Rinzai school; his teaching was to just sit. The Soto school proceeded on that assumption for many centuries in spite of the fact that Dogen's classic work, the *Shobogenzo*, or *The Treasure House of the True Dharma Eye*, is filled with all sorts of koans. Earlier in this century, a collection of 300 koans, handwritten in Chinese, was discovered. The compilation seemed to have been created by Dogen, though scholars had no real evidence to that effect until more recently. Now it seems certain that the manuscript is in Dogen's own hand, and there is little doubt that he selected and used these particular koans in teaching his monastics, and as source material for his Japanese *Shobogenzo*.

At Zen Mountain Monastery, in developing the training matrix, we combine the practice of both Rinzai and Soto schools. We use traditional koan study as well as the teachings of Master Dogen. The discovery of koans culled by Dogen provides us with an additional and tremendous opportunity to study koans he felt were especially important, many of which appear in no other collections. Many have been formally incorporated as part of our training.

In "One Bright Pearl," an essay in the *Shobogenzo*, Dogen refers to a teaching of Master Hsüan-sha who always used to say, "The whole universe is one bright pearl." One day a monastic asked him, "You have a saying, 'The whole universe is one bright pearl.' How can a student like me understand that?" Hsüan-sha replied, "What's the use of understanding that the whole universe is one bright pearl?" The next day he asked the monastic, "What's your understanding of 'the whole universe is one bright pearl?'" The monastic said, "What's the use of understanding that the whole universe is one bright pearl?"—simply repeating Hsüan-sha's reply to him from the encounter the day before. Hsüan-sha said, "I *know* that you're alive among the demons in the dark cave." In a sense, what Hsüan-sha was saying is that even in the monastic's delusion, even in his darkness, there is just this one bright pearl. Dogen comments, "Thus the bright pearl, existing just so and being beginningless, transcends changes and time and place. The entirety is brilliant light, one mind. When the bright pearl is the entirety, nothing hinders it. Round like the pearl, it rolls around and around. The merits of one bright pearl being manifested in this way, Avalokiteshvara and Maitreya therefore exist now, and the old Buddhas and new Buddhas appear in the world and preach the Dharma."

Dogen goes on to say, "When it is just so, it hangs suspended in space. It is hidden in the linings of clothing, it is held under the chin of a dragon, and worn in the hair topknot. All these are one bright pearl as the whole universe. It is its nature to be attached to the lining of clothing, so never say that it is attached to the surface. It is its nature to be guarded under the chin of a dragon, or kept in a topknot, so do not think that it is found on the surface. Though on the surface there may seem to be change or no change, enlightenment or no enlightenment, it is the one bright pearl. Realizing it is so is itself one bright pearl. The shapes, the sounds of the bright pearl are seen in this way. Saying to yourself, 'It is so,' do not doubt that you yourself are the bright pearl by thinking, 'I am not the bright pearl.' Confusion, doubts, affirmations and negations, these are nothing but ephemeral small responses of ordinary folks. However, still they are the bright pearl, appearing as small, ephemeral responses."

In talking about Zen practice, we frequently speak about letting go and trusting. Sometimes, though, the essence of trusting is not appreciated. To many people, to trust implies that somehow their expectations are going to be fulfilled. "Trust yourself" seems, then, to mean doing something so that everything will turn out as you expect. That's not what trust is about. Letting go and trusting, in and of itself, means no expectations. We say, "Do the best you can." But when you are still holding on to expectations, rather than really letting go, doing "the best you can" is still confined. It's confined within the limits of,

"This is all I can do; this is as far as I go." There's a tether attached. When you let go, "doing the best I can" has no limits, no expectations, no success, and no failure, just continuous practice. But to do that, we need to empower ourselves, we need to give ourselves permission to be the way we are, without holding onto anything—no ideas, no concepts, no positions.

We should keep in mind that there's not a single phrase, not one concept, teaching, or image in all of Zen practice that's not specifically designed to self-destruct at some time. The minute you hold on to any of it, it's gone. When you point to the absolute, the teacher will point to the relative. When you point to the relative, the teacher will point to the absolute. When you point to neither the relative nor the absolute, the sixteen-foot golden body of the Buddha is manifested in a pile of shit and rubbish. And that sixteen-foot golden body is nothing other than this one bright pearl that Dogen speaks of. Whatever you hold on to ultimately becomes a poison. Whether we're talking about the Precepts or about the Dharma, the minute you take hold of it, the medicine turns into the disease. When gold dust gets in the eyes it hurts, no matter how precious it is. When you meet the Buddha, *kill* the Buddha. When you meet the teacher, *kill* the teacher. That is the light of this one great pearl that fills the universe.

We look for approval. A student who did a writing workshop at the Monastery told me she was feeling very depressed about her writing. Then one of the teachers said, "You're really a good writer." Suddenly the student came to life, "*I'm a good writer.*" I commented, "Thank God she didn't say you're an awful writer." Actually that student immediately saw what her reaction was and learned from it how approval can become a nose-ring. It doesn't matter who puts that nose-ring there or what the nose-ring is—if it is in place, there is no freedom. In all my years of training with my teacher, he *never* approved me. He never said that I did a good job, or was a wonderful student, or was going to be a great teacher. The most I got out of him was a grunt, or "go deeper," or "not good enough." We have a tendency to get really attached to the opinions of people we give power to. We hear a physician say, "You have three months to live," and we believe him, fulfill the prophecy, and die. Our practice is self-empowerment. Nobody can do it for you, and the minute anybody tries, a nose-ring is created that can lead you away from taking responsibility for your own life.

It includes heaven and encompasses the earth. It is beyond the sacred and the secular. Revealed on the tips of a hundred thousand weeds—the wondrous mind of Nirvana, the exquisite teachings of formless form. The hundred-thousand weeds represent samsara or the realm of delusions—the greed, anger, and ignorance that often characterize life. Yet even this is the great bright pearl that encompasses the whole universe. Right here is the wondrous mind of Nirvana, the exquisite teaching of formless form that has been transmitted from generation to generation. *From deep within the forest of brambles, the light of the mani pearl is released.* The forest of brambles is a reference to all the restrictions and frustrations we experience, the confusion that seems to obscure our path. In this koan the brambles are expressed metaphorically, but you know what they are: "I can't sit." "I try to sit everyday, but I can't sit." "Every time I sit, I'm confused with all of this stuff that comes up, all of these desires that take over my life." "I can't write." "I can't do this." "I can't do that." Those are the brambles. Those brambles themselves, so tightly woven and intertwined, are a perfect, clear, brilliant sphere. They are that one bright pearl, emanating the light that fills the whole universe. To see that is to personally open the Dharma eye.

The main case is an exchange between Lu-tsu and Nan-ch'üan, who were peers, probably from two different lineages. *Lu-tsu said to Nan-ch'üan, "Nobody recognizes the mani pearl...."* I've added notes to each line of the main case, and for this line the comment is: "When you look at it, you're blinded." There are five kinds of blindness in Zen. There is the blindness of delusion, of just simply not knowing what is real. There is the blindness of a heretic, where we become so constricted by our own position that we're unable to see another point of view. There is the blindness of enlightenment—of no eye, ear, nose, tongue, body, or mind; no color, sound, smell, taste, touch, or phenomena; no world of sight, no world of consciousness. Poor dear, how will you get across the street? How will you take a meal, or take a breath? The fourth kind of blindness is the blindness of being attached to enlightenment, what we call spending one's life in a ghost cave. And then the fifth kind of blindness is transcendent blindness. What kind of blindness is Lu-tsu referring to in the koan? *"Nobody recognizes the mani pearl...."* When you look at it, you are blinded. To look at it, you need to stand outside it. That indicates being separate, and that's being blind.

Lu-tsu goes on to say, *"... but there is one in the storehouse of the Tathagata."* The note says, "Where did he get the news?" How did he find out about this? Does he know through his own experience, or did somebody tell him about it? Is he a believer, or someone who has penetrated the truth for himself? Lu-tsu then asks, "What is this storehouse?" In asking this question he reveals himself—obviously, he's a believer. The note says, "If you don't know what it is, why do you think there is one?"

Nan-ch'üan replies, "*Teacher Wang and yourself....*" The note says, "Not two, yet when the fish swims, the water gets muddy." Nan-ch'üan is also known as Wang, so he is referring to himself here. The note continues, "Not two, yet when the bird flies, feathers fall," referring to the traces and tracks left behind. The minute Nan-ch'üan opens his mouth, he creates mud, he leaves tracks. It's unavoidable. Leaving tracks is how the teachings point to what is real. And that's why we need to see what is real for ourselves—if we attach to the words and ideas that describe the reality, we miss the reality itself. So, don't attach.

Nan-ch'üan's reply continues, "*Teacher Wang and yourself, coming and going—it is nothing other than that.*" The note says, "Good news. But say, what is it good for?" Teacher Wang and yourself, coming and going—the whole universe is just this one thing. His response is like a hammer head without a place to fit a handle. It's useless. What will you do with it? Nan-ch'üan is presenting the absolute basis of reality: emptiness.

Then Lu-tsu asks, "*What about those who* don't *come and go?*" In other words, that's okay for me and you, for coming and going, but what about those who don't come and go, who don't fall into that activity? The note says, "There are many who still have doubts about this." Nan-ch'üan replies, "*They are the storehouse, too.*" The note says, "He keeps making piles of bones on level ground. Just don't talk about it." The phrase "piles of bones on level ground" is another frequently used image representing emptiness. We also call it "mountains level with the plain," or "flavorless talk," or just "bones," or "make a living in a ghost cave." All of these imply being stripped of intrinsic characteristics, the perfect circle of *shunyata*, forgetting the self, body and mind falling away. All of these, Nan-ch'üan is saying, are in the storehouse, too.

Lu-tsu goes on to ask: "*Then what is the pearl?*" The note says, "Give him the pearl. Hit him. It won't do to let him go." Still he searches for the storehouse. Still he looks here and there, outside of himself for this one bright pearl. When he asks, "*Then what is the pearl?*" Nan-ch'üan calls out, "Master Tsu!" The note says, "The whole universe calls out!" Lu-tsu answers, "Yes?" The note says, "The ten thousand Dharmas answer."

Calling and answering comes up repeatedly in the classic koans. Ch'ing-shui said to Master Ts'ao-shan, "I am poverty stricken, absolutely destitute. I have nothing. Please teach me." Give me something, make me rich. Ts'ao-shan responded, "Ch'ing-shui!" Ch'ing-shui said, "Yes?" And Ts'ao-shan answered, "You've just drunk three cups of the finest wine, and still you say your lips are not moist?" What are the three cups of wine Ts'ao-shan speaks of?

The National Teacher called out to his attendant, "Attendant!" "Yes, master?" answered the attendant. And the master said, "All along I thought it was I who had my back turned to you. Now I find that it is you who had your back turned to me."

What is the magic of that calling and answering? The whole universe calls out; the ten thousand Dharmas answer. The whole universe and ten thousand Dharmas are just two different names for the same thing. They're like two mirrors reflecting each other. Then why did Nan-ch'üan say, "*Go away. You don't understand what I mean.*" The note says, "Don't explain it for him. Let him go wrong for the rest of his life."

The truth cannot be explained. That is why all of the *upaya*, all of these teaching devices, are resorted to. The minute you say, "This is it," you've missed it. The minute you point to it, you separate yourself from it. When you look at it, you're blinded. Why? Because it can't be found anywhere other than where you sit. "This very life is the life of the Buddha. This very body is the body of the Buddha." Not my life … *your* life. What does that mean, "Not my life … *your* life?" How can you appreciate that?

So Nan-ch'üan tells Lu-tsu to, "*Go away. You don't understand what I mean.*" At that moment Master Lu-tsu has an insight. The note says, "Confined in prison, he increases in wisdom. Still, he will never attain it." Kashyapa Buddha sat on the Bodhi seat for ten kalpas, yet he never attained Buddhahood. Why? Ten kalpas, ten eons of doing zazen, and he never attained it. And in fact, Lu-tsu became one of the great teachers, so why am I saying he'll never attain it?

> *It illuminates itself,*
> *The solitary light of one bright pearl.*
> *No.… It illuminates the ten thousand things.*
> *See—there are no shadows.*

Think about it—what does it take to make a shadow? That's another phrase used frequently in Zen training— "He reveals his shadow, but hides himself." Or "The tree loses its leaves and doesn't reveal a shadow. Where does the light come from?"

> *When looking, who does not see?*
> *Seeing, not seeing—Bah!*
> *Riding backward on the ox*
> *Distant mountains endlessly unfold.*

Riding backward on the ox is an image used in Zen for freedom, the freedom to ride the ox any which way. Riding backward on the ox into the distant mountains is freely manifesting oneself in the world of ten thousand things. After all, that is where it counts. We have a tendency to see spiritual life as being an activity confined to spiritual places, whereas Dogen said, "To think the secular is a hindrance to the sacred only means that you understand that in the secular nothing is sacred. What you haven't yet understood is that in sacredness, *nothing* is secular." That's one bright pearl—the one bright pearl of Nanch'üan, the one bright pearl of Dogen, the one bright pearl that is the life of each one of us. So stop hoping; there is no hope. Stop looking; what you're looking for is is not outside yourself. Let go of everything and trust yourself. Our practice, in a sense, is giving birth, giving life, to that pearl because it exists in every one of us. It has always been there. But, please, don't believe me—see for yourself.

 THE TIME AND SEASON OF GREAT PEACE

Master Dogen's Three-Hundred Koan Shobogenzo, Case 103

PROLOGUE

Setting up monasteries and establishing the teachings is like adding flowers to brocade. When you take off the blinders and let go of the baggage, you have entered the time and season of great peace. If you can discern the phrase outside of patterns, the sword of Manjushri is in your hands. The Buddhas have not transmitted a single thing, the ancestors have all attained nothing, yet Zen students everywhere grasp at appearances, struggle over reflections. But say, "Since it is not transmitted, why so many koans?"

THE MAIN CASE

When Zen Master Kuei-shan was meditating, Yang-shan attended on him.[1] The Master said, "You recently became a successor of the Zen school. How is that?[2] There is someone who has his doubts about this."[3] And then he asked Yang-shan, "How do you understand it?"[4] Yang-shan said, "When I'm sleepy, I close my eyes and rest. When I'm feeling fine, I meditate. Therefore, I haven't ever said anything."[5] The Master replied, "To achieve this level of understanding is no easy matter."[6] Yang-shan then said, "According to my understanding, even being attached to this phrase is a mistake."[7] The Master said, "For someone it is a mistake, too."[8] Yang-shan said, "From ancient times until now, all the sages were just like this."[9] The Master replied, "There is someone who laughs at your answers."[10] Yang-shan said, "The ones who are laughing at me are my colleagues."[11] The Master asked, "How do you understand succession?"[12] Yang-shan walked in a circle around the Master, who was sitting in the high seat.[13] The Master said, "That lineage transmitted uninterruptedly from ancient times to now has been broken."[14]

THE CAPPING VERSE

The Buddhas have not appeared in the world,
Nor is there anything to be given to the people.
There is just seeing into one's own heart and mind—
This is the endless spring.

When Zen students are doing koan study, they need simply to be present. The minute they stop and try to figure out what they have learned in order to fit it into their reference systems, the whole thing begins to fall apart. But if students continue being intimate with the questions and develop their practice both in depth and breadth, at some point the pieces which didn't make sense suddenly fall into place.

During the past thirteen years many people who have entered training at Zen Mountain Monastery have broken through, experiencing *kensho*. Some have gone further and have clarified, to different degrees, what they've seen. To get a glimpse of the ground of being is not too difficult a thing to do, but when someone is going to take on the responsibility of teaching, his or her training needs to be exhaustive. That calls for a special effort and persistence. That is our tradition. It is not enough just to break through; you need to be clear before you can hope to impart strength to others. That's what creating successive generations means. Yet the whole endeavor is actually nothing but a giant cosmic joke, because essentially there is nothing to transmit and nothing to receive. That's what this koan is about. That's what this practice is about. We hear this principle all the time, but somehow we proceed as though there is something to attain.

Setting up monasteries and establishing the teachings is like adding flowers to brocade. To add flowers to brocade is to do something "extra." The brocade is already adorned, already beautiful. It doesn't need anything more. In a way, setting up monasteries and providing the teachings is also excessive. Recently, I watched a television documentary on Iraq's Saddam Hussein, detailing his skill in using the media and comparing and contrasting him with Hitler. They showed him with a big portrait of himself behind the desk and another portrait of himself on the desk facing the camera. *That's* excessive. I have often thought that pictures of food in dining rooms are extra. It's like hanging a painting of a flower in a garden. That is "adding flowers to brocade," because what we're looking for is already here.

When you take off the blinders and let go of the bag-gage, you have entered the time and season of great peace. This refers to letting go of the stuff we hold on to. Old people are bent over because most of them are carrying their lives with them. Everything we've ever done, every-thing we've ever experienced, we stuff into our "back-pack." Every twenty years or so we get a bigger backpack because we have more experiences to put in it. By the time we're sixty or seventy, we're bent over with the baggage. Let go of the baggage. Set it down. It sounds so easy to say; it seems so difficult to do. But actually, it's not so dif-ficult. When you do it once or twice, you begin to realize how easy it is to let go of yesterday and tomorrow and to be present in this moment. The moment is not complicat-ed. It contains nothing extraneous. There's no fear in the moment; fear has to do with the next moment. There's no expectation in the moment. Expectations have to do with the future. There are no regrets. Regrets have to do with the past. The moment is perfect, complete, and contains everything. It's where our life takes place. This is the time and season of great peace—simply right here, right now. Yet it seems so difficult to be where we are.

If you can discern the phrase outside of patterns, the sword of Manjushri is in your hands. To discern the phrase outside of patterns means to be able to act independently and freely, not to get caught in patterns of behavior, Dharma, or spirituality—not to be bound by any kind of conditions. Patterns tend to be repetitious and preconceived. The sword of Manjushri is the sword of wisdom and compassion. It can either kill or give life. One of its edges is the killing edge that eliminates and deprives. The other edge is the life-giving edge that nourishes and heals.

The Buddhas have not transmitted a single thing, the ancestors have all attained nothing.... This seems like an outrageous statement for a lineage based on transmission of the mind from generation to generation. In an unbroken lineage transmitted mind-to-mind, what is it that is transmitted? Did Ananda get anything from Mahakashyapa? Did Mahakashyapa get something from the Buddha? Was Ananda or Mahakashyapa lacking anything to begin with? Indeed, was the Buddha lacking anything? Are you lacking anything?

The ancestors have all attained nothing. I have deep gratitude for my teacher because he has given me absolutely nothing. I mean that. He used to say it all along. I would give him a birthday present and he would say, "Oh, thank you; I'm sorry I have nothing to give you." I'd say, "Oh Roshi, you've given me so much." And as I'd start saying that, he'd turn and walk away from me. I didn't know it, but I was putting him down by telling him that he gave me so much; that's the worst thing a teacher can do. His job wasn't to make clones; his job was to get us to see that each of us is as perfect and complete as the Buddha. And if word got around he was "giving," he'd be a laughingstock among Zen teachers. What could he possibly give that wasn't there to begin with?

When the Buddha realized himself, he said, "All sentient beings are perfect and complete, lacking nothing." Then what is all this business about transmission? Is this some kind of great hoax created by yellow-faced old Gautama? Why did he single out one person in that assembly of two thousand and say, "I have the all-pervading

True Dharma, incomparable Nirvana, the exquisite teachings of formless form. It does not rely on letters and is transmitted outside scriptures. I now give it to Mahakashyapa"? If you say it can be transmitted, then why was it transmitted only to Mahakashyapa? If you say it can't be transmitted, then what's the whole scenario about in the first place? *The Buddhas have not transmitted a single thing, the ancestors have all attained nothing, yet Zen students everywhere grasp at appearances, struggle over reflections.* This grasping at appearances is our tendency to follow after form. Struggling over reflections is looking outside the self, putting another head on top of the one you already have.

But say, "Since it's not transmitted, why so many koans?" Why so many talks? Why face-to-face encounter? Why eight areas of training, ten stages of practice? Why all the complications?

This case has to do with Yang-shan's succession. Yang-shan was a very brilliant Chinese master living during the T'ang dynasty, from 800 to about 890 A.D. He was nicknamed "Little Shakyamuni." Many people in very powerful positions were his students—officials, inspectors, and government representatives. Before he was twenty years old he had already called on Nan-ch'üan, the National Teacher, Ma-tsu, and Pai-chang. Eventually he was fully enlightened with Kuei-shan, and stayed with him for fifteen years. A koan in *The Book of Equanimity* deals with Yang-shan receiving the esoteric teachings of the ninety-seven circular figures, which became incorporated in his later teachings. It is said that Yang-shan burned the book which contained the symbols after he had read it once. The master who had given it to him lamented this, so Yang-shan created another copy from memory and presented it to him. He was a brilliant teacher and one of the great successors of Kuei-shan. He and Kuei-shan had a very close relationship; together they are responsible for creating the Kuei-yang School, one of the five houses of Zen. Yang-shan once said that the essence of the school was "two mouths without a single tongue." Evidently, Master Dogen was quite taken with both of them, because in his *Three-Hundred Koan Shobogenzo* there are many koans concerning the two. They're widely considered the ultimate example of master-disciple identification.

When Zen Master Kuei-shan was meditating, Yang-shan attended on him. The note I have added to the first line is, "A single mouth, no tongue." *The Master said, "You recently became a successor of the Zen school. How is that?"* And the note says, "Indeed, how is that? What succession are we speaking about?" It has never been transmitted, nor has it ever been received. *"There is someone who has his doubts about this."* When Kuei-shan says "someone," evidently this is a self-referential statement worded in an unusual way. The note comments, "All the Buddhas and ancestors since time immemorial doubt this also." This seems like a pretty emphatic statement—nothing to transmit, nothing to receive. If that's so, then what are we doing? This was the primary and central question that drove Master Dogen in his spiritual search, a question he began asking when he was fifteen years old: If we're all already enlightened, as the Buddha says, then why must we practice? Why must we do anything? It is not a new revelation to note that nothing has been transmitted, nothing has been received. This is the essence of Buddhism itself.

After saying he had some doubts about this, Kuei-shan asks Yang-shan, *"How do you understand it?"* How do you understand the transmission? The note says, "Diamond-thorned steel brambles, no ordinary monastic can leap clear of this." Keep in mind that Yang-shan's enlightenment experience with Kuei-shan had already happened. In fact, there probably were several such experiences over a course of years, each time further clarifying and refining his understanding, allowing it to mature and ripen. That process takes time; there's no way to accelerate it. Finally he was transmitted to, and yet here his teacher is still pecking at him.

I remember a very similar situation with my own teacher. It was in 1983. I was in Los Angeles for about a month completing the first phase of transmission. When it was completed and I was getting ready to come back to Mt. Tremper, I went to do a last dokusan before leaving. My teacher looked at me and said, "So, Daido, what will you bring back to your students in Mt. Tremper?" Watch out! Diamond-tipped iron brambles suddenly spring up! Should I say "Nothing"? Or, "My understanding"? Or, "Eyes horizontal, nose vertical"? In the course of my training, we'd been through all of those responses and hundreds of others. Indeed, how would you answer such a question?

He did the same thing to my Dharma brother after his transmission. When he started doing face-to-face interviews, our teacher got in the line and went in to see him. I asked him later, "What did he say?" He had said, "Teach me!" It never stops. As long as your teacher is alive, it continues, and long after your teacher is dead, it continues. Endless and continuous practice—how do *you* understand it?

Yang-shan said, "When I'm sleepy, I close my eyes and rest. When I'm feeling fine, I meditate. Therefore, I haven't ever said anything." The note says, "He holds up the sky and supports the earth. He's found his way amid the brambles. Still, it's difficult not to leave tracks." Definitely this is leaving tracks, footsteps in the sand. You can't move through the brambles without showing a sign of having passed through. *The Master replied, "To achieve this level of understanding is no easy matter."* The note says, "Neither difficult nor easy. The ancient teachings on the tips of a thousand grasses." The teachings are everywhere. There's no place they don't reach. *Yang-shan then said, "According to my understanding, even being attached to this phrase is a mistake."* The note says, "The good tracker will leave no traces." It is almost impossible to be trackless. It depends on how good the tracker who's tracking the tracker is. *The Master said, "For someone it is a mistake, too."* That is, "For me it's also a mistake to leave tracks." The note says, "When the fish swims, the water is muddied. When the bird flies, a feather falls."

Yang-shan said, "From ancient times until now, all the sages were just like this." The note says, "Like what? Is there anything to impart or not? He could have gotten out if he had kept his mouth shut, but he persisted." *The Master replied, "There is someone who laughs at your answers."* The note says, "It takes a fool to recognize a fool. Who would be laughing at these answers?" These answers are unquestionably the profound teaching of the Buddha-Dharma. When seen from the point of view of delusion, it seems like the jeweled palace. When seen with the enlightened eye, sometimes it seems funny. That's why there is so much humor in Zen—trying to protect the indestructible Dharma, trying to transmit that which is not transmittable, trying to receive that which cannot be received, trying to perfect that which is ultimately perfect, trying to complete that which lacks nothing. It's not so funny if you haven't seen it, but it's funny after you see it. That's why people laugh when they realize it. It takes a fool to recognize a fool. These two teachers are both in the same boat, both served up with the same indictment.

Yang-shan said, "The ones who are laughing at me are my colleagues." The note says, "It's all dirt from the same hole. What's the use of so much talk?" The word should be "peers"—the others who see with the same eye. Kuei-shan himself out of necessity must laugh. This is why in the *Mumonkan* collection of koans, Wu-men calls his teachers foolish and blind. Such comments are made from the point of view of realization. Wu-men is actually admiring them. It takes a lot of commitment to make an ass of yourself, and that's what both of these wonderful teachers are doing. They're like two kids sitting in mud throwing mud-balls at each other.

The Master then again persisted, "How do you understand succession?" The note says, "Again, he comes on directly. He wants everybody to know." This is what takes place in actual succession. What you read about lineage successions can be misleading and make you think that something is transmitted, that there is something to receive. There is nothing to get. There is a lot to get rid of —all our conditioning, ideas, and concepts. We've got to get rid of attachment and of non-attachment, of delusion and enlightenment.

Yang-shan walked in a circle around the Master, who was sitting in the high seat. The note says, "Deaf, dumb, and blind, he acts according to imperative." In the ceremony of transmission, circumambulation expresses the interpenetration of teacher and student, absolute and relative, enlightenment and delusion—of all the dualities that dominate our minds, our lives, and our actions. What Yang-shan did was symbolic of the 97 circular figures he was transmitted. So, why do I call it deaf, dumb, and blind? To use such words can be a positive or a negative statement. In a sense, all the Buddhas are deaf, dumb, and blind, in that they lack the ability to discriminate; they simply act in accordance with imperative. The imperative in this case is, "How do you understand succession?" Yang-shan should have turned over the high seat instead of circumambulating it, and driven that old man out into the forest with a stick. The Master said, *"That lineage transmitted uninterruptedly from ancient times to now has been broken."* The note says, "This is as it should be. What end will there ever be to it all?"

> *The Buddhas have not appeared in the world,*
> *Nor is there anything to be given to the people.*
> *There is just seeing into one's own heart and mind—*
> *This is the endless spring.*

This poem is transparent; there is very little concealed in it. The key word is perhaps "appeared." No enlightened ones have ever appeared in the world. There is no truth to be given to the people. People and Buddhas are not two separate things. Buddha-nature is the nature of all sentient beings, and the nature of all sentient beings is Buddha-nature—your nature, my nature. It's already there. It may be covered by layers of conditioning, but it's there, and the purpose of our practice is to uncover it completely. A "breakthrough" is a simple discovery. Enlightenment is seeing it through and through, seeing what has always been there, before you were born, before the Buddha was born. When you see it, you see the endless spring. You live the endless spring, the time and season of great peace. To be enlightened is to be in harmony with your life, with the life of the universe. It doesn't mean that there are no difficulties, only that there is no struggle. It doesn't mean that there is no pain, only that you know how to function in it. It doesn't mean that there are no brambles or barriers, but that you find your way through them with ease. The endless spring is the birthright of each one of us.

You've got to trust yourself and empower yourself. Keep in mind that it's not enough to just sit and wait for enlightenment to happen, because it doesn't happen. Nothing happens to you. What you do and what happens to you are the same thing. Sometimes I wish there were more I could do. My teacher would have done it for me, his teacher would have done it for him, and that's what the transmission would have been. But that's not the way it is. He had to do it for himself. I've got to do it for myself. And you have to do it for yourself.

FOUR

DECLARATION OF INTERDEPENDENCE

The Blue Cliff Record, Case 54

PROLOGUE

Transcending life and death, actualizing Zen spirit, he casually cuts through iron and nails, lightly moves heaven and earth. Tell me, whose doing can that be? Listen to the following.

THE MAIN CASE

Yün-men asked a monastic, "Where have you recently come from?" The monastic said, "From Hsi-ch'an." Yün-men said, "What words has Hsi-ch'an offered lately?" The monastic stretched out his hands. Yün-men hit him. The monastic said, "I had something to tell you." Yün-men now stretched out his own hands. The monastic was speechless. Yün-men hit him.

THE CAPPING VERSE

Controlling the head and tail of the tiger,
Exerting invincible influence.
Over the four hundred provinces,
How precipitous he is!
The master says, "One further word, I leave it open."

On July Fourth of each year we celebrate the
Declaration of Independence and with it our liberation,
our freedom. During the signing of the Declaration of
Independence, Benjamin Franklin made the comment,
"We commit our sacred honor, our fortune, and our lives
in signing this." And that was true. All the signers of that
historic document had a great deal to lose. They were very
wealthy, powerful people. They were leaders in their communities, owned property, and were highly respected.
They would have done well whether or not religious and
political suppression continued. They would have done
well in any kind of circumstance, but for them that wasn't
the point. In signing the Declaration of Independence,
they were jeopardizing everything, including their lives. If
it had not worked—if the British had been victorious—
they would have lost their property, been arrested and, in
all likelihood, executed. And yet they signed their names,
taking a great risk, and putting their lives on the line.

The risk they undertook is the same one that always
accompanies the decision to realize independence.
Freedom never arrives easily. It comes at a high price—
especially spiritual freedom. But what does spiritual freedom mean? It means we have to give up all the "stuff" we
cling to. It means we have to let go of our attachments.

Basically, that is the function of a Zen teacher: to take away all the things we hold on to, to pull the rug out from under us, to knock out the nails and collapse the structure. If we are holding on to anything, we are hindering ourselves.

People usually misunderstand non-attachment as not caring: "Zen Buddhists are nihilistic; they don't care about things." But there can't be real caring until there is letting go. If you are attached to something, you end up controlling it, manipulating it and, most significantly, separating yourself from it. You can't hold on to something unless it is something other than you. When there is no separation, there is no attachment, no holding, and nothing to hold on to, no one to do the holding. In reality, there can't really be love until there is letting go. Non-attachment doesn't mean not loving; it doesn't mean not caring. It means not attaching.

Buddhism is now in an environment where religious freedom is guaranteed by law—not just in this country, but in the West in general. In the East, Buddhism has often been at the mercy of emperors, shoguns, or whoever happened to be controlling the country at the time. It now exists in a political milieu where there is a long-standing legal guarantee of free access to and practice of religion. Because of this, we have an incredible opportunity as American Buddhists. We don't have to worry the way our predecessors did about offending the politicians or the power structure. It is a great gift and a great challenge.

What exactly is freedom? People sometimes think that freedom is simply license: anything goes, do whatever you want. But that's not real freedom; it's just self-centeredness. "I do whatever I want whenever I want because I'm so free." This is a dangerous trap. The "I-do-what-I-want" kind of freedom is just another form of oppression in that it is based on the skin-bag illusion: "Who I am is this bag of skin, and everything outside of me is the rest of the universe." That basic separation creates all our illusions and difficulties.

What I would like to see is a *Declaration of Interdependence*. It's not impossible; some great leaps in consciousness have already taken place regarding how we take care of our environment, our politics, and our society. I'd like to propose a declaration of interrelatedness, an acknowledgement of the co-origination and interpenetration of all things: interdependence with other nations, with the environment, with one another, with our children, and with our parents. Such a declaration would recognize the interdependence of the sacred and the secular. On the mountain ... in the world ... one reality, the great, all-pervading Diamond Net of Indra.

Interdependence is the meaning of actualized Zen spirit. In his introduction to this koan, Master Yüan-wu says, *He casually cuts through iron and nails, lightly moves heaven and earth.* Who is such a person? I ask *you*: Who is such a person? In a sense, Yüan-wu is speaking of Yün-men. So you might answer, "Yün-men." And if you say so, that's the way it is. But don't sell yourself short. Yün-men doesn't have anything you don't have. We are all fully equipped and basically free. The limits are our own limits, the cage is our own cage. You constructed your cage, and you are the only one who can free yourself of it. Ultimately, freedom is in your hands. Ultimately, the whole universe is in your hands, whether you realize it or not.

Yün-men asked a monastic, "Where have you recently come from?" The monastic said, "From Hsi-ch'an." Yün-men said, "What words has Hsi-ch'an offered lately?" The monastic stretched out his hands. Yün-men hit him. The monastic said, "I had something to tell you." Yün-men now stretched out his own hands. The monastic was speechless. Yün-men hit him. What is going on here? First of all, Yün-men is using what we call "the probing pole"—testing the understanding and sincerity of the student. People wonder how such qualities can possibly be tested and revealed. My question is, how can you possibly hide them? How can anybody hide where he or she is? There is no place to hide. Everything we do, everything we say, reveals us. This is why whenever new students appear in the classic koans, the master tests them, tests the depth of their understanding and clarity.

How else can the process start? How else can the teacher know where the teaching needs to begin? There are many levels of clarity. The teacher has to know how clear and genuine the student is. It's one thing to come to a monastery; it's quite another to be a student, to be involved in the search, to have entered the Way. And again, there are the words and ideas that describe it, or the belief systems that support it, and then there is the reality itself.

Yün-men immediately asks the monastic, "Where have you come from?" Where are you coming from? What is your understanding? The question also asks quite literally where the student last trained. The monastic could answer any number of ways. He could do so very subtly, the answer appearing as casual, ordinary conversation. Much of what occurs in the koans happens under the surface; there are subtleties involved. This is particularly true of the koans as originally written in Chinese. Because of the multiple meanings Chinese characters have, there is the potential for a wonderful richness in the koan. English language has a tendency to nail things down, to make them specific and exact.

Of course, life is not so exact. Things are constantly shifting. Everything is in a constant state of becoming, including ourselves. That perpetual flux frustrates and makes very problematic any attempted attachment. The instant you hold on to something, saying, "I've got it!" it changes, just like that. It changes and you change. What can we possibly hold on to? From moment to moment everything changes and evolves. This is where so much pain and suffering comes from, because the "wonderful thing" we were attached to doesn't exist anymore. The princess that we married is no longer a princess, or the prince has turned into a frog. Unless we move with the flow, we become stagnant and full of anxiety. The only thing that remains constant is the idea, the thought that we hold on to. We limit ourselves and become miserable.

"Where have you recently come from?" Master Yüan-wu who commented on this collection of koans added notes to clarify the main case. The note to this line of the koan reads, "Don't say 'Hsi-ch'an'; a probing pole. Don't say 'East, West, North, or South.'" *The monastic said, "From Hsi-ch'an."* The note: "As it turns out, he's too literal. At that moment the monastic should have given him some of his own provisions." The monastic should have revealed to Yün-men his own realization of the truth. *Yün-men said, "What words has Hsi-ch'an offered lately?"* The note: "I want to bring it up, but I fear it would startle you, teacher." *The monastic stretched out his hands.* This is what the words and phrases are at Hsi-ch'an. Note: "He's been defeated. He took in a thief and got his house ransacked. This will inevitably cause people to doubt." The thief the monastic took in was Yün-men. What is the thief's intent? To steal everything that is precious to this monastic, to take whatever it is that he's holding. Whatever it is that's most dear and most precious, Yün-men's going to take it.

And this monastic let him in his house by the answer he gave.

Yün-men hit him. The note says, "He acts according to the imperative." The monastic should be hit. Why should the monastic be hit? What's the point of the hitting? There are many different ways that hitting was used during this period of Zen history. It was used to make a point. It was also used as a sign of disapproval. And sometimes it was used to indicate approval. How can hitting be understood if that's the case? That's why people were very confused about Te-shan. If you answered affirmatively, he'd give you thirty blows of the stick. If you answered negatively, thirty blows of the stick. If you answered neither affirmatively nor negatively, thirty blows of the stick. Were all the thirty blows the same? What was the message? How did you know what this meant? After Yün-men hit him, the monastic said, "I had something to say." I'm still talking, he says. I haven't finished. The note: "So you want to change your plea?"

That "Wait a minute, I had something to say" is an attempt by the monastic to vindicate himself. In a way, it's almost an acknowledgment of defeat in this Dharma combat. Yün-men's response was to extend his hands. When he did that, the monastic was flabbergasted. The note says, "What a pity." The monastic was then silent; Yün-men hit him again. This was a punishing blow, a disapproving blow. Up to this point, Yün-men had been going along with the monastic, responding to him. We call it "following the waves." It's like a mother with an infant. The baby totters away and the mother goes right behind it. The infant doesn't know the mother is there; the mother is ready to protect the infant, while also allowing it a sense of freedom.

It is said that whenever Yün-men responded, the

"Three Phrases" were always present: *following the waves,* responding according to the circumstances; *cutting off the myriad streams,* taking away all possible intellectual interpretations, whatever is being held on to; and *encompassing heaven and earth,* including everything in totality. All three of those are in this koan and in all of Yün-men's koans.

In talking about how Zen teachers work, we often use the image of a lioness who pushes her cubs off the precipice and will only raise the ones who can climb back up. The jungle is a challenging place where only the strong and well-trained will survive. They are the ones the mother concentrates on. It seems cruel, but there is only so much anyone can do for anyone else. That's why we say there are no Zen teachers and nothing to teach. There is nothing that anybody can really give to you. It's got to happen from within yourself and your own practice.

While camping in the Catskills, I witnessed a terrific wind storm one morning. Two tiny birds fell out of a tree. I think they were members of the wren family. They weren't quite ready to fly, so the mother had a problem. She had two very vulnerable live babies on the ground. She had to do some fast teaching. The entire day was about that mother getting the young birds airborne.

Of course, they didn't realize the danger. The mother did, and she was so concerned about taking care of the young ones that she completely ignored me. I held a video camera two feet away from one of the birds, and she would fly right by me, bring an insect to it and urge it to fly. She would move away with the insect, and when the baby bird would try to reach for it, she'd give it the bug, and then flutter up a tree and call to it—*cheep-cheep! cheep-cheep!* Back and forth they would go. The bird on the ground would do this for a while, and then, just like a baby, it would get tired and stick its head under its wing and go to sleep.

The mother would go berserk. This was no time to go to sleep! She would call and call, and when that didn't work, she would bring another insect down. After a while, the baby bird tried to fly up the trunk of the tree. It would grab on and flutter a little bit, but would soon flop to the ground. The mother would start the process all over again.

If that mother could have flown for those babies, she would have. There was nothing she could do except to help them realize their own power, to help them realize that they had all the equipment necessary to do what needed to be done. But they had to learn how to use their equipment. It is the same with us. The Buddha-nature is the nature of all sentient beings. Perfect and complete. No one lacks it. But unless you know about it firsthand, unless you know how to use it, it doesn't do you any good. So you go to your grave never appreciating it, never realizing it.

There's a similar scenario in the movie *The Earthling*. The plot involves an elderly man who has a few weeks to live and decides to go back to his birthplace in Australia, to die in the little wilderness cabin where he had been raised. It is a long journey taking a couple of weeks. Meanwhile, a family of American tourists, a mother and father with a very spoiled ten-year-old boy, are exploring the outback in an RV. Suddenly, in a terrible accident, the parents are killed when their car rolls off a cliff. Only the boy survives, totally helpless, like those birds.

The old man finds the boy, and initially is angry that this has happened, that he is now burdened with responsibility for the boy. He can't turn his back on it. He knows that he is too weak to carry the boy out. The old man will not last the journey. He will die before they reach safety and the kid will starve to death. The cabin he is heading towards is in the middle of nowhere. Within a week he will be dead and the kid will be on his own, this kid who knows nothing about survival. He has to teach him, and he has to do it quickly. How?

What he starts doing seems like the cruelest thing possible. He ignores the boy. The kid is in shock, can't even talk, and the old man just ignores him. The kid follows after him. The man catches a fish and eats it. He leaves the bones, the scraps, but he won't give any meat to the kid. When the kid begs for it, the old man chases him away. He keeps moving on, and the kid keeps following. The kid keeps asking for food, but the old man won't give him any. So the kid eats the scraps from the bones. As the days pass, the old man says to the kid, "Watch what I'm doing. Learn how to build a fire. I'm not going to show you how to do it. Find out how to do it for yourself." In one way it is really awful, but what you begin to see in the man's actions is an incredibly deep compassion. Real compassion, not do-goodedness. Do-goodedness would have been to try to take care of the kid. The old man would have failed and the kid would have been at the mercy of the wilderness. This was complete, selfless compassion.... and that's a very different kind of mentality and attitude. The man was totally identified with the boy; he knew what had to be done, and he knew he couldn't do it for him. The kid had to do it. And he had a week. By the time they get to the cabin, the kid knows how to find his direction in the wilderness, how to build a shelter, how to make a fire, how to catch fish—how to survive and how to get out of there. The man dies, the boy buries him and sets off on his own. The lesson is complete.

The lesson for the birds was no different. The mother couldn't do it for her fledglings. In Zen training it is no different. The teacher can't do it for the student. Buddha can't do it for the student. The only one who can do it is you. And the reason why only you can do it is that the barriers are created by you. The cage, the restrictions are created by each one of us. We alone have the power to put an end to the struggle. The teacher can use all kinds of skillful encouragement, just as the mother used the insects and the chirping and the fluttering around. The woodsman did the same thing with the boy. But that's as far as it goes. Ultimately, the whole matter rests with you. If you don't empower yourself, you become dependent on whatever the source of power is. The only kind of empowerment is self-empowerment. The only kind of liberation is self-liberation.

Why did Yün-men hit the monastic? What is this extending of the hands? What does it mean? When the monastic said, "I had something to say," why did Yün-men spread his hands? This practice is not a charade. It can't be accomplished by imitating the honchos. It can't be accomplished by memorizing the sutras or by passing koans. Ultimately the lotus must bloom in the fire—in the kitchen, the nursery, the marketplace, and the office as well as in the Buddha Hall.

We should be grateful for the opportunity of coming into contact with this wondrous Way, for the chance to practice and to do so with others. We should really appreciate ourselves and each other. We should let it work, let it manifest. Give it half a chance and you will understand what is meant by "cutting through iron and nails, moving heaven and earth." You will be able to combust your lives with ease, with the same ease that you grow your hair or draw a breath.

That freedom is not something you "get." It cannot be acquired. This is the key point. Freedom is something that you have. It doesn't matter whether you're in a prison, a concentration camp, or a free country. That inherent freedom cannot be given and cannot be taken away. It is yours. It is you. But if you don't realize it, you can't use it. Please realize it. This life is too important to waste.

FIVE

CHAO-CHOU'S MU

Gateless Gate,
Case 1

THE MAIN CASE

A monastic once asked Master Chao-chou, "Has a dog the Buddha-nature or not?" Chao-chou said, "Mu!"

COMMENTARY

In studying Zen, one must pass the barriers set up by ancient masters. For the attainment of incomparable satori, one has to cast away one's discriminating mind. Those who have not passed the barrier and have not cast away the discriminating mind are all phantoms haunting trees and plants.

Now tell me, what is the barrier of the ancient masters? Just this Mu—it is the barrier of Zen. It is thus called "the gateless barrier of Zen." Those who have passed the barrier will not only see Chao-chou clearly, but will go hand in hand with all of the great masters of the past and see them face to face. You will see with the same eyes that they see with, and hear with the same ears. Wouldn't it be wonderful? Don't you want to pass the barrier? Then concentrate yourself into this Mu, with your 360 bones and 84,000 pores, making your whole body one great inquiry. Day and night work intently at it. Do not attempt nihilistic or dualistic interpretations. It's like having bolted a red-hot iron ball. You try to vomit it but cannot.

Cast away your illusory discriminating knowledge and consciousness accumulated up until now, and keep on working harder. After awhile, when your efforts come to fruition, all the oppositions, such as in and out, will naturally be identified. You will then be like a dumb person who has had a wonderful dream: they only know it personally, within themselves. Suddenly you break through the barrier; you astonish heaven and shake the earth.

It is as if you had snatched the great sword of General Kan. You kill the Buddha if you meet him; you kill the ancient masters if you meet them. On the brink of life and death you are utterly free, and in the six realms and four modes of life you live with great joy, a genuine life in complete freedom.

Now, how should one strive? With might and main work at this Mu, and be Mu. If you do not stop or waver in your striving, then behold, when the Dharma candle is lighted, darkness is at once enlightened.

THE CAPPING VERSE

The dog! The Buddha-nature!
The truth is manifested in full.
A moment of yes-and-no:
Lost are your body and soul.

To give a talk on Mu seems almost like carrying coals to Newcastle. There are several excellent commentaries on this koan by various teachers. Still, there are so many people working on Mu that it feels appropriate to give this case a thorough going over. The general instructions for working with Mu apply to all other koans, both those from the ancient collections that make up our formal koan study, and the koans of everyday life, the barriers that we seem to come up against spontaneously in living our lives. What follows are very rough guidelines, because each person necessarily evolves his or her own method for working with a koan. In the trial-and-error process of doing zazen, sitting on the dokusan line, going to face-to-face teachings, one begins to develop a way of communicating with the intuitive aspect of consciousness, and that is a very personal and idiosyncratic process.

Mu is usually the first koan used at this training center. For most students it represents the first opportunity to personally engage a koan. It is introduced after students have been working with the breath for about a year, and have found their bearing. It marks entry into the second stage of spiritual training. People in the first stage are getting oriented, learning how to sit, moving past the barrier of pain, and beginning to develop *joriki*, the power of concentration.

One of the key prerequisites to working with Mu is established through the initial work with the breath. It is essential to lay that firm foundation of experiencing the breath completely, staying focused. That focused concentration builds the power of *joriki* and allows access to *samadhi*, true one-pointed concentration. *Joriki* taps our physical, mental, and emotional reserves, and opens up our spiritual capacities. We have an incredible physical power that we never use. You see it demonstrated in extraordinary situations. When a 10-year–old boy weighing less than 90 pounds lifts a car off the chest of his father, where did that burst of strength come from? Or when a mother picks the back wheels of a truck off her child pinned underneath it? Physiologically, that power comes from adrenalin. In cases of emergency, in times of extreme stress, the body gets pumped up with adrenalin. This increases muscle strength, visual acuity, and reflexive responses. The capillaries pull back from the surface of the skin so that if you're cut you don't bleed as profusely. It's a highly intensified state. When it passes, the adrenalin is still there, and you remain shaky for a while.

That power is always available. We just don't know how to access it except in those automatic responses to acute stress which are beyond our control. In modern times this has become very debilitating. The stress factor we experience during an argument with a boss or a spouse fills us with the power great enough to deal with a saber-toothed tiger, but we usually can't do anything about it except to sit with the stress, unable to process it. People end up hurting themselves with it.

The same power and intensity become freely accessible in a positive, healing way when we develop *joriki*. There's a karate student who comes to the Monastery, a young woman who probably weighs no more than 110 pounds. There's nothing particularly extraordinary about her physique. She has regular skinny arms like the rest of us and is not at all muscle-bound. Yet she breaks two cinder blocks with her elbow. If you examine her elbow, it's an old-fashioned elbow. There are no calluses on it, no swelling. She can leap into the air—what looks like seven feet up—and with her foot break three boards held by a student who stands on the shoulders of another student. She's less than 5 feet tall. Where does that ability and focus come from? How do you tap into it?

It's the same with mental power. *Joriki* begins to open up our mental clarity, the ability to see with a broad perspective and the ability to penetrate complexities. We also develop emotional stability, an acute awareness of other beings, and other people's feelings, of what they're projecting, what they're communicating beyond words. Most importantly, spiritual power emerges out of *joriki*. It unblocks and opens up the intuitive aspect of consciousness, the right hemisphere of the brain.

The human form is absolutely magnificent when it's fully developed and engaged. Most of us, even geniuses and special people, go through life using only a small portion of our human potential. According to scientific studies, we only use some five percent of our brain on the average. Even Einstein used only a small part of his capacity as a human being.

It is difficult to fully appreciate what incredibly powerful resources we have when fully developed. When we take that potential and turn it into wisdom and compassion, what a wonderful creature the human being can be. We all have the potential to do it, but it is a very rare occurrence. It is within the grasp of each one of us to fully realize the Buddha-nature. In spite of using so little of our potential, we accomplish so much. Still, human achievements are a little lopsided. We know about the distant planets, the vast reaches of space, and the subatomic particles. We know about computers and light-speed communication. We can access and harness nuclear energy. We have mastered complex mathematics, and revolutionized medicine. Yet we know precious little about the most vital of matters—the nature of the self, of who we are, of what our life is, of how to live it. That is what our practice is primarily and ultimately about. To study the Buddha Way is to study the self, to find out who we are.

It is only when the student has cultivated sufficient *samadhi*, and there is the beginning of "falling away of body and mind," that Mu is introduced. You work with a koan the same way you work with the breath. Your attention is in the *hara*, in the viscera, and that's where you put Mu, that's where you put any koan. The *hara* is the physical and the spiritual center of the body. Each time you inhale, the diaphragm pulls down and the belly rises. Your lungs fill with air and you fill yourself with Mu. On the exhalation your total concentration goes to Mu itself, so you exhale Mu. Inhale Mu, exhale Mu. In taking the powerful energy developed through *joriki* and directing it at a koan, you have the necessary ingredients to break through, to see the koan.

What automatically and immediately happens during the early stages of practice is that we go into our usual, deeply ingrained mode of problem solving. How do we solve a problem? All of our education and most of our experiences teach us to use the left hemisphere of the brain, the domain of linear, sequential thought. We try to figure things out. In the process of working with a koan, we end up exhausting our habitual way of using the mind. Koans are specifically designed to frustrate and short-circuit the intellect. You can't solve a koan by linear, sequential thought. It takes an intuitive leap. It takes activation of an aspect of consciousness that we rarely use, that is largely dormant and underdeveloped. Our educational system is one of the finest in the world, and we've attended very thoroughly to the left hemisphere of the brain; but there is another, direct and intuitive half to our life that is far more important and relevant than that which can be accessed using only linear, sequential thinking.

It is not only in exploring spiritual areas that the direct, intuitive aspect of consciousness is necessary. It also plays a significant role in art and science. All of the great scientific discoveries were made by an intuitive leap. When Newton came forth with calculus, he developed it as an afterthought. When he shared with a friend his theories about the existence of a previously unnoticed planet that he had intuited, the friend said, "Can you prove it?" Newton said, "I think maybe I could," but since the mathematics of the day couldn't handle the task, he invented calculus. Einstein rode a light beam into space with his brilliant mind in order to develop the theory of relativity. The proofs came later. But you don't read about those intuitive leaps. It's hard to describe them in scientific journals, in technical jargon. In a scientific journal, you have to be scientific. After the discovery is complete, you have to communicate it to other people, so you make it logical. You condense the vast appreciation into a linear explanation. Then the students come along and think that this is the way you do science, logically. Very little science is done in a linear, sequential way. Most formidable barriers are penetrated with one incredible leap, with a profound shift of consciousness.

When students start working with Mu, they first try various intellectual responses. It's important to exhaust them so that they can be put to rest and gotten out of the way. What usually follows, if the students have been reading Zen literature, are all kinds of crazy presentations—crazy talk, crazy gestures, crazy actions. This, too, exhausts itself. It may take a while but eventually the person becomes ready to get down to business. Then we start really working on the koan. Finally there comes that quantum leap. In subatomic physics, when you put energy into an electron, it doesn't change its orbit until the energy reaches a certain threshold that is sufficient for the particle to jump to the next energy level. It does that in a quantum leap, not gradually or partially. Something similar to that quantum leap happens with a breakthrough in koan study. But before it happens, a lot of energy needs to be generated. It takes an instant for water to go from non-boiling to boiling. The shift represents but a fraction of a degree in temperature, but you've got to put a lot of kilocalories per molecule into the pot of water to bring it to that threshold, so the boiling can happen. The development of *joriki* and the early experiences of *samadhi*, cultivated in the first stage of training, are likewise essential in order to effectively work with a koan, any koan, but particularly Mu.

Historically, Mu dates back to the great Master Chao-chou. Chao-chou was an extraordinary teacher who lived during the T'ang Dynasty, the Golden Age of Chinese Zen. He was a student of Master Nan-ch'üan. He first came to Nan-ch'üan as a young boy. He was ordained at a very early age, as was usual during those days, and studied Buddhism. Then, when he was about 18 years old, he again visited Master Nan-ch'üan. The time was somewhere around the later part of the 700s. When Chao-chou got to see Nan-ch'üan, the Master wasn't feeling well and was resting in bed. As Chao-chou approached him lying in bed, Nan-ch'üan, as is always the case, immediately started testing him. "Where have you been recently?" he asked Chao-chou, the usual opening question. Chao-chou said, "At Zuiso." Zuiso, literally translated, means "auspicious image." Nan-ch'üan said to him, "Did you then see the auspicious image?" Chao-chou responded, "I didn't see the image, but I have seen a reclining Tathagata." Nan-ch'üan sat up in bed, looked at him carefully and said, "Do you already have a master to study under or not?" Chao-chou replied, "I have." Nan-ch'üan said, "Who is he?" At this Chao-chou came closer to Nan-ch'üan, and bowing to him, said, "I'm glad to see you are so well, in spite of such a severe cold." Nan-ch'üan recognized his unusual character, and accepted him as a disciple. Immediately, Nan-ch'üan knew he was dealing with someone remarkable. Chao-chou carried out his studies under Nan-ch'üan, and while still very young came to full realization. He continued studying with Nan-ch'üan, and many of the koans that involve Chao-chou took place at Nan-ch'üan's monastery. He was with his teacher until he was 57 years old. At that time, Master Nan-ch'üan died. The great persecution of Buddhism was just beginning in China.

After Nan-ch'üan's death, Chao-chou stayed on for a few more years at that monastery, and then, in his sixtieth year, he started off on a journey that was to take him all over China to various temples and monasteries. Setting off on the pilgrimage, Chao-chou said, "I'll go anywhere to study under anyone, no matter how young, if they've got something to teach me, and I'll go anywhere to teach anyone, no matter how old, if I have something to teach them." He continued the journey until he was 80 years old. At 80 he finally settled down in the village of Chao-chou, where he began teaching. He taught from age 80 to 120.

I remember when I first started reading these koans and saw that Chao-chou lived to be 120 years old, I thought that maybe they just didn't keep good records in those days. I thought, people just don't live to be 120 years old; it must have been an exaggeration because he was such a special teacher. But actually, people do live to be that old. NBC News every morning announces birthdays of people over 100 years old, and recently they introduced a man who is 121, alive and well.

The extraordinary thing about Chao-chou is his beginner's mind, his student attitude. After all those years studying with Nan-ch'üan, and being his attendant, being with him all the time, he was still ready to keep on learning. Nan-ch'üan was one of the great masters of the period, one of the 84 enlightened disciples of Ma-tsu. Chao-chou worked with him for 40 years, and then went out to study, polish, and clarify his understanding further with other teachers during his twenty-year-long journey. He finally settled down only when he was 80, and then taught for another 40 years. As far as I've been able to find out, and I'm not positive about this, he did not have any successors. I can imagine it would be pretty difficult to satisfy a teacher like that with your understanding. An extraordinary human being.

In this koan, a monastic comes to Master Chao-chou and says, "Has a dog Buddha-nature or not?" Clearly, this monastic would have been aware of the fact that all sentient beings, without exception, have the Buddha-nature. He was either a seasoned adept, who was asking a question that was unapproachable, or a monastic who was very confused about it. The koan does not say too much about the monastic. He simply asks the question. Chao-chou, before the words are even out of the monastic's mouth, answers, "Mu." "Mu" literally means "no." It's a negation, and people attach to that, looking for some kind of meaning. But we should keep in mind that Chao-chou, as is recorded in *The Book of Equanimity*, goes further into this question and offers seemingly contradictory responses. A monastic asked, "Does a dog have Buddha-nature or not?" Chao-chou said, "Mu." The monastic continued, "All sentient beings have Buddha-nature—why does a dog have none?" Chao-chou replied, "Because he still has impulsive consciousness." On another occasion, a monastic asked Chao-chou, "Does a dog have Buddha-nature or not?" The Master answered, "U"—"Yes." The monastic said, "Having the Buddha-nature, why is he in such a dog body?" Chao-chou answered, "Knowingly, he dares to be so." I deal with the complexities of these two questions and answers in the next chapter. Here, it is important to appreciate that a simple search for meaning is not sufficient to grasp Mu.

In order to really penetrate the koan, you must enter the state of mind of this particular student. Imagine that instead of being a Buddhist monastic he was a Catholic who had spent many years in a monastery, studying the scriptures. At some point he started to struggle with a question deep inside himself. The great doubt arose. It might have surfaced as an inquiry into God's existence. To put the gnawing doubt to rest, the monastic started an overland journey to Rome. It was a difficult trip to a distant part of the country, through mountains, rivers, and valleys. He risked his life in the undertaking. When he arrived in Rome to have the audience with the Pope, he was made to wait. He had to get through the barriers, the barrier gates. Finally, he found himself face to face with the Pope and asked the fundamental question that's at the heart of the teachings of his religion. "Father, is there a God?" The Pope looked at him and said, "No." Can you imagine the state of the monastic's consciousness? That's what it was like for this monastic who knew from the scriptures that all sentient beings have the Buddha-nature. All things have the Buddha-nature. Yet Chao-chou, the great teacher, as clear as a master could be, says no, the dog doesn't have it.

Anyone who works on this koan, needs to approach it and treat it as a question of life and death. That's one of the reasons why the entry barriers exist, to determine if clear, driving motivation is present at the outset. Unless it's a question of life and death, working with a koan is almost a waste of time. It becomes some sort of a clever riddle. The koan is not a riddle. This Mu goes to the heart of our very existence. In a sense, it's like saying that the ten thousand things, the whole universe, every planet, every star, every sound, every atom, every molecule, every thought, every color can be reduced to this one thing, and we provisionally call it Mu. What is Mu?

The instructions Wu-men gives for working on Mu are applicable not just to Mu, but to any koan. He says in his commentary, *In studying Zen, one must pass the barriers set up by ancient masters. For the attainment of incomparable satori, one has to cast away one's discriminating mind. Those who have not passed the barrier and have not cast away the discriminating mind are all phantoms haunting trees and plants.* Although the koan Mu is only one line long, Wu-men's commentary goes on for several paragraphs. This is very unusual for the *Gateless Gate* collection. For Wu-men, this was an important koan. He spent six years investigating Mu before he broke through it and had a great *satori*. He named his collection *Gateless Gate* and also called Mu itself the gateless gate, the no-gate barrier. To him seeing Mu was a pivotal experience.

Those who have not passed the barrier and have not cast

away the discriminating mind are all phantoms haunting trees and plants. Not to realize one's own true nature is to live one's life as a ghost, not having any real substance. It means continually struggling with all of one's baggage. The illusion that the self is something separate and distinct from the rest of the universe is the basis of *duhkha*, suffering, the first of the Four Noble Truths which formed the first teachings of the Buddha. Master Dogen calls them the Four Wisdoms. The First Wisdom is that life is suffering. How extraordinary that he chose to start turning the wheel of the Dharma with that statement. It has always fascinated me how simple, absolutely true, and fundamental this statement is. The Second Wisdom is that the cause of suffering is due to what we call thirst, or desire, and that thirst or desire is based on the illusion that the self is separated from the thing it desires. When you realize that there's no separation, then you realize that there is nothing to attain. There is no inside or outside. Desire becomes an absurdity. Your way of relating to things becomes intimate and completely personal. The Third Wisdom is that it is possible to put an end to suffering. The Fourth Wisdom is how to do it. In the practice of Zen, passing through the barriers set up by the ancient masters is the Way. "What is the barrier of the ancient masters?" Just this Mu. *Muuuuuuuuuuuuuu.* With the whole body and mind *be* Mu.

Wu-men says, *Those who have passed the barrier will not only see Chao-chou clearly, but will go hand in hand with all of the great masters of the past and see them face to face.* To see Mu means to forget the self, and to forget the self is to be enlightened by the ten thousand things. The ten thousand things include not only the whole phenomenal universe of the present, but also the past and the future. Once we free ourselves from the bag of skin, there are no boundaries in any direction or dimension. We see Chao-chou face-to-face, the Buddha face-to-face, the past seven Buddhas face-to-face, Maitreya Buddha face-to-face. We walk hand in hand with every ancestor. We're as boundless as the universe itself, as boundless as being and time itself. That's why I say this Mu is the heart of the great matter. That's why it was so incredibly important for Master Wu-men to share this with his descendants.

You will see with the same eyes that they see with, and hear with the same ears.... Then concentrate yourself into this Mu, with your 360 bones and 84,000 pores, making your whole body one great inquiry. Don't be misled by the ancient Chinese physiology. They just didn't know how many bones and pores people had. It doesn't matter. These numbers mean the whole being. It means to absorb Mu into every cell, every molecule, every atom of yourself.

Day and night work intently at it. Do not attempt nihilistic or dualistic interpretations. It's not something outside of you and neither is it nothing. It is something, definitely and precisely something. Something that you should get to know intimately, something that you should get to know with the whole body and mind. *It's like having bolted a red-hot iron ball. You try to vomit it but cannot.* You try to swallow it, but you can't. You can't go forward, you can't go back.

Cast away your illusory discriminating knowledge and consciousness accumulated up until now, and keep on working harder. Let body and mind fall away. That's why it's so important to have developed the sound footing in *joriki* and *samadhi*. The power of concentration then becomes a very important edge that you use to work unwaveringly on Mu.

After awhile, when your efforts come to fruition, all the oppositions, such as in and out, will naturally be identified.

You will then be like a dumb person who has had a wonderful dream: they only know it personally, within themselves. Suddenly you break through the barrier; you astonish heaven and shake the earth. It is as if you had snatched the great sword of General Kan. You kill the Buddha if you meet him; you kill the ancient masters if you meet them. You don't put another head on top of yourself, on top of the one you already have. You already know; you've realized that you yourself are the master of your existence. But more important than even that is the realization that what you do and what happens to you are the same thing. Therefore, what you've realized is responsibility. You're responsible not only for your life, but for the life of the whole universe, for the life of all the Buddhas and ancestors past, present, and future.

When you realize that responsibility, nothing that you encounter or do is a burden. You're not carrying the whole universe, trying to support it. You *are* the whole universe. You realize freedom, because you can no longer blame anyone. You can no longer be a victim. You can no longer say, "She made me angry," because you know through your own experience that only you can make you angry. That is extremely liberating. There is nothing you can do when someone else makes you angry, but there is definitely something you can do when you realize that only you can make you angry. That realization gives you power. That's what it means to realize yourself. Literally, what *kensho* means is to see the nature of the self. It's not this bag of skin. That's the smallest part of who you are. The bag of skin comes and goes. The bag of skin that sits there now is not the same bag of skin that was there when you were three months old. Nothing about it is the same —you don't look the same, you don't act the same, you don't feel the same, you don't think the same. The apparent temporal continuity of the self is part of the illusion of selfness. Self is an idea, and when you break past that idea and realize Mu with the whole body and mind, the self is forgotten, and you astonish the heavens and shake the earth.

It is as if you've snatched the great sword of General Kan. You kill the Buddha if you meet him; you kill the ancient masters if you meet them. There is nothing outside yourself. You contain the Buddha, the ancient masters, the ten thousand things. There's no place to put this gigantic body. That's why it becomes so very personal. This planet and its inhabitants, the people, the flora, the fauna—it's all very intimate. *On the brink of life and death you are utterly free, and in the six realms and four modes of life you live with great joy, a genuine life in complete freedom.* Once and for all you break the cycle of birth and death. What is it that's born? What is it that dies? When you realize the nature of the self, the true nature of the self, you understand what the Buddha's teaching really means when it says that birth is the unborn, and death is the unextinguished.

Now, how should one strive? With might and main work at this Mu, and be Mu. How do you be Mu? *Muuuuuuuuuuuuuuu.* With the whole body and mind. Every thought—Mu. Every action—Mu. Mu sits, Mu walks, Mu works, Mu bows, Mu chants. Nothing outside it. The last thought before you fall off to sleep—Mu. The first thought upon waking up—Mu. These instructions are for a person working full time in a monastery. When you're working on it away from the monastery, outside of a sesshin, it is important just to follow Mu, to maintain contact with it. If you were to work on it with this kind of depth, day and night—walking, sleeping, working, eating—it could become dangerous. You could hurt yourself.

If you try to drive a car and do Mu, you can run into problems. You need to do what you're doing while you're doing it. And when it's time to practice Mu, you need to be able to do Mu with the whole body and mind. When it's time to work with a chain saw and cut wood, be with the chain saw cutting wood. Otherwise, we'll have pieces of you to work with.

If you understand how to work with Mu, you basically understand how to work with any koan. I'm not talking just about the classical koans that come to us from ancient collections, but also the *genjo-koans*, the koans that we face in everyday life. We come up against them all the time, and most of the tough barriers we confront as our everyday-life koans are not problems that can be solved rationally. They're not questions that you can access with linear, sequential thought and come up with an answer. They demand an intuitive leap. Most of the stuff that we struggle with is emotional. We're very attached to and invested in it. It's hard to make that intuitive leap. It takes training. It takes practice. Knowing how to work with a koan means chewing it up, digesting it, and assimilating it into the whole body—every cell. Only then can you make that intuitive leap that's beyond discriminating consciousness.

The student needs to infuse the koan with great faith, faith in one's self, faith in one's ability to penetrate the koan, to see it. Faith in the process he or she is engaging, a process that's been handed down for 2,500 years. Alive and functioning, this process has guided thousands of men and women though the centuries to great realization. Great faith needs to be coupled with great doubt. It must be just as boundless, just as vast and without edges. It must be a constant questioning: Who am I? What is life? What is truth? What is reality? What is God? These questions are no different from What is Mu? What is the sound of one hand clapping? What is your original face? They all deal with the ultimate nature of reality. They all have to do with the ground of being. The cutting edge that is applied to the dynamic tension between great doubt and great faith is provided by great determination. In the words of the great Master Bodhidharma, "Seven times knocked down, eight times get up." Nothing is going to stop you. It doesn't matter how long it takes, it doesn't matter how much effort needs to be put into it—you're going to do it. No question about it. Indeed, if you have great faith, great doubt, and great determination, sooner or later, you'll see it. If you truly have great doubt, great faith and great determination, realization is just a matter of time. These are the three pillars upon which our practice rests.

Determination must be unstoppable. But it can take many different forms. For some people it needs to be ferocious. Some people come into practice ferocious, and they practice Mu ferociously. Some people come into practice gentle, and they practice Mu gently. It doesn't always have to be like a big boiler about to explode. It depends on the individual's personality. It's the same with encouragement. With some people, the more you poke at them, the more it gets them going and they break through. With other people, if you push them hard, they crumble. The process needs to be approached skillfully. There are no generalizations. If there were generalizations, we could publish a cookbook—15 steps to enlightenment. That's why we need teachers. Everybody is unique and the teachings are dealt with one-to-one, face-to-face.

Great determination is like a flowing river; just like the waters of this mountain inevitably finding their way to the great ocean—there's no way to stop them. Rain falls and the rain fills Basho Pond. The pond overflows and feeds Esopus Stream. The water works its way down to the Hudson River. One day people decide to build a dam. The Ashokan Valley, which was a little village, is flooded. The level of the water keeps on rising. A great lake appears. No matter how high the dam is, the Esopus continues to fill it. It always finds its way to the Hudson River, and from the Hudson River into the great ocean. It does it as tumbling torrents. It does it as a gentle stream. Either way is okay. But it is unstoppable. There's no way that anything is going to prevent you from breaking through that koan.

While students are working with the first koan, the student-teacher relationship is at the stage where the teacher has pulled back and is withholding support. Students must find their own practice. Here, great faith, great doubt, and great determination become indispensable. At the beginning of training, during the first year or so, when the student is working on the breath, the teacher is supportive, positive, and encouraging. But if that continued, all one would end up with is a dependent student, not a free person. Sooner or later the dependent framework has to be dismantled, but that only makes sense and is appropriate when the student is strong enough to stand on her or his own two feet. At such a time the teacher pulls out the rug. Down goes the student. If necessary the teacher again becomes supportive and encouraging. When the student is strong enough to be standing, out comes the rug again. Down the student goes. This process is repeated until the time when the rug gets pulled and the student doesn't fall. Each time the student enters the interview room, the teacher is demending, "What is it? Don't tell me! Show me!" The students have only themselves to turn back to. They fall back on their own resources. It's self-empowering, and little by little the students discover their own source.

Nobody can fly for you. You have to do it yourself. Every mother bird knows when the time comes for the fledglings that she's been feeding for weeks to leave the nest. She sits on a nearby limb, holding a worm, enticing them to the edge of the nest. They're hungry, chirping and crying. And she just sits there as if she doesn't have a drop of compassion or love in her heart. Her little ones are fluttering and getting all excited, and she's just dangling the worm. Finally they can't take it anymore, and they leap out of the nest, and the minute their wings hit the air—flight happens. They didn't even know they had wings. They don't know anything about flying or aerodynamics. They never read a book. Sometimes one or two birds won't respond to the encouragement, and the mother will actually push them out to get them airborne. They need to fly to live. She can feed them, she can take care of them and keep them warm, but there comes a point when they have to take over and fly by themselves. So it is with the human species. Our unbounded freedom is inherent. We're born with it but we need to discover it; not in books, not listening to lectures, but in our experience. No one can give it to us, because we already have it.

When you are confronting a teacher who has withdrawn support, you can plunge into depths of great doubt. That's what gulping down that red-hot iron ball is all about. It's stuck in your throat. Great determination and great faith keep driving you back into the interview room. Rejection sends you away. More doubt. You go deeper. Nothing and nobody can stop you, because you're convinced that you're going to see it. You *know* that you're going to see it. Finally, the emotions are exhausted, and the intellect comes to its extreme. There's not a crack left for discrimination to enter. It's a very intense spiritual state of mind. When it's hot, the whole universe is hot. When it's cold, the whole universe is cold. When you see, you see intimately, with the whole body and mind. When you hear, you hear intimately, with the whole body and mind. No discrimination. There's no seer, no thing that the seer sees. There's no hearer, no thing that the hearer hears. There's just hearing completely, seeing completely. No room for thought.

In that state, Wu-men says, keep on going straight forward. "The illusory discriminating consciousness accumulated up until now" refers to our dualistically working mind. No trace of it remains. You become transparent, lucid, like a clear crystal. Subject and object, inside and outside, being and nonbeing are all reduced to one thing. And even this One ceases to be any longer, because there is no knower, and no thing that the knower knows. The witness disappears, the witness that sits there all the time with you saying, "This is a good sitting. The last one wasn't so good. The next one's going to be better. You're doing fine. You're doing poorly. What are you going to say in interview? Well, you'd better think about it."

Finally, Mu is awakened to itself. Wu-men describes the experience of someone who has broken through that barrier. You will then be like a dumb person who has had a wonderful dream: they only know it personally, within themselves. *Suddenly you break through the barrier; you astonish heaven and shake the earth.* It's called attaining incomparable *satori*, or dying the Great Death. When you die once, you can never die again. It's the death of the ego, the death of the idea of a self. When your eye is open, just as Wu-men said, all beings on earth have opened their eyes. Or as Buddha himself proclaimed at his own enlightenment, "All sentient beings and I have simultaneously realized the Way."

It is as if you had snatched the great sword of General Kan. You kill the Buddha if you meet him; you kill the ancient masters if you meet them. On the brink of life and death you are utterly free, and in the six realms and four modes of life you live with great joy, a genuine life in complete freedom. It may be more accurate to say that the sword of General Kan is the sword of Manjushri. You snatch the sword of Manjushri, the weapon of wisdom and compassion, away from him. Wisdom is to realize the self. Compassion is the activity of that realization in the world. There's no way that one can exist without the other. They're interdependent, mutually arising. Now you find the sword in your own hands.

At the moment of breaking through the barrier, the world, oneself, and everything changes. It's like one who was born blind acquiring sight. Being absolutely free, you are now able to see and hear everything, just as it is. Wu-men says, "Mount Sumeru jumps up and dances." Only when you experience it yourself can you really appreciate what Wu-men is saying. In a sense, nothing changes, absolutely nothing changes except your way of perceiving it, your way of perceiving yourself and the universe. The view is no longer based on the dualistic separation of self and other, and that little change is incredibly profound. The permutations and combinations that are the result of that shift are staggering. It takes a lifetime of practice to realize them completely, to appreciate what it means to have seen Mu. All of the rest of the koan system, all 700 or 2,000 of the cases, are simply a process of refining what's originally seen in Mu.

MASTER WU-MEN'S POEM:

The dog! The Buddha-nature!
The truth is manifested in full.
A moment of yes-and-no:
Lost are your body and soul.

The dog! The Buddha-nature! What else do we need? As it is, just as it is, it's Mu. As they are, just as they are, nothing but Mu. *The truth is manifested in full.* Wu-men continues, *A moment of yes-and-no: Lost are your body and soul.* If even a single thought comes up, heaven and earth are separated. People misunderstand this line to mean that discriminating thinking is of no value. Thinking is one of the most important qualities of human consciousness, this ability to use our minds in a rational, logical way, to deduce and to communicate. But it is only one aspect of our being. We should appreciate that thoroughly. There is a whole other dimension of consciousness.

All negativity arises out of dualistic thinking, out of the separations and categorizations that we have created. When viewed with the eye of compassion, when viewed with the eye that doesn't discriminate, they are seen in a very different, spacious way. When both of those domains are fully activated and are working simultaneously, in balance, our way of manifesting ourselves in the world is completely transformed. The world doesn't change. Discrimination is going to continue, but we learn how to be free within that, how to function without hindrance in the mind. No hindrance and therefore no fear; no anxiety, greed, anger, or ignorance. It is important to know how to discriminate. If you don't, you won't be able to get across the street without getting hit by a car. You won't be able to use a chain saw, because you might cut off your leg, seeing no distinction between it and a branch of the tree. But at the same time, we need to know the limits of discrimination. We need to appreciate that it is just one mode of functioning. The truth of this great universe is that there is no separation. What you do to others, you do to yourself. There is no way to affect one aspect of this universe without affecting the totality of it, no matter how small or insignificant the part. In birth not a single speck is added to this great universe, and in death, not a single speck is lost from this universe.

So how will you work with Mu? Be Mu. Be the koan. Be the breath. Be your life. To study the Buddha Way is to study the self, to study the self is to forget the self, and to forget the self is to be enlightened by the ten thousand things. To be enlightened by the ten thousand things *is* Mu. Cast off body and mind, self and other, and enter into Mu. Be it. Take off the blinders. Unload the baggage. Make yourself free. No, not make yourself free—realize that, right from the beginning, from the beginningless beginning, you have been free. What a wonderful gift it is to be born human. Do you see? *Muuuuuuuuuuuuuuuu.* What else can be said?

CHAO-CHOU'S DOG

The Book of Equanimity, Case 18

PROLOGUE

> *A gourd floating on the water—push it down and it turns. A jewel in the sunlight—it has no definite shape. It cannot be attained by mindlessness, nor known by mindfulness. Immeasurably great people are turned about in the stream of words—is there anyone who can escape?*

THE MAIN CASE

> *A monastic asked Chao-chou, "Does a dog have Buddha-nature or not?" Chao-chou said, "Yes." The monastic said, "Since it has, why is it then in this skin bag?" Chao-chou said, "Because he knows, yet deliberately transgresses." Another monastic asked Chao-chou,*

77

"Does a dog have Buddha-nature or not?" Chao-chou said, "No." The monastic said, "All sentient beings have Buddha-nature—why does a dog have none, then?" Chao-chou said, "Because he still has impulsive consciousness."

The Capping Verse

A dog's Buddha-nature exists, a dog's Buddha-nature does not exist;
A straight hook basically seeks fish with abandon.
Chasing the air, pursuing fragrance, cloud and water travelers—
In noisy confusion they make excuses and explanations.
Making an even presentation, he throws the shop wide open;
Don't blame him for not being careful in the beginning—
Pointing out the flaw, he takes away the jewel;
The king of Chin didn't know Lian Xiangru.

Every once in a while I like to present this koan and air it out for the benefit of the people working on Mu. In the *Gateless Gate* collection of koans, Wu-men deals with the bare-bones version of this case: *A monastic asked Chao-chou, "Does a dog have Buddha-nature or not?" Chao-chou said, "Mu."* Mu here means "no." That's the end of it. That's all that Wu-men chose to introduce as the first koan.

The Book of Equanimity contains the above, expanded record of the exchanges between Chao-chou and the monastics. In fact, in the compilation of Chao-chou's writings, these two instances are not even listed together. They're two different encounters. Combining them into a single koan is a useful way of dealing with one of Chao-chou's teachings.

It is also vitally important to engage Wu-men's distilled version of the koan. Doing so serves as the cornerstone of the koan practice in our lineage. In the Korean lineage Mu is the only koan students work with, studying its various permutations. Students working with a koan like Mu, or any koan for that matter, have to throw themselves totally into the koan, with the whole body and mind. They have to become the koan, losing themselves completely in this Mu. What is wonderful about Mu is that it's completely ungraspable. When the teacher says to be Mu, the student has no idea what this Mu is. How can I be it? It's not tangible or accessible. The other formal introductory koans—"the sound of one hand clapping" and "your original face before your parents were born" have the same attributes.

To really work with a koan and do it effectively means thoroughly immersing oneself in every aspect of the koan. I have a feeling that in the West "Chao-chou's Mu" has nowhere near the same impact that it had in China during Chao-chou's days, or even nowhere near the impact it would have had in Japan, with a Japanese Zen practitioner. You have to appreciate the fact that the monastic in this koan did a lot of traveling to get to Chao-chou to ask this question. For him it was an incredibly important question. His very existence hinged on it. He risked his life journeying across China to reach this eminent authority and lay himself open in his doubt. Our way of dealing with authority in the West is very different from the way it is dealt with in the East. When the Pope says something, some people believe it, some people don't, and some people argue about it. In the case of great master Chao-chou, whose reputation was known all over China, when he said something, it was taken quite seriously.

The monastic is asking a question that fills him with immense doubt. This is not an idle inquiry. The sutras say that every sentient and insentient being has Buddha-nature. He wants to know whether a dog has Buddha-nature. Chao-chou says, "No." For many Americans, Mu is an important koan because it's the first koan, and usually it represents a breakthrough. The question seems not so significant. I don't think there are many people in the West who lose much sleep over whether a dog has Buddha-nature. But this monastic did. And you have to put yourself in his body and mind, as well as that of Chao-chou to fully appreciate the monumental tension and the vitality of this koan. That's why Master Soen Sunim always asks his students, "I don't want to know about Mu. I want to know what Chao-chou was thinking before he said, 'Mu.'" How could you respond unless you're the body and mind of Chao-chou himself, the body and mind of the monastic?

There is a tendency among practitioners to turn koans into riddles or intellectual exercises, to deal with them on a very superficial level. For a koan to be fully engaged it has to become relevant to your life. You have to see the relevancy of the questions being brought up. If you see that, if you can switch places with the monastic or the teacher, or whomever or whatever is involved, then you'll see the importance of the koan in your own life. But if the koan remains an abstraction, a mental preoccupation, then its full impact doesn't touch you. It touches your mind, but it doesn't touch your life. You may develop a koan fluency and eloquence, but with no real depth, no real penetration to the heart of it.

The prologue says, *A gourd floating on the water—push it down and it turns.* The prologue and the capping verse are speaking about the koan itself. They're telling you what it is about. *A gourd floating on the water—push it down and it turns.* That's the resiliency of the gourd. When you poke at it, it just rolls over, slips away and pops up again to the surface. You can't sink it. You can't fix it. It's free and has no abiding place. It doesn't attach to anything. That's Chao-chou, free and unhindered, like a dragon following the wind, riding the clouds.

A jewel in the sunlight—it has no definite shape. Another translation says, *A diamond in sunlight has no definite color.* And it's true. If you look at a diamond as the sun passes by, as the light shifts, it changes. The sun changes, the diamond changes. Is the cause the sun or is it the diamond, or is it both? Or perhaps it's neither. What's the true color of the diamond?

It cannot be attained by mindlessness, nor known by mindfulness. No-mind—mindlessness. No eye, ear, nose, tongue, body, or mind. Mindlessness is just blank consciousness. It doesn't function. Yes-mind—mindfulness. Mindfulness practice is very conscious, very present, moment-to-moment awareness, but it still doesn't have the power to cut the roots of delusion. What's the reality of neither the yes-mind nor the no-mind, of neither affirmation nor denial?

The final line says, *Immeasurably great people are turned about in the stream of words—is there anyone who can escape?* The Hakuin system of koan study divides the koans into five groups. First are the *dharmakāya* koans, koans concerned with the absolute basis of reality. The second group contains the *kikan* koans on differentiation. Then there are *nanto* koans—koans that are difficult to pass through. There are also koans concerned with words and phrases, and how we get stuck in language. Finally there are the *goi* koans, pertaining to the Five Ranks of Master Tung-shan. In our lineage, the seven hundred koans taken up during the course of complete training are not broken up that way. They're all mixed together. But there is a lot of attention given to koans on the use of words and phrases. These are the places where we really stick. Examples abound. A monastic shows up, walks around his teacher's seat in a circle, rattles the rings on his staff, and the teacher says, "Right!" The monastic then goes to another teacher, does exactly the same thing, shakes the staff, and the teacher says, "Wrong!" "Why? The first teacher said I was right. Why do you say I'm wrong?" "He was right. You're wrong," the teacher responds. Why was he wrong? Why did one say "yes" and the other say "no?" Why did Master Fa-yen say, "One has it, one has not" when two monastics followed his instructions to the letter and did exactly the same thing, responding in precisely the same way? Why did Chao-chou say to one monastic that a dog has Buddha-nature, and to another monastic that he does not?

When we established Zen Mountain Monastery in 1980, there was an old man who used to hang out around the property. His name was Mr. Wilson. He had a dog, a big black Labrador mix that followed him every place he went. We couldn't find out much about Mr. Wilson from Mr. Wilson. He was somewhat incoherent, a bit eccentric. So I called up the property's previous owners and described him. They said, "Oh, he comes with the place."

Mr. Wilson was always smiling. He had a beautiful smile—no teeth, but a smile that would light up his face. And he loved to walk. That's all he did from dawn until dusk. He'd get up in the early morning and he would walk, just walk and walk and walk. We'd see him in

Kingston or along the highways. We would always see him walking, with the dog close on his heels. We used to call the dog Ms. Wilson.

Mr. Wilson was a World War II veteran. What I gathered from the locals is that he evidently suffered some sort of injury in active combat. As a result he was a "little off." He would tell us incredible stories about gorillas and elephants that he saw in the field and chased back into the woods. He felt that was his job, to come around and make sure that the wild animals didn't get into the building. That dedication created a problem. He would start his rounds at five o'clock in the morning, so during morning zazen we'd hear the door open and Mr. Wilson come into the kitchen to make himself coffee. He would turn on the gas but then forget to put a match to it. The smell of gas would drift up into the zendo. One morning when I woke up in the parsonage, he was in the living room.

We decided that since he wanted coffee, he could come in and have coffee, but he couldn't heat it. He would have to take it cold, the way it was. (This was in the days before automatic coffee makers.) And he had to earn it. We would say, "Bring some wood for the fire," and he would come in carrying two sticks. When we gave him a hard time about it, he'd say, "Well, my job is to chase the gorillas away." So, there was something sensible about that.

As our relationship with Mr. Wilson deepened, a controversy arose in the sangha. One group of people didn't want him in the building. They were afraid of him. He looked like a Bowery bum. His clothes were bedraggled and his hair was unkempt. He had a home, but his veteran's checks were controlled by his brother and his brother's wife. He lived with them and they would give him only twenty-five cents a day, so he was always bumming.

He would go to Phoenicia, stop at different diners and get free cups of coffee. Besides walking, he loved coffee and he loved cigarettes. The group in the sangha that didn't want him coming around was concerned that he was going to start a fire or hurt himself and we would be liable for him. There was another group that thought that he was just a poor old derelict and we should show compassion and take care of him. And so the argument grew, becoming almost continuous and splitting the community.

I could not help but get involved. So to the group that didn't want him around I started selling Mr. Wilson as the Han-shan of Tremper Mountain. I said, "You know, they felt the same way about Han-shan. Everybody thought that he was a bum, but he was a deeply enlightened being. Mr. Wilson is a deeply enlightened being. If you don't believe it, talk to him." And they would ask him questions like, "Mr. Wilson, what's truth?" and he'd laugh and say, "You got a cigarette?" They'd give him a cigarette and he'd say, "Got a light?" and they'd persist and he'd say, "Can I have a cup of coffee?" He would do Dharma combat with them. Word spread in the sangha that Mr. Wilson was very wise and special.

To the other group I would say, "This guy's a bum. He's dangerous. He should get a job. Why has he got to panhandle? Why can't he earn a living? He's strong enough. You ask him to bring in some wood and he brings in two sticks—he's lazy." The rift grew. The two groups went at each other, back and forth, for the first year-and-a-half after the Monastery was founded. It was our first major sangha koan. And you should have heard the fighting over it! Just like in the famous koan in which Nan-ch'üan's community fought over a cat, our sangha fought over Mr. Wilson. Nan-ch'üan held up the cat and challenged his community: "Say a word of Zen or I will kill the cat!" Here, no one could kill the "cat" in a year-and-a-half, and no one could save it either. The "cat" just kept getting into everybody's craw—the "yes" people and the "no" people at each other's throats.

It all ended one afternoon during a February blizzard. Mr. Wilson was on one of his walks when a car hit and killed him. Then Ms. Wilson showed up at the Monastery. She didn't know where to go. The family didn't want her. Actually, she wasn't even Mr. Wilson's dog. She just followed him. So she arrived and the controversy flared up again. It was as if the karma had been transmitted. There was a group that didn't want the dog hanging around here, and another group that wanted the dog. The second group would feed her on the sly, so the dog always kept coming back for food, of course. Then one day a bodhisattva from Maine showed up. He lived here for about six months, took consistent care of Ms. Wilson, and when he moved back to Maine he brought her with him. She lived a long and happy life with him and died just last year.

Using poison to get rid of poison, seeing a cage he builds a cage. The first monastic in this koan says to Chao-chou, "*Does a dog have Buddha-nature or not?*" and Chao-chou answers, "*Yes.*" "Since it has, why is it then in this skin bag?" You can tell by this second question what this monastic is thinking. "*Because he knows, yet deliberately transgresses,*" Chao-chou replies. The second monastic: "*Does a dog have Buddha-nature or not?*" Chao-chou says, "*No.*" The monastic continues, "All sentient beings have Buddha-nature—why does a dog have none, then?" Again, you can see where this monastic is coming from by the question that follows Chao-chou's "No." Chao-chou responds, "*Because he still has impulsive consciousness.*" All dogs have Buddha-nature, all beings have Buddha-nature.

Why doesn't a dog have it? Because of his karmic consciousness, because of his karma, because of the cause and effect of his dog nature.

What is going on? In both instances, Chao-chou reveals the truth. He doesn't lie. It's as if he were answering just to annoy the monastics. The verse says, *A dog's Buddha-nature exists, a dog's Buddha-nature does not exist.* The two statements are obviously not the same, but both are true. How is it? Is there or isn't there Buddha-nature? Do humans have Buddha-nature?

The next line states, *A straight hook basically seeks fish with abandon.* This refers to a story in another poem about a man who was fishing with a straight hook. When somebody asked him how he expected to catch anything with that, he answered, "I'm only interested in a fish with abandon." A fish that has no fixed place, a fish that's free and easy, willing to practice at the edge, to take a chance, to take a risk. In the great ocean of billions of fish, only a handful have that degree of abandon. Here's my straight pin for you: there were really two dogs. One had the Buddha-nature and the other didn't. And the question is, which one had it and which one did not? This is not a riddle. It's a real, bottom-line question. Which one had it and which one did not have it? Only a fish with abandon can see it. Abandon words and ideas. Abandon eye, ear, nose, tongue, body, and mind. Abandon yes. Abandon no. Abandon body and mind. Abandon Buddha-nature. Abandon abandoning.

Every single thing that we hold onto, no matter how small, separates us from the entire universe. We need to see, though, that it is not the thing itself, but the process of holding onto it that is the separation. A single thought, a single feeling, a single idea—if we attach to it—separates us from the myriad things. It doesn't mean not having thoughts, feelings, and ideas. It means not attaching to them, not recreating and sustaining them moment to moment after they pass. When we separate from the totality of being, we separate from ourselves, from our own Buddha-nature.

Every time a thought arises in working with Mu, there is you and there is Mu. Every time you move, you re-establish and reinforce the idea of a self. And when you do that, everything else is distinct and separate. When you've merged completely with Mu; when you are Mu with every thought, every breath, every action; when Mu sits and walks and chants and bows without reflection; then Mu fills the whole universe. But let one thought —"I see it!"—settle in, and the intimacy is gone. The reality is no longer there. What remains are the words and ideas that describe it.

So, what happens when you abandon eye, ear, nose, tongue, body, and mind? What happens when you abandon "yes" and "no," body and mind, Buddha-nature? What's left? Everything. The whole universe, but with no abode, no fixed place. That's the nature of life. That's the nature of each one of us. But if you "chase the air pursuing fragrance," then all you are creating is noisy confusion, making excuses, explanations, and justifications.

In noisy confusion they make excuses and explanations. Making an even presentation, he throws the shop wide open. "He throws the shop wide open" refers to Chao-chou exposing everything. He is not being divisive with this. *Don't blame him for not being careful in the beginning.* This was not a rehearsed script. Chao-chou didn't figure this out. He didn't say, "Oh, they're going to pick two of my koans and put it in a collection, so let me show both sides." He was just responding to the circumstances.

Chao-chou had somebody come up to him with great

doubt, wanting to know if a dog had Buddha-nature, and he said, "Yes, he does." "Then why is he in that smelly skin bag?" "Because he dares to offend," Chao-chou answered. Another monastic filled with great doubt came and asked, "Does a dog have Buddha-nature or not?" and Chao-chou said, "No, he doesn't." "Everything has Buddha-nature. How come a dog doesn't?" "Because of his karmic consciousness." What was Chao-chou getting at? He wasn't searching for the right answer. He wasn't thinking, "I told the first monastic 'Yes,' I have to be consistent and tell this one 'Yes.'" He was teaching both of these monastics. He was treating poison with poison. He was curing sickness with sickness. He was building a cage because he saw a cage. What's the cage he saw? What's the cage he built?

Don't blame him for not being careful in the beginning. He didn't reflect on what he was going to say. He just said it. He responded to the situation. He wasn't responding in a Buddhist context. He wasn't quoting the sutras. He was responding to the needs of a human being, right at the very instant, in both instances. He gave answers which, when placed side-by-side, seem to contradict each other. Yet both are absolutely, unequivocally true and consistent with the Buddha-Dharma.

The poem says, *Pointing out the flaw, he takes away the jewel.* Both of these monastics came to Chao-chou with a little gem, a little jewel, and Chao-chou, being the expert thief that he was, said, "Look! This is not really a jewel. It's got a flaw in it." And he stole it. He didn't physically take it away, but he made it useless to them. It was no longer a jewel. They were walking around with this wonderful thing that they thought they had, reflecting, "Isn't this gem wonderful?" But when they took it to the jeweler, they suddenly found out it was fake. It was not a diamond. It was made out of glass. And that ends that. Only someone with the gigantic heart of a bodhisattva can do something like this.

What are your bags of treasures? Whatever they are you've got to unload the pack, put it down, take off the blinders, strip everything away, and get to what has always been there—the ground of being, beyond the conditioning, beyond words, beyond Buddhism and Buddha-nature. Where is that? What is that? See it, and then live it.

SEVEN

ORDINARY MIND IS TAO

Gateless Gate, Case 19

THE MAIN CASE

Chao-chou once asked Nan-ch'üan, "What is the Way?" Nan-ch'üan answered, "Ordinary mind is the Way." "Then should we direct ourselves toward it or not?" asked Chao-chou. "If you try to direct yourself toward it, you'll go away from it," answered Nan-ch'üan. Chao-chou continued, "If we don't try, how can we know that it is the Way?" Nan-ch'üan replied, "The Way doesn't belong to knowing or to not knowing. Knowing is illusion. Not knowing is blank consciousness. If you really attain to the Tao of no doubt, it's like the great void, vast and boundless. How then can there be right and wrong in the Way?" At these words, Chao-chou was suddenly enlightened.

COMMENTARY

Questioned by Chao-chou, Nan-ch'üan immediately showed that the tile is disintegrating, the ice is dissolving, and no communication whatsoever is possible. Even though Chao-chou may be enlightened, he can truly get it only after studying for thirty more years.

THE CAPPING VERSE

Hundreds of flowers in the spring, the moon in autumn,
A cool breeze in summer, and snow in winter.
If there is no vain cloud in your mind,
For you everyday is a good day.

This koan is a very important koan in our training. As far as I'm concerned, it may be the most important koan that we work with. It appears among the koans of the fourth stage of training, but we also do it again at the end of practice. It needs to be very clearly understood, in all of its nuances.

There are many questions that come up in this koan. Foremost, what is the Way? What is ordinary mind? What does it mean, "When you direct yourself toward it, you move away from it?" What is it that doesn't belong to knowing or not knowing? Did Nan-ch'üan know when he said that? What is the Tao of no doubt? Is that knowing? What's the great void? What about the place of right and wrong in the Tao? What does Wu-men mean when he says that the tile is disintegrating? When Chao-chou was enlightened, what did he see? Why does Wu-men say it'll take him thirty more years to get it? If he was enlightened, didn't he get it? Get what? What is it? What does it mean, "Every day is a good day?" If the truth transcends affirmation and negation, what is a good day?

One of the aspects that makes this koan so vital and critical is that it's very easily misunderstood and can give rise to *buji* Zen, self-styled Zen. When Nan-ch'üan says "ordinary mind," what does he really mean? Is it the same mind that you always had? If so, then why was Chao-chou enlightened? Didn't he have an ordinary mind when he was asking questions of Nan-ch'üan? Suddenly he's enlightened and he has an ordinary mind. Is it the same mind that he had before he was enlightened?

Master Shibayama gets right to the heart of these questions in his commentary on the koan. He says, "If the Way or the Tao is literally everyday mind as it is, then farmers and householders and fishermen and everybody would all know it, and we would not have to wait for saints and wise ones to teach us." Then he goes on to say, "This means we have to transcend our ordinary mind to attain the true ordinary mind, and in order actually to transcend our dualistic ordinary mind, sincere searching and hard discipline are required. When we've broken through the barrier where our ordinary mind is not at all ordinary mind, we can for the first time return to the original ordinary mind, which Nan-ch'üan upholds."

Yet, the ordinary mind is not to be found anywhere other than where we sit. It's not something that arrives from the outside. But it's one thing to know, believe, or understand that it is always there, and quite another to realize its presence, to realize the ordinary mind with the whole body and mind. That realization is transformative. It changes the way you perceive the universe and the way you perceive yourself. To know it, believe it, or understand it, adds more information, but doesn't cut the roots of delusion. How do you realize it?

We live at a time of many great conflicts—conflicts that exist on the personal level and on the multinational level. There is the rape of the individual and the rape of this great earth itself. As we turn to our institutions to look for solutions, in most instances we find that they have failed us. Somehow they don't seem to provide satisfactory answers. Somehow they seem to be in as much conflict as everyone and everything else. As a result, many people have been searching for alternative means of resolving their doubts, often turning to exotic Eastern traditions, gurus, and spiritual teachers. Among those Eastern masters are both charlatans and genuine teachers. Of the 300 teachers of Zen in this country, there are little more than a dozen who have been authenticated by their own teachers and by their own lineage. The remainder, some 285 of them, are self-appointed and sell delusion under the guise of enlightenment.

Spiritual con-artists perpetuate *buji* Zen. Whenever you sell something that you don't have, you are participating in a con game. When you advertise something that you don't have, that's a con game. When you sell something that's valueless, that's a con game. Material con-artists, if apprehended, go to jail. There are laws that protect us from their abuses. Spiritual con-artists, on the other hand, can get away with it because we don't have laws that really deal with them. So spiritual seekers must really look into what it is they're asking for, and what is being promised to them. You must know beyond any doubt that if a teacher tells you that he or she has something to give you, it is time to run for your life. You're dealing with a charlatan. The truth is that you lack nothing. Everything you seek you were born with and you'll go to your grave with. En route, you may realize it or you may not, but the fact remains—it's with you.

Although there are all these charlatans around, in Zen tradition a system has been in place for thousands of years for finding out whether or not you're dealing with an authenticated teacher. The system centers on Dharma sanction or Dharma transmission. It is an authentication that is always documented. It's not public, but it's documented. It's not the same as graduating from a university and hanging up your shingle and starting to practice your profession. There are records kept, and the sanction comes from someone who has been authenticated. In seeking a teacher, there's nothing wrong with asking to see these documents. If you walked into a doctor's office and a diploma was not displayed, you'd ask for it, particularly if you were going in for surgery. You'd want to know that you're dealing with a bona fide, trained, experienced physician. It's the same with the teachers in your spiritual life. There's a way to find out about their status.

Most of the dubious teachers are not badly motivated people. Strictly speaking, they are not charlatans. They do not want to try to hurt a student deliberately. Some of these people have enormous hearts and are filled with good intentions. They really want to help, and they believe that they're doing the right thing. But they are often misguided and may not yet clearly understand it. One of the ways that the misunderstanding occurs is when someone says, "Everything I do, anything I do, is Zen, is the Tao, is my practice." Everybody does that. Children do it. Babies do it. Old people do it. The birds and the bees do it. So what makes it enlightenment? What is it that Chao-chou realized?

When Shibayama says, "When we have broken

through the barrier where our ordinary mind is not at all ordinary mind, we can for the first time return to the original ordinary mind," he literally means that the everyday, ordinary mind, as it is, without dualism and discrimination, is the Tao. And that reveals itself in everything we do. Every single action, if it comes from a self-centered point of view, is missing the point of this koan. In a sense, we can say that it's nothing special, because it's the way the mind has always worked. But what we've got, and what we're calling ordinary mind is our conditioned ordinary mind. Conditioned ordinary mind is very different. It's like a computer. It's already got everything in it, all the data, all the ways to respond to circumstances, all the triggers that trigger selfishness, anger, and fear. Those qualities don't appear unless there's a self. Anger, greed, and ignorance are all conditioned ordinary mind. And so is holiness and sacredness.

Under the dragon mask of enlightenment is enlightenment. When we pretend, when we act ordinary mind, what we're doing is essentially obscuring the truth that's right underneath it. It's here, and yet we miss it. That's the point that makes this koan so difficult. That's the slippery ground that makes us grab for words and think "that's it." If it's something we already have, why do we have to do anything? Why do we have to seek anything? That's the fundamental question. That question motivated Master Dogen through most of his search. And it took a long time before he finally broke through and saw the Tao of no doubt.

How could it be that we have the ordinary mind, and yet it's not functioning? How can it be that we have it, and yet we need to realize it? What does it mean to realize it? The story of the ugly duckling poignantly clarifies these questions. The ugly duckling was born ugly. Even the egg he broke out of was ugly. His didn't look like all the other eggs. The mother duck wondered about this odd-looking egg, but being a good mother, she just did her job and took care of her responsibility. She hatched all the eggs and out of that one egg came the ugliest duckling she ever saw. But it was hers and she reared him with the others. As they grew up, the other ducks always made fun of the ugly duckling. He wasn't the right color, had a tiny, narrow beak, and couldn't walk like a duck—he didn't have that waddle that ducks hold in very high esteem. He was very clumsy. And he was big and gawky, much bigger than the other ducks. So they were always laughing at him. The ugly duckling got more and more withdrawn and despondent. As the days went on, without any kind of approval, the ugly duckling became miserable. Eventually, even his mother barely tolerated him.

He tried to imitate the ducks. He attempted to quack, and what would come out sounded like a honk. Everybody would laugh. He would try to waddle, and would trip over himself, and they would all jeer at him. At the peak of his alienation and desperation, he wanted to die.

One day, while he was drinking in the pond, he saw his own reflection and cried. Then he saw another reflection exactly like it. He looked up, and there was another ugly duckling, just as ugly as he was. And at that moment he realized that he was not a duck at all. He was a swan! At that moment of realization, he became perfect and complete, lacking nothing. But he was always perfect and complete, lacking nothing. He was born that way. But until he realized it, he was miserable trying to be something else. Suddenly, at that moment, he realized that everything he did was perfect swan nature, Buddha-nature. He didn't have to think about it. He didn't have to analyze it, or judge it, or imitate it, or understand it, or believe it. Each gesture, each movement was the perfection of the swan. That realization was transformative, even though his true nature was always there.

It is easy to imagine other creatures of the forest trying to help this poor ugly duckling. The wise old owl might have said, "Look, you're young. Don't worry about it. Somebody will love you. Just deal with it, grunt and bear it. It'll be all right." The wolf might have added, "You're in the wrong group. You actually don't belong here. Think about joining another community." The rabbit might have told him, "It's your sex life. That's why you're so miserable." And on and on. Would that have nourished? Would that have helped? Everybody would have offered all kinds of solutions. But until the realization happens, no words, no beliefs, no understanding can do it. Something else connected, and the whole lineage of swans back to the original swan was manifested in this one being, perfect and complete, lacking nothing. That's what this ordinary mind is. It's the Buddha-mind. It's the Buddha-nature. It's the nature of all sentient beings. But it doesn't function until it's been realized. How do you realize it?

It is clear. "This is it" doesn't reach it. Not knowing doesn't reach it. Knowing doesn't reach it. "Everything I do" doesn't reach it. "Chopping wood, carrying water" doesn't reach it. Those are simplistic conclusions. They don't work in the dokusan room and they don't work in life. Those conclusions ultimately reinforce arrogance, anger, greed, and ignorance. We need to do something else. Zazen is the entry point. Koans are the devices. The eight gates of training are all skillful means to help us, step by step, get to that ground of being that's perfect, complete, and ordinary. And to realize it.

That search takes place within samsara itself, within

the arrogance, anger, greed, pain, and fear that make up daily life. We have to climb the mountain we call practice. When we finally get to the peak, there's the edge. We reach the apparent limit of our practice. It is here that we must take the leap, forgetting the self, even if for a moment, letting go enough to get a glimpse, to see it. But it's not over with the leap, as we quickly find ourselves on the ledge again, clinging for our dear lives, not wanting to let go completely.

When I was in the Navy, one of the training tests we had to pass was to climb a 60-foot tower, which was the height of the deck of most ships in those days, and, wearing a life-jacket, jump into a swimming pool below. This was supposed to simulate an evacuation drill in case one had to abandon ship. Simple enough. You just had to jump. It didn't look so bad when you were on the ground looking up, but once you climbed the ladder and looked down, the pool looked like a little tiny postage stamp. It seemed you could easily miss it. In reality, it was a huge Olympic-size pool. At the diving board on the top of the tower, an old bosun's mate waited with a long pole padded on the end. He would goose anybody who hesitated or froze. Everybody had to do it. You didn't get through Naval boot camp until you did that jump. There were no discussions, options, or alternatives. We were all apprehensive but there was one guy who was really frightened. When he got to the end of the board he started screaming and wanted to back out. Along came the bosun's mate with the prod. Earlier, the pool had been used for some kind of party and was strung with banners all over the place. There were flags and decorations hanging from wires running across the hall. When the bosun's mate pushed him, the guy went off the end of the diving board and grabbed the nearest wire. And there he was, hanging and screaming his bloody head off, "Help! Help! Help! Help!" In the pool everything echoed tremendously. Everybody got very quiet. There was just this one guy yelling. There was nothing anybody could do. You couldn't even put a ladder up to get him. He had to let go, and he wasn't about to let go. So he held on. Everybody just waited. Nobody else could jump. We had to wait. And we waited. The crying and yelling and begging got weaker. He couldn't stay there for the rest of his life. Finally he let go, yelling all the way down until he hit the water.

Sometimes we do something similar in our practice. We get to a certain point and then we grab on and don't want to let go. And it takes a little bit of prodding. That's the ledge—clinging to the wire. When you let go, you learn to fly. You can't fly while you're holding on. You can't fly when you're sitting on the ledge. You have to let go to learn to fly. Learning to fly is the sixth stage of our training. The seventh stage is learning to use the wings twenty-four hours a day, without reflecting on it. When that swan got ready to fly, it flew like a swan. If you've ever seen a swan take off in the wild and ride the wind, it makes a duck look stupid by comparison. Ducks are constantly fluttering their wings, looking frenzied. Swans have magnificant aerodynamics and grace. In the eighth stage you've got to give up the wings. The ninth stage is what we call the Tao of no doubt, and the tenth stage is "in the world," no trace of wings, no trace of flying, perfect and complete, lacking nothing. Ordinary mind.

Zen practice is a serious business. It's the business of life and death. It's not a trivial or casual undertaking. It's not something to play at or to take lightly. It's a profound teaching that transforms lives, if you're willing to engage it. You can try to get away with playing at Zen, but that will not impart any strength to you or to anyone else.

"What is the Way?" *"Ordinary mind is the Way."* *"Then should we direct ourselves toward it or not?"* *"If you try to direct yourself toward it, you'll go away from it."* All Nan-ch'üan is saying is that ordinary mind is right where you stand. This is the same advice the ugly duckling needed. What you're looking for, you already have. If you try to be something else, to do something to get there, the very activity separates you from it. The very effort, the very thought separates you from it. Just the mind moving separates you from it. Chao-chou didn't understand. He said, *"If we don't try, how can we know that it is the Way?"* Nan-ch'üan replied, *"The Way doesn't belong to knowing or to not knowing."* Knowing is illusion. It's being caught up in all the words and ideas that describe reality. Not knowing is blank consciousness—no eye, ear, nose, tongue, body, or mind. It doesn't work, it doesn't function, it doesn't heal, it doesn't nourish, it doesn't love, it doesn't feel. *"If you really attain to the Tao of no doubt, it's like the great void, vast and boundless."* How can you speak of it in terms of right or wrong? That's when Chao-chou saw it. That's when he realized himself.

In the commentary, Wu-men says, *Questioned by Chao-chou, Nan-ch'üan immediately showed that the tile is disintegrating, the ice is dissolving.* The constructs are falling apart. The game is disintegrating. *No communication whatsoever is possible.* What does that mean, "no communication?" If communication always refers to an exchange between A and B, why is there none between Chao-chou and his teacher Nan-ch'üan? Because there's no A and B. It's all one reality. That's what he saw. That's what he realized. He let go of the self that separated him from his teacher, from the Way. He died the Great Death, the death of the ego, the death of the self.

Even though Chao-chou may be enlightened, he can

truly get it only after studying for thirty more years. Thirty more years was not accurate. Chao-chou was 20 years old at this point. He had already been a monastic for a number of years. He knew all of the teachings, found Master Nan-ch'üan, and came to realization at 20 years of age. Then he continued studying with Nan-ch'üan until he was 60 years old—40 more years of training. And then, after his teacher died, he went on a pilgrimage, from age 60 to age 80, 20 more years, learning wherever he went. Finally, at age 80, he settled down and began to teach.

When we look at the progressive steps in the spiritual journey—the search, climbing the mountain, the edge, the leap, the flying, learning to use the wings, giving up the wings—we should realize that we are part of a continuum. It doesn't end at any point. We mark the steps along the way. When a student has completed the first third of their training, we mark that occasion with a ceremony called *shuso hossen.* This is a way of clarifying what we're doing, and a way of avoiding *buji* Zen. One of the reasons for *buji* Zen is that people don't know where they are in their training. They see something, possibly a hallucination, and they think, "This is it!" and suddenly they become self-appointed teachers. As I look back I can recall so many times during this Dharma journey when I said to myself, "Now I've got it! This is it!" only to find out two months later that this wasn't it. And two months later, again the same process. It must have happened a hundred times if it happened once. Without a teacher or a structure or a matrix to work in, it's very easy to delude oneself into thinking that something has been seen.

So we mark the significant points of passage. We acknowledge a student when two-thirds of the training is finished, at the completion of the sixth stage. Then again as the student moves into the eighth stage of training, giving up the wings, we recognize him or her as a Dharma holder. At that point, a student has received "the intent to transmit" from the teacher. We say, "The message has been transmitted, but has not yet been manifested completely." Then that student begins learning to be a teacher. The eighth stage is to die the Great Death. The ninth stage is to return to the world. The ordinary mind begins to function. We mark that by the transmission of the Precepts, and the student becomes either a priest, in the case of a monastic, or a Dharma minister, in the case of a lay person.

And then the tenth stage—in the world, no trace of wings or flying. The lay practitioner receives Dharma sanction. The monastic receives Dharma transmission. Now the student is independent, and teaching independently. But training is still not over. It continues. That's what Wu-men is referring to here: "... he can truly get it only after studying for thirty more years." That thirty years means practicing continuously and courageously. It's not just for a period of time. Some of the students who, having completed their studies, are confirmed by sanction or transmission may become heads of lay training centers or monasteries. There's further training associated with taking the high seat to become spiritual director of a center or with ascending the mountain to become abbot of a monastery. A lot more training is required after transmission. At least in this Monastery and order, all of it is a way of authenticating the training of the students, so we don't become part of spiritual deceit. The bottom line is that the practice never ends. It is constantly being refined. The teachings are everywhere. That's the place where the rivers chant the 84,000 hymns, and the mountains proclaim the Dharma. That's the place of the teachings of the insentient.

Hundreds of flowers in the spring, the moon in
autumn,
A cool breeze in summer, and snow in winter.
If there is no vain cloud in your mind,
For you everyday is a good day.

We can say, "Hundreds of flowers in the spring, the moon in autumn, a cool breeze in summer, and snow in winter. If there is no self, ordinary mind is the Way."

The extraordinary thing about this koan is that an ordinary person realizing it becomes a sage. A sage realizing it becomes an ordinary person. This is the continuous practice of the Buddhas and ancestors. It's from here that our own ceaseless practice emerges. We attain the Way and we heal and nourish all sentient beings.

EIGHT

LIN-CHI'S GREAT ENLIGHTENMENT

The Book of Equanimity, Case 86

PROLOGUE

> Even with a head of bronze, a forehead of iron, the eyes of a god, the pupils of a dragon, the beak of an eagle, the jowls of a fish, the heart of a bear and the guts of a leopard, under the diamond sword no plan is accepted and no measurement is possible. Why does it have to be like this?

THE MAIN CASE

> Lin-chi asked Huang-po, "What is the truly essential great meaning of the Buddha's teaching?" Huang-po immediately hit him. This happened three times; then Lin-chi left Huang-po and visited Ta-yü. Ta-yü asked, "Where have you come from?" Lin-chi said, "From Huang-po." Ta-yü said, "What did Huang-po say?" Lin-chi said, "Three times I asked him about the truly

105

essential great meaning of the Buddha's teaching, and
three times I was beaten with a stick. I don't know if I
had any fault or not." Ta-yü said, "Huang-po was so
kind. He did his utmost for you, and still you come and
ask if there was any fault or not." At this, Lin-chi was
greatly enlightened.

THE CAPPING VERSE

Nine-colored phoenix, thousand-mile colt
The wind of reality crosses the pipes
The spiritual work goes into action.
Coming on directly, the flying lightning is swift:
When the clouds of illusion break, the sun is alone.
He grabs the tiger's whiskers—
Do you see it or not?
This is a brave and powerful person of great stature.

There is quite a bit of humor in Zen training, and
there are subtle differences in its expression and style in
traditional Rinzai and Soto Schools. From the point of
view of the teacher and the teachings, the real humor in
Zen is often missed because we usually engage koans only
superficially. When you look at the surface of this koan of
Master Lin-chi's enlightenment, for example, it sounds a
little bit like a comedy routine by the Three Stooges or
the Marx Brothers. Underneath the surface, though, there
is profound teaching going on, and seeing that is the key
to appreciating how the koan works, and where its real
humor comes from. The humor of it isn't where we normally tend to think it is.

In the prologue we hear that ... *under the diamond*

sword no plan is accepted and no measurement is possible.
The diamond sword is the sword of Manjushri, the sword
that both kills and gives life. It kills by taking away everything we hold on to; it gives life via its capacity to be
nourishing, positive, supportive. The sword is used sometimes for one purpose and sometimes for another. But
why is "no plan accepted"? This seems to be one of the
biggest problems most of us run into, and inevitably, we
get down to this question in the face-to-face teaching.
There is nothing wrong with making a plan. The problem
is that once we've made a plan we attach to it, and in so
doing lose all freedom and flexibility.

In the same way, there is nothing essentially wrong
with measurement and evaluation, except that they
become things we hold on to. People are constantly measuring themselves. The most difficult thing to let go of at
the beginning of Zen practice is the witness, the internal
voice that says, "Now I'm doing it well. Now I'm doing it
poorly. So-and-so is sitting better than I am. When will I
be enlightened?" The measurements actually are a waste of
time and ultimately don't mean anything. By getting stuck
in them we create barrier after barrier for ourselves. As
long as that witness is reflecting on what we're doing in
zazen, then what we're doing is witnessing. It's not yet
the falling away of body and mind. So when people come
into dokusan and tell me how "body and mind fell away,"
I ask, "How do you know?" Because you can't *know*
unless there's still a witness.

What this koan is about—indeed, what our lives are
really about—is whole body-and-mind intimacy. That
means no witness and no separation: seeing form with the
whole body and mind, hearing sound with the whole body
and mind. Another problem with planning and measuring
is that they involve expectation, and one of the characteris-

tics of having expectations is that things never turn out the way we expect them to. So don't expect. Take things as they come. Allow them to be as they are. What that means is trust. Trust yourself. In its most perfect sense, trusting yourself simply means having no expectation. It means giving yourself permission to be the way you are, to succeed or to fail. That's very empowering and very liberating. When you trust yourself, you are free.

In this koan, Lin-chi asks Huang-po, "What is the ultimate meaning of Buddhism?" At that, Huang-po hits him. This happens three times. It's important to appreciate that, as a religious event, this is as significant as what took place in the realizations of Saint Theresa of Avila, Saint John of the Cross, or Mary Baker Eddy. It is as significant as the experiences of Luther or Moses. All of these people had a religious experience that transformed their lives, and so it was with Lin-chi. Usually these events tend to be quite sober. The experience of Lin-chi seems to have another, different dimension, the surface of which appears to be humorous. It takes a certain state of mind to begin to hear what is going on.

To appreciate the koan more fully, it's important to see the context in which it took place. Lin-chi was one of an assembly of monastics at the monastery of the great master Huang-po. Huang-po was part of the lineage that traced itself through Pai-chang, who had earlier received the teachings from Ma-tsu. Huang-po was a fierce character. He stood seven feet tall in a country where the average height was under five-and-a-half feet. There was also a huge callus, a lump, in the middle of his forehead, that he got from bowing all the time. This made him appear even more intimidating.

Lin-chi came to this monastery and practiced for three years but never went to dokusan, never went face-to-face with his teacher. One day the head monastic said to him, "How long have you been here?" Lin-chi said, "I've been here three years." "Have you ever asked for instruction?" Lin-chi said, "No." This happens at our monastery, too. Sometimes it's a way of evading the issue, avoiding confrontation, just sitting there and looking good. Don't shake the tree, don't stir the pot. Sometimes fear does it; sometimes it's understanding that does it. Being afraid can keep us stuck on our seat; thinking we have all the answers can do the same thing. The historical record does not clarify what was really going on with Lin-chi while he spent three years in a monastery without engaging his teacher. That they let him get away with it for such a long period of time is surprising.

When I first went to Los Angeles to begin intensive training with my teacher, I couldn't stand the services they did. I had been training in a traditional Rinzai-style monastery and the services there were very few, but even those I couldn't tolerate. What I was reacting to was my Catholic upbringing. In Los Angeles it seemed as if every time I turned around there was another service. I developed the habit of slipping out the back door as soon as the temple bell started ringing. I figured I was making up for it in the other things I did. I justified it by telling myself that it was okay as long as I sat "better" than everybody else, and that if I snuck out the side door nobody would mind. Besides, I thought, nobody would notice my absence. At that time there were hundreds of people practicing at this zendo. Who was going to notice me sneaking out the side door? Well, *everybody* did—everybody knew it! Apparently they would poke each other and say, "There goes Daido!" The head monastic was going to grab me, but Roshi told him to let me go. I thought I was invisible to the sangha.

The background details of this koan provided in *The Book of Equanimity* commentary are helpful in seeing what is happening. It seems that Lin-chi had been getting away with never asking for instruction. He tells the head monastic that he simply doesn't know what to ask. The head monastic says, "Why don't you go and ask Master Huang-po what the cardinal principle of the Buddha-Dharma is?" Nothing much, right? Being a good monastic, Lin-chi goes in and before he has finished asking the question— POW! Old Huang-po slugs him. He gets up and goes back to sit in the zendo. The head monastic later asks him, "How did it go?" "Well," Lin-chi says, "before I even finished talking, he hit me. I don't understand." The head monastic says, "Then go ask him again. Be persistent!" Lin-chi gets up and goes back in, and asks the same question. Again, before it's out of his mouth—POW! Huang-po hits him. Lin-chi comes back out and sits down. Again, the head monastic asks what has happened. Lin-chi says, "He hit me again." "Be persistent. Go ask him again." A third time he goes in—POW! And when he comes out he says to the head monastic, "I'm leaving. It was very kind of you to send me to the master. Three times I asked him and three times I was hit. I regret that some obstruction caused by my own past karma prevents me from grasping his profound meaning, so I'm going away for a while."

The head monastic, who was a wonderful "grand-mother" and *really* wanted Lin-chi to see it, says, "Well, if you're going to go away, you should take leave of the teacher; you shouldn't just walk out. Go back and tell him that you're going." Before Lin-chi gets in to see the master, the head monastic goes in and talks with Huang-po: "There's a young man, the one who's been questioning you.... I think there's something very special about him. If he comes in to take his leave, please handle him expediently. In the future, with training, he should become a great tree which will provide cool shade for the people of the world." When Lin-chi later came to take his leave, Huang-po told him, "You shouldn't go anywhere else other than to Ta-yü's place by the river. He's sure to explain things for you."

Very little is known about Ta-yü other than that he was a hermit who spent his days living in the mountains. He was a student of Huang-po, though it's not verifiable whether he formally received transmission from him. He was, however, a clear-eyed monastic with deep understanding, and a good teacher. Following Huang-po's instructions, Lin-chi arrives at Ta-yü's hermitage. Ta-yü says, "Where have you come from?" Lin-chi says, "I've come from Huang-po's place." "What did Huang-po have to say?" asks Ta-yü. "Well, three times I asked him what is the truly essential great meaning of the Buddha's teaching, and three times he hit me. I don't know whether I was at fault or not." Ta-yü should have just hit him, but he doesn't. Instead he says, "Old Huang-po is such a grandmother that he has utterly exhausted himself with your trouble. And now you've come here asking whether you're at fault or not." At these words, Lin-chi attained great enlightenment. What did he see?

Lin-chi then says, "Oh, there isn't so much to Huang-po's Dharma." At that point Ta-yü grabs him by the arms and says, "You bed-wetting little devil. You just finished asking whether you're at fault or not and now you say there isn't so much to Huang-po's Dharma. What did you see? Speak, speak!" Lin-chi immediately hits Ta-yü three times on the side and shoves him away. Ta-yü says, "Huang-po is your teacher; it's none of my business. Go back to him." Lin-chi leaves Ta-yü and goes back to Huang-po. Seeing him coming, Huang-po says, "What a fellow—coming and going, coming and going. When will it end?" Lin-chi responds, "It's all due to your grand-motherly kindness," and presents his teacher with a cus-tomary gift. "Where have you been?" Huang-po asks. "Recently you did me the favor of sending me to see Ta-yü," says Lin-chi. "What did Ta-yü have to say?" Huang-po asks. Lin-chi tells the story and Huang-po says, "How I'd like to get my hands on that fellow and give him a good dose of my stick." Lin-chi says, "Why say that you would like to? Take it right now!" And—BAM!—he hits Huang-po. Huang-po says, "You lunatic, coming back here and pulling the tiger's whiskers!" Lin-chi then gives a great, penetrating shout: HAAAGHH! "Attendant!" Huang-po calls out, "Get this lunatic out of here and take him to the monastics' hall." Lin-chi then took his place in the assembly and eventually became the most important successor of Master Huang-po.

That this whole koan is centered around hitting often makes people wonder about Zen training. There are many stories about teachers striking monastics—clearly there is something going on there, some kind of teaching. People sometimes conclude from this that hitting is a basic char-acteristic or technique of Zen. Actually it isn't, any more than slapstick is generally characteristic of American come-dy. There was a time when Charlie Chaplin, the Three Stooges, and Abbott and Costello were popular. Hitting and falling down and acting ridiculous largely defined comedy forty or fifty years ago, and then slapstick drifted out of fashion. Today, comedy has taken on other dimen-sions. Similarly, there was a period in Zen training when hitting was a very important method, particularly in this specific lineage, but then it faded. You don't find accounts of hitting in the teachings of Dogen, for example, or Tung-shan, or most of the other great masters.

We need to see what's going on at the core of this koan. Three times Lin-chi asks the meaning of the Buddha-Dharma; three times Huang-po hits him. The old man was getting redundant. Was he saying that the "answer" was to hit? As a reference, there's the classic example of Master Te-shan. If a monastic answered a question affirmatively, he would give him thirty blows of his stick. If he answered negatively, he would give him thirty blows of his stick. If he answered neither affirmatively nor negatively: thirty blows. If he didn't answer: thirty blows. His monastics didn't want to go into the dokusan room with him. You could do nothing without incurring thirty blows. What was that about?

In studying these exchanges, you need to remember that until you've felt the sting of the question, you won't appreciate the sting of the answer. Is being hit the answer, and if so, where is its meaning? I can save you a lot of time with this question. There is no meaning whatsoever. Don't even waste your time looking for it. The same imperative is given to students working on the koan Mu or the koan on the sound of one hand clapping. There is no meaning whatsoever to Mu. Don't bother to present *meanings.*

To clarify another possible misconception, being struck is not a punishment. It's not done out of anger. Hitting needs to be appreciated as an ultimate act of compassion. The first time I walked into a Zen monastery, I sat and got more and more angry because of my own pain. I hated the whole experience. At the time I didn't realize what the source of the anger was. I thought I was getting angry because of all the things going on in the place that I considered wrong. The next thing I knew, a monastic got up and started walking up and down the aisles hitting people with a stick. At Zen Mountain Monastery, we give a nice long explanation about the function of and procedure for receiving the *kyosaku*, but at that monastery nobody explained anything. I grew up on the streets, in a ghetto, and nobody hits me. Yet here was this guy walking down the aisle getting closer and closer with the stick. I knew there was going to be a fight, maybe the first rumble ever in a Buddhist monastery. I was set on it: if he took that stick to me, I was going to deck him. And not only that, I was going to go after the old man and deck him too. Then I was going to kick over the Buddha image. There I sat, boiling with emotions, trying to be "peaceful." I didn't know that you had to ask for the *kyosaku* before anyone would use it on you, so the monastic walked right by me. But in just the two or three minutes that it took him to slowly come up the aisle, I had worked myself up into quite a frenzy.

The hitting in this koan is also different from the kind of practice that once was common among Catholic monastics who used self-flagellation to reach greater spiritual depth by trying to feel the pain and the suffering of Christ. That is not what Huang-po was doing. He wasn't trying to inflict suffering on Lin-chi; he was trying to get him to see something. What was it? What was it that Huang-po was really giving Lin-chi?

The commentary on this koan says, "The treasury of the eye of the true teaching perished in the blind donkey. Huang-po was too kind, Ta-yü was too talkative." After Lin-chi became a master and had been teaching for many years, he began to prepare for his death. Terminally ill, he was in bed, and all his disciples gathered around him. He looked up at his primary disciple and said, "Please don't let my Dharma be extinguished." The disciple answered, "How could I let your Dharma be extinguished?" This was a wonderful response to that question. Indeed, how can you? That, in a sense, is another kind of a joke. We do a service each week to protect the imperishable Dharma. It reaches everywhere; where will it go? Where did it come from? How could it possibly be extinguished? Like this very life itself, it is unborn and inextinguishable. Lin-chi said, "Many years from now, when someone asks you what the teachings of Master Lin-chi are, what will you tell them?" The disciple gave a great shout, in the tradition of Lin-chi's years of teaching. The shout was Lin-chi's answer to "What is the Buddha?" The shout was his answer to "What is the truth?" The shout was his answer to all the questions, just like the thirty blows of the stick was Te-shan's answer. Lin-chi looked his disciple right in the eye and said, "To think my true Dharma will be extinguished with this blind ass." And then he died.

What Lin-chi was doing was approving his disciple. What the old hermit was doing when he called Lin-chi a "bed-wetting little devil" was approving him. When Lin-chi came back after his pivotal meeting with Ta-yü and told Huang-po what had taken place, Huang-po's response was, "Ta-yü was too talkative; wait until I see him, I'm going to give him a beating." To this Lin-chi said, "Why wait?" and hit Huang-po. Huang-po's response was to laugh. That laugh was at once an approval and an expression of joy. For a teacher, seeing a disciple connect with this incredible Dharma is probably more important than the teacher's personal enlightenment experience. That's what Huang-po was expressing. That laughter was the laughter of a parent who sees his or her child make it. When he follows his laugh with, "This lunatic comes to grab the tiger's whiskers," this is also approval. What was it that Lin-chi saw that allowed such a transformation to take place? For three years he's sitting in a corner of the zendo, afraid to go into dokusan, and now he comes back from his meeting with Ta-yü and socks the old man in the head. What kind of a teaching is that? Is it that we should all run around hitting people? You had better be *sure* of what you're doing before you come into dokusan and hit me. I'm still a street kid!

Kuei-shan once asked Master Yang-shan, "Did Lin-chi get Ta-yü's power or Huang-po's power? Whom did he really succeed? Who brought him to enlightenment?" Keep in mind what happened in the encounters. Huang-po hit Lin-chi three times. Lin-chi hit the old hermit monastic three times. Huang-po says he'd like to hit Ta-yü, to which Lin-chi responds by hitting Huang-po, and asking, "Why wait?" What Lin-chi was doing was revealing the mutual identity of the three of them—intimacy, whole body-and-mind intimacy.

There's a eulogy poem that was written for Ta-yü:

> *Bitter and harsh, biting like a dog,*
> *He opened the Lin-chi of the north and made him a*
>   *great tree.*
> *He pushed Yün-men over the precipice cliff.*
> *His words were like dry firewood.*
> *His reason cannot be systematized.*

Later, Lin-chi said to an assembly, "At my late teacher's place, I asked about the ultimate meaning of Buddhism three times and three times I was beaten. It was like being brushed with a branch of mugwort. Right now I'm thinking of another beating. Who can do it for me?" At that point a certain monastic came forth and said, "I'll do it." Lin-chi held up his stick to hand it to him, and as the monastic reached for it, Lin-chi hit him. Another master said of this, "Lin-chi's letting go was a bit dangerous, but he gathers in exceedingly fast." This is taken up in the line we looked at earlier: "The treasury of the eye of the true teaching perished in the blind donkey. Huang-po was too kind; Ta-yü too talkative." Those are words of praise for these three men. The true teaching perishing in the hands of the blind donkey refers to Lin-chi's approval of his successor.

Huang-po was incredibly kind. His kindness was that of a parent who compassionately disciplines a child. This is worlds apart from the horrors of child abuse. There are times when a spanking works, times when it's an important way of giving. I think I only spanked my kids twice. Once was when my two older sons (who are now in their mid-thirties) were eight and ten years old. We had a pond near the house, and an autumn freeze of a few days froze the surface of the pond. Then it snowed a little, which covered the pond nicely, but the ice was still thin. My sons were on their way out to play in the snow when I said, "Don't go to the pond. It's dangerous. Stay off the surface of the pond until I say it's okay. It's going to take a couple of months yet." A half-hour later I looked out the window and they were on the pond. Luckily, they were light enough for the ice to support. I ran out and immediately gave them both a good wallop on the behind. I wanted them to remember that this was a life-and-death matter, and for a life-and-death matter, I was willing to whack their behinds. During those days, all the psychologists said you should never do that to kids. They would have argued that my kids would be brain-warped because of that incident. But that spanking was one of love, not anger. It came completely out of deep concern, and not self-centeredness. There are times when severe but loving action communicates directly and immediately something that can't be talked about, something that is beyond words and ideas.

In the verse there is the line, *The wind of reality crosses the pipes.* This is basically a reference to playing a bamboo flute. "The space between heaven and earth is like a bamboo flute." Like a lute or a dulcimer, a bamboo flute has a wonderful sound potential in it, but without excellent fingering the sound can't come out. The music is constantly present, perfect, and bottomless—but if you don't know how to use the flute, it will not make the beautiful sound. So it is with all of us. All sentient beings are perfect and complete, lacking nothing. Yet if you don't know that truth personally and intimately—if you haven't examined yourself and gotten beyond the layers and layers of conditioning that separate you from your true self, you go to your death thinking that there is something wrong, that you have missed something. We think that we should have attained something that we haven't. Yet, it's *all* here. The life of each one of us, just as it is, is the life of a Buddha. But if you don't see it, you can't use it.

In a sense, the striking hand of Master Huang-po and the stick of Master Te-shan are no different from the touch of the autumn wind when you really feel it. The sound of Lin-chi's shout is really not different from the sound of the valley stream when it is really heard. All these things are a form of intimacy, whole body-and-mind intimacy. When you are really intimate with yourself, you are intimate with the ten thousand things, with the whole phenomenal universe. There is no longer any separation.

> *If you still don't get it, then look—*
> *Just look at September! Look at October!*
> *Hundreds of thousands of gold and yellow leaves*
> *Fill the mountain streams.*

NINE

STRIKING THE MORTAR, SHAKING THE SIEVE

Transmission of the Light, Case 34

PROLOGUE

*The sound of the striking of the mortar still rever-
berates throughout the whole universe. Can you hear it?
Each of you has the ancient mirror, all the myriad
forms: long, short, square, round, past, present, and
future. Each and every thing appears in it. Have you
seen it? Right now it fills the dragon palace, it fills the
ten directions. Can you hear the sound of the rain? Can
you see the spring flowers? Then enter the gate right
there.*

THE MAIN CASE

*Hui-neng was working hard in the rice refining
hut of Obai. One night Hung-jen entered the hut and
asked, "Has the rice become white?" Hui-neng said,
"Yes, it has, but it has not yet been sifted." Hung-jen*

119

*struck the mortar three times with his stick. Hui-neng
sifted the rice with a winnow three times and entered the
ancestor's room.*

THE CAPPING VERSE

*The sound of striking the mortar
is loud beyond the empty blue sky.
The moon is sifted white by the clouds,
and the evening is deep and serene.*

Hui-neng is probably the most extraordinary teacher
in the history of Zen Buddhism. The Sixth Ancestor after
Bodhidharma, he's responsible for the spread of Zen
throughout China and the beginnings of all the major
schools of Zen, two of which survive down to the present
day here on this mountain.

Master Hui-neng came from the southern part of
China, considered by most Chinese of that time to be the
homeland of the "barbarians." He was a lay person, not a
monastic, and in the cited case he was very young, probably eighteen or nineteen years old. He had no schooling
whatsoever, had never sat zazen, never studied Buddhism,
and yet he went on to become the Sixth Ancestor of Zen.

Hui-neng's training and teaching took place in the
seventh century, prior to what is known as the "Golden
Age of Zen." In fact, we can attribute much of what the
Golden Age came to be to the outstanding accomplish-
ment of this man. His father was evidently a bureaucrat
who was demoted and sent to the southern frontier
region. There he died after just a few years, leaving the
young boy to be raised by his mother. The family was

extremely poor and Hui-neng contributed to their modest living by cutting wood and selling it in the marketplace.

One day in the market he heard a monastic reciting the *Diamond Sutra*. When the monastic reached the line, "You should activate the mind without dwelling on anything," Hui-neng experienced deep enlightenment. He asked the monastic, "What scripture is this? Who did you learn it from?" The monastic told him it was the *Diamond Sutra* and that he learned it from Master Hung-jen in the northern part of China.

Hui-neng returned home and told his mother he intended to seek the truth. He then left home, traveling first to another province, where he became friends with a very educated man whose mother-in-law was a Buddhist monastic. The mother-in-law used to recite the *Nirvana Sutra* every day. After hearing her recite one day, Hui-neng suddenly started expounding the Dharma. The monastic picked up the sutra and started asking him questions about it. She handed him the book, but he said, "I can't read; would you read it to me and ask me what you'd like to ask?" The monastic said, "If you can't read, how can you understand the meaning?" Hui-neng said, "The subtle principles of the Buddha are not bound up in the written words." Startled, the monastic started telling people around town about the young man's natural wisdom. It wasn't long before people were coming in droves to pay their respects. An old temple near the area was rebuilt as a teaching site for him and very quickly it became a sanctuary. Hui-neng was still less than twenty years old.

One day Hui-neng said, "I'm seeking the great teaching; why should I stop halfway?" and soon left the temple to continue his search. (One wonders how many people today, having experienced great enlightenment, having hundreds of followers surrounding them asking for their wisdom, would suddenly decide they needed to complete their training?) He started traveling north. Along the way he met another Zen master and asked for instruction. This master recognized from Hui-neng's demeanor that he wasn't an ordinary person. He told Hui-neng that the Indian monastic Bodhidharma had transmitted the Mind Seal, that it had been handed down to Hung-jen, and that what he should do is go to Hung-jen's monastery. After being referred to Hung-jen this second time, Hui-neng began the journey to his monastery in the far north.

Hung-jen was held in very high regard by all of the emperors, officials, and intellectuals in that part of China. His monastery was huge. Over a thousand monastics were practicing there when Hui-neng, this young illiterate woodcutter from southern China, came knocking on the door. When I first read about Hui-neng's initial meeting with Hung-jen it reminded me of St. Francis' calling on the Pope. If you recall, he too arrived looking very ragged after having walked from one end of Italy to the other on his pilgrimage. The church officials wouldn't even let him in, but when finally he did receive an audience, the Pope immediately recognized the caliber of the young man's spirit and gave him what he was asking for. That was the beginning of the Franciscan order.

Hung-jen asked Hui-neng, "Where are you from?" Hui-neng replied, "The south." The Ancestor said, "What are you seeking?" Hui-neng said, "I just seek to be a Buddha." The Ancestor said, "You southern monkeys have no Buddha-nature. How can you attain Buddhahood?" And then this young illiterate replies, "As far as people are concerned, there is north and south, but how could that apply to the Buddha-nature?" The Fifth Ancestor instantly knew that there was something very special about Hui-neng. He ordered him to work pounding rice in the monastery mill. Hui-neng bowed and went to work. (Again, can you imagine that happening in this country in the twentieth century? Hui-neng's "reward" upon being recognized as a person who has clearly realized enlightenment is a lowly job—and he just bows and goes right to work!)

For a long time after this initial meeting, Hui-neng worked diligently in the rice shed. None of the other monastics knew who he was. He looked like a poor layman that the master had taken pity on and given a job. He was allowed to sleep in the rice-pounding quarters, was very quiet, and did his work. He didn't run around expounding the Dharma, showing everybody how much he knew; he revealed it in his actions and just did his work.

Hung-jen, realizing that the time for the transmission of the Dharma had come, said to his community, "The truth is hard to understand. Don't uselessly memorize my words and take that as your only responsibility. Each of you should freely compose a verse. If the meaning of the words is in accord with the truth, I'll transmit to you the vestment of the teachings."

At that time Shen-hsiu was the head monastic at Hung-jen's monastery. He was, in fact, highly evolved in spiritual matters. When people read this account they often think that Shen-hsiu was some kind of dummy. He wasn't. Shen-hsiu also later received transmission and started a lineage branch that continued for many years. He was the eldest of over a thousand monastics at the monastery and very well-versed in the spiritual and mystical teachings. He was admired by all the monastics, and it was generally assumed that he would receive the transmission. Because of this, none of the other monastics even attempted to meet Hung-jen's challenge.

Shen-hsiu tried to compose a verse, but found that he had a great deal of difficulty; he felt held back somehow. It's said that he kept breaking out in a sweat as he worked on it. Over a period of days he tried repeatedly to present his verse to Hung-jen. Finally, he just posted it on the wall outside the Fifth Ancestor's room without signing it:

> *The body is the tree of enlightenment.*
> *The mind like a bright mirror stand.*
> *Time and again diligently wipe it.*
> *Don't let it gather dust.*

When the Fifth Ancestor saw the verse, he knew that it was by Shen-hsiu and he praised it: "If later generations practice in accord with this, they too will recognize excellent results." (If you listen carefully to these words, you will see that they are not approval. Hung-jen is saying that the verse is not bad, but neither does it quite reach it.)

Here we can see some incredible *upaya*—skillful means—unfolding. Hung-jen had a community of a thousand monastics. In China at that time, in order to be a monastic you had to be very highly educated and probably from an important family as well. The elite of the civilization resided in the monasteries, similar to the way it was in Tibet prior to the Chinese invasion. Monasteries were the centers of learning. The career choices available to young men at that time were essentially to go to a monastery, to work in government, or to become merchants. If you were an intellectual, being a merchant wasn't very exciting, so it was the monastery or government. As a result, the monasteries blossomed. Shen-hsiu was the *creme de la creme* of that monastery. The Fifth Ancestor asked everybody to memorize his verse.

In the meantime, down at the mill, the ragamuffin from the south heard the monastics talking about the poem, and asked, "What writing are you talking about?" One of the monastics said, "Don't you know? The Ancestor is seeking a successor for the teaching and asked everyone to compose a verse. This is the verse of Shen-hsiu, the head monastic. The teacher praised it highly; he surely will pass on the transmission to him." Hui-neng, of course, couldn't read it and had to ask the monastic to recite it for him. Hui-neng was quiet for a minute after hearing it, and then said, "It's nice alright, but it's still missing something." The monastic laughed and said, "What do you know about this? You're a rice pounder. Don't talk crazy!" and just walked away.

That night Hui-neng had one of the servant boys who worked in the rice-pounding shed accompany him to the hall outside the Master's room and asked the boy to write this verse next to Shen-hsiu's:

Enlightenment is basically not a Bodhi tree.
Nor has the clear mirror a stand.
Fundamentally there is not a single thing.
Where can the dust collect?

Everyone who saw this verse the next day praised it. They were all convinced that some living bodhisattva had created it and put it there. (Hui-neng hadn't signed his verse either.) When the Fifth Ancestor read it, he knew immediately that it was by Hui-neng but said, "Who composed this? This is by someone who hasn't perceived his real nature yet!" He pulled the verse off the wall, tore it up and threw it away. Because of his actions, the whole community ignored Hui-neng's verse, figuring, "Well, the teacher knows. It must not be the verse of a great bodhisattva. There must be something wrong with it."

That night, the Fifth Ancestor secretly came to the mill where Hui-neng was working and asked him, "Has the rice become white?" Hui-neng said, "Yes, it has, but it has not yet been sifted." The Fifth Ancestor hit the mortar three times with his stick; Hui-neng sifted the rice three times. The Ancestor told him—and this saying is something that continues to this day in the transmission ceremony—"*The Buddhas, for the sake of the one great matter of the appearance of the enlightened knowledge in the world, guide people in accord with their capacities. Eventually there came to be teachings of ten stages, three vehicles, sudden and gradual enlightenment, and so on. Moreover, the Buddha transmitted the unexcelled, extremely subtle esoteric real treasury of the Eye of the Right Teaching of Complete Enlightenment to his senior disciple, Mahakashyapa. This was handed on until it reached Bodhidharma, in the twenty-eighth generation. He came to China and found the great Master Hui-k'o. It continued to be transmitted until it came to me. Now I pass it on to you, this treasure of the teaching and the vestment which has been handed down. Preserve the teaching well, and please, do not let it be cut off.*" Kneeling, Hui-neng received the vestment and the teaching, and said, "I have received the teaching. To whom should the vestment be imparted?" In other words, "I have the teaching. What's the vestment for?" (The vestment is the Buddha robe.) The Ancestor said, "A long time ago when Bodhidharma first came to China, people didn't believe, so he handed on the vestment as an indication of having attained the teaching. Now faith has developed, and the vestment has become a source of contention. So let it stop with you, and don't pass it on. Now you should go far away and conceal yourself until the appropriate time to teach comes. It is said that the life of a person who has received this vestment hangs like a thread."

Hui-neng said, "Where should I hide?" The Ancestor said, "When you come to Wei, stop and hide there for a while." He suggested that Hui-neng hide because he knew that if the monastics found out about the transmission they would be enraged, and that probably this young woodcutter from the south of China would end up losing his life at their hands. Hung-jen wanted to protect him. People always ask me, "But they were monastics. Why would they do something like that?" Indeed!

Master Hui-neng bowed and together they went down the mountain to the river. Hui-neng said, "You should go back now. I've already realized the Way and should ferry myself over." The Fifth Ancestor said, "Though you have attained the Way, I will still ferry you over to the other shore." He then took the pole, put Hui-neng in the boat, and brought him across the river. Then Hung-jen returned to the monastery alone.

The community had no idea that any of this had taken place. But the Fifth Ancestor stopped lecturing, didn't go into the dokusan room anymore, and stopped giving Dharma talks. When the monastics asked him what was going on, he said, "My Way has gone." Someone asked him, "Who's got your vestment and teaching?" The Ancestor said, "The able one got them." Then the community began to figure it out; "able" was the meaning of Hui-neng's name, and he had also disappeared. When they realized he had gotten the vestment, a group of them set off to get it back. They couldn't have this illiterate southern layman who was just a boy running around with the robe of Bodhidharma. After some time searching for Hui-neng, most of them gave up because the journey took them very deep into the mountains.

One of the monastics, however, a former general by the name of Ming, persevered until he finally overtook Hui-neng. As Hui-neng saw Ming approaching, he put the robe down on a rock. Ming tried to pick it up, but somehow he couldn't do it. Even though he tried with all his might, the robe wouldn't budge, and Ming began to tremble and sweat. He fell to his knees and said, "I have come for the teachings, not for the robe. Please teach me, lay brother." Hui-neng said, "Think neither good nor evil. At that very moment, what is your original face?" Hearing these words, Ming experienced great enlightenment and began sobbing in gratitude, bowing to this youngster— now Sixth Ancestor—and asked, "Is there any further secret meaning behind what you have just said?" Hui-neng said, "What I have just told you is not secret. If you look into your mind, the secret is in you." Ming said, "When I was at the place of the Fifth Ancestor, I didn't realize myself. Now that I've received your teaching, I'm like the person who drinks water and knows for himself whether it's cold or hot. You are my teacher." Hui-neng said, "If it is as you say, then the Fifth Ancestor is both your teacher and mine." Again, you can see Hui-neng's modesty; he wasn't all puffed up. He simply realized himself down to the bones and marrow.

After that, Hui-neng concealed himself for nearly sixteen years. Then one day he appeared inconspicuously at a local monastery. He heard two monastics arguing about a flag. They were having a philosophical discussion about whether it was the wind or the flag that was moving. Hui-neng said, "It's neither the wind nor the flag; it's your mind that moves."

The master of the temple later heard about this exchange, and sent for Hui-neng. Seeing that there was something extraordinary about him, the temple master asked where he was from and from whom he'd received the teachings. Because he had now completed his time in hiding, Hui-neng told the master the story. Immediately the temple master resigned his abbacy, turned the temple over to Hui-neng, and became his disciple. (Again, what an extraordinary event. Can you imagine such a thing happening these days?) The temple master told the entire assembly of his students, "I'm an ordinary mortal, but now I've met a living bodhisattva." A few days later several famous priests were assembled and formally ordained Hui-neng.

Many students began to gather around him. Hui-neng was touted as the fulfillment of a several hundred-year old prophecy predicting that a very enlightened layman would appear and receive the Precepts at this particular location. A year after he began teaching, however, he said to the community, "I don't want to stay here. I want to go back to my old hiding place." The former abbot of the monastery and more than a thousand monastics and lay people escorted him back to where he had emerged. Years later he became the Chinese National Teacher for a short time at a famous national temple, and is said to have had many successors. The two that we know best are the ones whose lineages have survived: Ch'ing-yüan and Nan-yüeh. At the age of seventy-six, Hui-neng passed away while sitting.

Of course, the heart of this story is the transmission of the teaching. When the Fifth Ancestor said, "Is the rice white yet?" he was using the grains of rice to indicate the spiritual sprouts of truth, the life roots of sages and ordinary people. They grow by themselves; they don't need to be tended, hoed, cultivated, or fertilized. When they're husked and polished, they can take on no defilement. Yet even so, they have not been sifted and strained. If you sift and strain them, you'll comprehend inside and out, you'll move up and down, forever free—husks removed, everything extra removed. But removing the husks is only one part of it; the rice still needs to be sifted. You still need to sift the husks to get the white grains.

The Fifth Ancestor knocked on the mortar three times, Hui-neng shook the sieve three times, and the Way was transmitted. Ever since that time of the knocking on the mortar and the sifting of the rice, the transmission has never stopped. It has continued endlessly.

No scholastic understanding, no scholastic teaching and yet Hui-neng heard. "The mind that doesn't dwell on anything" arose in him after hearing just one line of the scripture. He had no experience in formal Zen training, and yet his mind was like a clear mirror. The transmission was carried out in the middle of the night. The lifeline was passed on. It didn't necessarily depend on years of effort, even though it is clear that Hui-neng was diligent. But this enlightenment can't be measured in terms of length, distance, time, or level of education. Master Keizan, who collected the records of the enlightenment experiences from Shakyamuni Buddha to his own teacher seven hundred years ago, wrote the closing remarks for this koan:

"This spring for ninety days I have spoken this way and that way, commenting on past and present, explaining the enlightened ones with both coarse words and soft speech, entering into the subtle and minute, falling into two and three. I've defiled the Way of Zen, and brought out the disgrace of the school. Due to this I think you people have all understood the principle and have gained strength.

But it seems you have not personally accorded with the meaning of the Zen founders. The practice is not like that of the sages of the past; we are lucky to be able to meet like this. If you work on the Way single-mindedly, you will be able to master it, but many of you have not yet reached the other shore. You still can't see into your inner sanctum. The time of the Buddha is in the distant past. Your work on the Way is not yet complete, and physical life is impossible to guarantee. How can you procrastinate? The end of this spring retreat is almost at hand. How could you arbitrarily memorize a word or half a phrase and call that my teaching? Would you bring out a mere bit of knowledge, half an understanding and call that what we are conveying here? Even if you have fully attained that power, the disgrace of this house will still be exposed. How much more so if you wrongly expound the Way? If you want to truly arrive at this realm, you should not fritter away the time, and should not use your body and mind arbitrarily."

Do you know what the disgrace of this house is? It is that each of us already has what Keizan is speaking of. It can't be given to us. It can't be received by us. There is nothing to transmit and nothing to receive. "Nothing" doesn't indicate a void; it means that no "thing" can go from me to you—because we're already filled with it completely.

> *Knock, knock, knock;*
> *Swish, swish, swish.*
> *Countless generations of Buddhas have come forth—*
> *Do you understand it?*

TEN

NAN-CH'ÜAN'S PEONY

The Blue Cliff Record, Case 40

PROLOGUE

When the action of the mind is stopped and swept away, an iron tree will bloom. Can you demonstrate it? Even a crafty person will come a cropper here. Even if they excel in every way, they will have their nostrils pierced. Where are the complications? Listen to the following.

THE MAIN CASE

Lu-hsüan, while talking with Nan-ch'üan, said, "Chao has said that heaven, earth, and I are of the same root. All things and I are of one substance. Isn't that absolutely fantastic?" Nan-ch'üan pointed to a flower in the garden, called Lu-hsüan to him and said, "People these days see this flower as though in a dream."

THE CAPPING VERSE

*Hearing, seeing, touching, and knowing are not one
    and one.
Mountains and rivers should not be viewed in a
    mirror.
The frosty sky, the setting moon at midnight;
With whom will the serene waters of the lake reflect
    the shadows in the cold?*

This koan is an example of a *nanto* koan. What makes *nanto* koans hard to realize completely is that the point of the koan is very subtle. You need to get deep within the interweaving layers of the koan in order to perceive its intricacies. Usually the subtlety is nicely hidden, and whether one sees it or not makes all the difference in the world as to how the koan is understood and presented.

"Nan-ch'üan's Peony" appears in the *The Blue Cliff Record* as Case 40, and in *The Book of Equanimity* as Case 91. Students encounter some of the koans in three or four different places in their training as they progress through the stages of spiritual development. Sometimes a koan is first introduced among the miscellaneous koans in the third stage. Then it reappears in the fifth stage, in the *The Blue Cliff Record*. Then again in the sixth stage, in *The Book of Equanimity*. Each time it is expected that the student's understanding of the koan will have matured. There's no answer to a koan. Since the response to a koan is a state of consciousness, there may be a hundred different ways to present a koan. Each individual will present it uniquely. What is important is what has been seen and how deeply and clearly it has been seen.

If you compare the translations of koans as they appear in the various collections, you will notice obvious surface differences. This can be misleading. It just so happens that there are five different translations available for this particular koan. We have an in-house translation of *The Book of Equanimity*, and the published Thomas Cleary version. There's an in-house version of *The Blue Cliff Record*, Thomas Cleary's *The Blue Cliff Record*, as well as a translation by Sekida. All the versions agree in content, although their phrasing is quite distinct. In studying koans, a practitioner, by understanding the koan, should be able to see which translation is in error and which is accurate.

The prologues, with their different styles, say essentially the same thing. *The Book of Equanimity* states: *Yang-shan uses a dream state to make the real; Nan-ch'üan points to the awakened place to make the unreal. If you know that awakening and dreaming are fundamentally empty, you'll finally realize that the real and the unreal transcend duality. Tell me, with what kind of eye is this person endowed?*

Compare this with the prologue in *The Blue Cliff Record*:

When the action of the mind is stopped and swept away, an iron tree will bloom. Can you demonstrate it? Even a crafty person will come a cropper here. Even if they excel in every way, they will have their nostrils pierced. Where are the complications? Listen to the following.

The main case is presented pretty much the same way in both collections, but the verses appear very differently. The poem in *The Book of Equanimity* says:

*Subject and object penetrated illuminate the roots of
  nature.*
Busily appearing and vanishing, the gate is seen.
*But in the time outside the kalpa, what question could
  there be?*
Fixing the eyes before you, wisdom is subtly present.
*When the tiger growls, the lonely wind stirs around
  the rocks.*
*When the dragon intones, the flying clouds are
  certainly obscured.*
Nan-ch'üan smashes the dream of his fellow man.
*He tries to acquaint them with the stately Maitreya's
  nobility.*

And in *The Blue Cliff Record*:

*Hearing, seeing, touching, and knowing are not one
  and one.*
*Mountains and rivers should not be viewed in a
  mirror.*
The frosty sky, the setting moon at midnight;
*With whom will the serene waters of the lake reflect
  the shadows in the cold?*

Although they sound very different, both prologues
and verses are basically making the same point. There are
as many ways to express a koan as there are people
expressing it, just as there are thousands of ways to express
a sunset, an apple blossom, or a feeling. But the key to
every koan is the truth that underlies its expression.

In Yüan-wu's introduction, he says, *When the action
of the mind is stopped and swept away, the iron tree will*

bloom. He is trying to show us something. He's talking about the falling away of body and mind. In a sense, he's talking about intimacy. *When the mind is stopped and swept away,* in other words, when there is no mind, *the iron tree will bloom.* "The iron tree will bloom" is an expression of the unimaginable, just as is "Stone woman giving birth to a child in the night" and "Blue mountains walking over water." All of this sounds impossible and absurd. But it only becomes impossible and absurd when we've separated ourselves from it. When we're looking *at* it, subject and object are two separate things. Then it doesn't make any sense at all.

Even a crafty person will come a cropper here. Yüan-wu is pointing out that one may act as if one understands, but the person whose understanding is purely conceptual and not based on personal experience will be exposed at the point when he or she tries to show what Yüan-wu is talking about. Yüan-wu is also telling us a little bit about what's going on in the koan. The student here, Lu-hsüan, is still intellectualizing. He's got everything up in his head. He is still operating logically and hasn't yet experienced or expressed the intimacy to Nan-ch'üan's satisfaction.

The Book of Equanimity says: Yang-shan uses a dream state to make the real, Nan-ch'üan points to the awakened place to make the unreal. The first line is a reference to another koan in which Master Yang-shan had a dream of going to Maitreya's heaven. Maitreya is the Buddha of the future. There he was given the third seat in the assembly of monastics, a place of status. A venerable monastic stood up, struck the table with a gavel and said, "Today's talk will be given by the monastic of the third seat." Yang-shan got up, also used the gavel, and said, "The Buddha-Dharma of the Mahayana goes beyond the four propositions and hundred negations. Listen carefully." Then he took his seat again. What Yüan-wu is saying is that Yang-shan used the dream to reveal the real essence of the Mahayana, not its theoretical underpinnings.

Nan-ch'üan points to the awakened place to reveal the unreal. Lu-hsüan, while walking with Nan-ch'üan, said, "Chao has said that heaven, earth, and I are of the same root." True, no question about it, heaven, earth, and I are of the same root. *"All things and I are one substance."* Perfectly true. "Isn't that absolutely fantastic?" Lu-hsüan added but Nan-ch'üan wouldn't accept it. He found a flaw in it and called Lu-hsüan over. He pointed to a peony in the garden and said, *"People these days see this flower as though in a dream."* That's Nan-ch'üan pointing to the awakened place to reveal the unreal.

The best way of working with a koan is to really chew it up, to really be intimate with it. Don't treat it as some kind of riddle or puzzle, or as some kind of exam. Put yourself completely into it and be the koan through and through. To do that you need to know something about the background of the people mentioned in the koan. Usually the compilers of the collections will tell you something about them. Nan-ch'üan, for example, was one of the greatest masters of the T'ang Dynasty. He was a successor of Master Ma-tsu who had eighty-four enlightened disciples. Of those eighty-four, he regarded Nan-ch'üan as one of the best. He was born in 748, and at the age of 19 became a monastic. He died at the age of 87. This koan takes place towards the end of his life, when he was well into his 80s. Ma-tsu once said of Nan-ch'üan, "The sutras are in the hands of Hsi-t'ang, Zen is in the hands of Pai-chang, but only Nan-ch'üan surpasses the world of things." So here is this wonderful old teacher Nan-ch'üan in the ripe, mature years of his life. Lu-hsüan was a government official and a student of Nan-ch'üan. He had been studying with Nan-ch'üan for quite a while. In fact he came to realization and some insight while with Nan-ch'üan. One day, Lu-hsüan said to Nan-ch'üan, "I've raised a goose in a bottle, and it has gradually grown too big to get out without damaging the bottle or injuring the goose. How would you get it out?" Nan-ch'üan said, "Lu-hsüan!" Lu-hsüan answered, "Yes, Master." Nan-ch'üan said, "It's out." Lu-hsüan had an opening experience as a result of that dialogue.

In this koan, the two of them are going for a little walk, having what appears to be a casual exchange. This is an example of one type of a teacher-student interaction. There is the very direct, one-to-one encounter of the dokusan room, which comes out of the context of zazen. There are discourses such as this one, which arise from the point of view of the realized koan. Dharma combat is sort of like a public dokusan. *Mondo* is a question-and-answer session between teacher and students which has a distinctly intellectual flavor. And there are the casual encounters of working together and being together every day, captured by this koan.

Lu-hsüan, in addition to being a Zen student and a government official, was a scholar who loved to study Buddhist history and theory. He especially appreciated the discourses of Dharma Master Chao. Chao was a scholar in fifth–century China. In one of his pieces he described his sense of intimacy with the whole universe. *Heaven, earth, and I are of the same root. All things and I are of one substance.* Basically, it was an expression of his understanding. Lu-hsüan, having some insight and being well informed about the scholarly aspects of Buddhism, used this quote as a wonderful example of the merging of subject and object. It's a poignant statement on the unity of things, the oneness of this reality. *Heaven, earth, and I are of the same root. All things and I are of one substance.*

To see the koan is to be the koan. The only way you can be the koan is to forget the self. It's the idea of the self that separates us from everything; from each other, from our lives, from the ten thousand things. It's the illusion of the self that separates us even from our own personal barriers. When you encounter a barrier, whether that barrier is a traditional koan or a koan of everyday life, a koan of anger, fear, anxiety, or pain, resolve it by being it. The way we respond to obstacles is to want to move away from them, to turn and go the other way. The more aggressive among us will try to bang our heads against the walls, to push against them by using force. But the only way through the barrier is to be the barrier. When you are the barrier, there is no barrier, and the only way you can be a barrier is to forget the self. The only way you can be the pain is to forget the self; the only way you can be the fear is to forget the self.

In his poem, Chao was affirming the fact of no separation. We create the separation with the idea of self. Buddhism is based on *anatman*, no self. It's one of the aspects that makes Buddhism unique among the world's religions, and it has a powerful and profound impact on Buddhism's moral and ethical teachings. All the Precepts are based on no self. The life of the Buddha is based on no self. Most other religions, past and present, confirm the idea of a self, and it's that idea that separates us from each other and the ten thousand things. Finding this concise expression of the unity of the ten thousand things, Lu-hsüan was impressed with it. He said, "*Isn't that absolutely fantastic?*" Somehow, Nan-ch'üan didn't approve. You can imagine the scene. Nan-ch'üan in his eighties, hobbling along with this very young, enthusiastic student, a very important person in China, filled with his insight, overflowing with all the information he's gathered from wonderful Buddhist texts and poems that he's been studying. And Nan-ch'üan pulls him over to a flower, points to it, and says, "*People these days see this flower as though in a dream.*" What is Nan-ch'üan saying? Clearly he wasn't approving, but what was he teaching? Lu-hsüan was talking about what Chao had experienced. He could have expressed it in a very different way. He could have expressed his own understanding, but he didn't choose to do that, or wasn't able.

One old master said, "The ultimate person is empty, without form, yet none of the myriad things are not his own doing." In other words, we create the ten thousand things, we are the ten thousand things. Who can understand that the myriad things are one's own self? Another master said, "Heaven and earth and the whole world is just this one self. When cold, it's cold throughout the whole heaven and earth; when hot, it's hot throughout the whole heaven and earth. When it exists, all throughout heaven and earth it exists; when it doesn't exist, heaven and earth do not exist. When affirmed, all throughout heaven and earth are affirmed. When denied, all throughout heaven and earth are denied." Heaven, earth, and I are of the same root. A teacher asked, "Tell me what root do they share? Which body do they have in common?"

Nan-ch'üan could have ignored Lu-hsüan's comment. It's not that Lu-hsüan was wrong in what he said. But it wasn't live Zen. It had the stink of Zen in it. That's one of the sicknesses of Zen. There are many. There's even the sickness of having no sickness at all. What kind of a person is that? Is it someone who's real, alive and breathing? Nan-ch'üan, answering this way, was breaking up the nest Lu-hsüan was beginning to create for himself. The nest was his collection of ideas. It's very easy to have some kind of insight and immediately grab onto it. We begin explaining it to ourselves. Before long we're explaining it to others, and it loses all of its life. Nan-ch'üan is trying to prevent that from happening. He points to the flower, exclaiming, "*People these days see this flower as though in a dream.*" A commentator on this koan said, "This is like leading Lu-hsüan to the edge of a ten thousand–fathom cliff and giving him a push, causing his life to be cut off." "Causing his life to be cut off" is killing the ego, killing the idea of a self so that the statement he was mouthing could become a living reality.

Nan-ch'üan says, "People these days see this flower *as though* they were in a dream." He doesn't say, "People see this flower in a dream." What does he mean when he says that? Why is the example of a dream important? He could have said, "People these days don't really see this flower." He was pointing to the possibility of intimacy. What does it mean to intimately see a flower? And what does it mean to see a flower in a dream? In Buddhist psychology, there are six senses, not just the five that we are familiar with from Western psychology: sight, sound, smell, taste, and touch. In Buddhism, mind is also considered an organ of perception, a sense organ. We sense the universe with the mind. We create reality through the interaction of the object of perception, the organ of perception, and human consciousness. The total spectrum of human experience is based on that—the organ of perception, the object of perception, and consciousness coming together. If any one of the components is missing, the thing doesn't exist.

Your eye sees the stick; therefore eye, stick, and consciousness create the visual reality of its existence. Take away the stick, and even though eye and consciousness are there, it doesn't exist. Even though the stick is there, if the eye doesn't function, the stick doesn't exist. And even though eye and stick are present, if consciousness is not, the stick doesn't exist. The line from *Heart Sutra*, "No eye, ear, nose, tongue, body, mind; no color, sound, smell, taste, touch, phenomena," points to that cessation of existence.

The object of perception for the mind is thought. Mind, thought, and consciousness create a reality that's as real as this or as unreal as this. When we sleep, we sometimes dream. A dream can be very vivid and real. There you are in the dream being pursued by one of your demons. You're frightened and running. You break out into a sweat, you're panting, out of breath, unable to get enough oxygen. Suddenly you wake up, and dripping with sweat, you realize it was a dream. It didn't really happen. It was all in your mind. Well, so is this experience a creation of the mind. We create the universe, we create the dream.

In view of that, what was Nan-ch'üan saying when he was pointing to that flower and saying, *"People these days see this flower as though in a dream"*? Dogen speaks of seeing form with the whole body and mind, of hearing sounds with the whole body and mind. He says that when one does that, one understands intimately. What he means when he says that one understands intimately is the state of enlightenment itself; no separation of subject and object. The reality of what Chao said, "The ten thousand things and I are of the same root, the myriad forms and I are the same substance" is the reality of no separation. Nan-ch'üan is warning Lu-hsüan, "It's up in your head." How is it when there's intimacy?

The Buddha says to regard all existence as transitory. The whole *Diamond Sutra* speaks of existence as an illusion. But the Buddha Way is not about existence, nor is it about non-existence. It transcends both existence and non-existence. As one master said, "If you know that waking and dreaming are fundamentally empty, that they have no fixed characteristics, then you'll finally realize that real and unreal, dream and not dream, transcend duality. They're beyond those dualities." The truth is beyond dualities. If you really realize the dream, then you and I, the ten thousand things, the whole universe are a dream, and there's nothing outside that dream. And that's exactly the same as there being no dream at all. But Nan-ch'üan said, "People see this as though in a dream." He didn't say, "In a dream." It's not called a dream, and it's not called not a dream, nor is it called neither a dream nor not a dream. Then what is it?

Referring to Shakyamuni's holding up the flower on Vulture Peak and the transmission of the Dharma from generation to the generation, Master Dogen calls them "explaining a dream within a dream." He also says that Hui-k'o's prostration and attaining the marrow from Bodhidharma is also "explaining a dream within a dream." In other words the Dharma, the teaching, the transmission, are just explaining a dream within a dream. Is that what this is? Is that what our existence is? If everything is a dream, then what is real? What is reality?

Lu-hsüan had a wonderful understanding of Chao's poem, but unfortunately it was a dream, it was all up in his head. It was an idea, a mental construct. How is it when the action of the mind has stopped? When the mind doesn't move, when there is no mind, what happens to you and me and the ten thousand things? What happens to the peony? What happens to the pain, the barrier, the koan Mu? Where do they go? Where did they come from? How did they get there? When there is no mind, there is no sight, sound, smell, taste, or touch. There is no color, no phenomena; there is no world of sight, no world of consciousness. That's the intimacy of seeing form with the whole body and mind, of hearing sound with the whole body and mind.

In the verse, Hsüeh-tou says,

> *Hearing, seeing, touching, and knowing are not*
> *one and one.*
> *Mountains and rivers should not be viewed in a*
> *mirror.*
> *The frosty sky, the setting moon at midnight;*
> *With whom will the serene waters of the lake reflect*
> *the shadows in the cold?*

A master talking about this passage said, "Mountains and rivers should not be seen in a mirror. If you say that they are seen in a mirror, and only then illuminated, then they're not apart from where the mirror is." Mountains, rivers, and the great earth, plants, trees, and forests—do not use a mirror to observe them. If you use a mirror to observe them, then you make it into two parts; self and other, this and that, me and you, self and the barrier. Just let mountains be mountains, rivers be rivers. But if mountains and rivers are not seen in a mirror, then tell me, where do you see them? How do you see them? Do you understand?

And what about old master Nan-ch'üan? How do you speak of such a person? Where does he abide? In intimacy there is no reflection, no understanding, no knowing, no analysis, no judgment, no categorizing. It's hard to trust that. One of the biggest handicaps in koan study is our irrepressible need to intellectualize any new insight. We want to hold onto it and personalize it. That's the

145

equivalent of trying to take the spring breeze, put it in a jar, and label it "spring breeze." It is then no longer the spring breeze. It has lost everything that made it alive and vibrant. So it is with a koan. You need to make it your own, beyond any answers and labels. Whole body and mind, so integrated with every cell in your body that you don't even know it's there. It works the way your heart works. It just beats. It just grows, like your hair grows. It's just trust. Whom do you trust? Who else is there? What else is there? There is only yourself. To trust yourself means to be intimate with yourself. To be intimate with yourself means that the self fills heaven and earth and the ten thousand things. There is nothing outside it. That's what Lu-hsüan was missing. That's what Nan-ch'üan, out of deep compassion for his student, was trying to point to. With whom will the serene waters of the lake reflect the shadows in the cold? I ask you.

ELEVEN

YÜN-MEN'S TWO SICKNESSES

The Book of Equanimity, Case 11

PROLOGUE

A bodiless person suffers illness. A handless person compounds medicine. A mouthless person takes meals. A non-receiving person has ease and comfort. Tell me: for incurable disease, what is the treatment?

THE MAIN CASE

Attention! The great Master Yün-men said, "When the light doesn't penetrate completely, there are two kinds of sicknesses. When wherever you are is not quite clear and there are things in front of you, that is one sickness. Even though you thoroughly penetrate the emptiness of all Dharmas, there still somehow seems to be something. In this also, the light has not yet penetrated completely.

Again there are two kinds of sicknesses in the dharmakāya. *Though you reach the* dharmakāya, *because Dharma attachment is not forgotten and a view of self still persists, you plummet into the* dharmakāya *side. That is one sickness. Though you penetrate through this, if you are negligent it is still no good. Even after a minute examination, when what inadequacy could there be, this is also a sickness."*

THE CAPPING VERSE

Multitudes of shapes allowed to be as is—
Boundless, thorough liberation still obstructs the eye.
To sweep out this garden, who has the strength?
Concealed in one's heart, it of itself gives rise to
*   feelings.*
Steeped in gathering autumn lies a boat upon blue.
Illumined by snowy reed flowers stands a pole with
*   lights suffused.*
An old fisherman with a skewered perch thinks of
*   going to the market;*
Carefree, a leaf sails over the waves.

Amid the unfolding of our lives is a great variety of sicknesses. It is very easy to get caught up in them. Many of them become apparent at the very beginning of our practice and manifest themselves as the sicknesses of delusion, inadequacy, and separation. As we proceed through our training, we seem to solve one type of sickness only to create another. Ultimately, the whole point of practice is to be able to recognize, deal with, and practice these various sicknesses.

One thing that always amuses me is how we invariably come down with an illness in the middle of our ninety-day Ango intensive retreat here at the Monastery. Somehow, in the middle of Ango when things get especially tough, everybody gets sick. Then by the end of spring a sense of well-being and joy returns. Everybody is happy. All the physical ailments are gone, the atmosphere is filled with vigor, the birds are nesting, the grass is green again, and flowers are all over the place. Everybody is full of life, just loving every moment of the day. And this is also sick, sick, sick—because it is another kind of holding on. It is in the attachment, in that tendency to hold on, that the sickness happens. Yasutani Roshi used to say that if you sit in a big, beautiful, comfortable chair that is all covered with glue, after a while it becomes painful. You become attached to the chair, you can't walk anymore, your behind begins to hurt. Anyone who has been on a ten-hour flight knows how it hurts to be in a comfortable chair.

Every night we chant, "Sentient beings are number-less; I vow to save them. Desires are inexhaustible; I vow to put an end to them. The Dharmas are boundless; I vow to master them. The Buddha Way is unattainable; I vow to attain it." Again—sick, sick, sick. This is delusion within delusion, or an expression of a dream within a dream. It is knowing full well that there are no sentient beings, yet vowing to save them. But that's the delusion, that's the sickness. A wonderful sickness it might be, but it is, nonetheless, a sickness.

Master Yün-men is an extraordinary teacher and, like the great Master Chao-chou, he is known for his beauti-fully subtle teaching words, for his "turning words." The thing about subtlety, though, is that on the surface there doesn't appear to be anything going on. If you dig, you're going to miss it; you'll inevitably go too deep, and that's not where the point is to be found. Yet if you look only at the surface, you'll also miss it. Simply to scratch just beneath the surface is how the point will be found in this koan. And when you see it, it is incredibly fulfilling, incredibly complete. That is Yün-men's style and the style that later came to characterize the Yün-men school.

Yün-men had his first enlightenment experience with Master Mu-chou. He was struggling with a question and went to Mu-chou for guidance. When Yün-men knocked on Mu-chou's door, Mu-chou opened it, looked at him, and then just as Yün-men started to ask his question, slammed the door right in his face. Of course, Mu-chou was responding to his question. Yün-men went away and continued his zazen but soon came back again to visit Mu-chou. Again Mu-chou opened the door, but the minute Yün-men opened his mouth to ask a question, he slammed the door on him. Yün-men went away again and sat. The next time he visited Mu-chou he was determined to get inside, so when Mu-chou opened the door, instead of asking his question Yün-men stuck his foot in the doorway. Mu-chou slammed the door, breaking Yün-men's leg. Yün-men let out a scream of pain and at that moment, in the midst of that scream, he realized himself. He then continued his studies with Master Hsüeh-feng and ultimately succeeded him. That very rough treatment by Mu-chou may be why Yün-men became the gentle teacher with words. He didn't resort to yelling, or punching students out, or slamming doors on their legs, but rather used words to reveal the Way.

In the prologue to this koan, Wan-sung basically tells us what the point of Yün-men's teaching in the main case will be. He tells us about the sicknesses that are described in the koan: *A bodiless person suffers illness. A handless person compounds medicine. A mouthless person takes meals. A*

*non-receiving person has ease and comfort. Tell me: for
incurable disease, what is the treatment?*

The bodiless person is one whose body and mind
have fallen away: "no eye, ear, nose, tongue, body, or
mind," as we chant in the *Heart Sutra*. And that, in itself,
is a kind of sickness. A handless person is a person who
uses hands freely but has no sense of doing it. This is the
"empty hand" of karate, and empty hand means empty
mind. So this handless person is making the medicine. The
mouthless person taking meals also has a particular kind of
sickness. As one teacher pointed out, "Take notice that
the mouthless person is taking a meal, not the medicine.
They're so sick they don't even know they need medicine." That's the sickness.

The non-receiving person who has "ease and com-
fort" points to the fact that to receive is, in fact, to suffer.
The minute you separate yourself, there is suffering. To
give is also to suffer. Many schools of Buddhism resort to
non-receiving. But to avoid receiving is to run away from
receiving, and that's simply being attached to non-receiving. To avoid receiving is not yet enlightenment. Where
there is no giver and no receiver, receiving is distinctly different. To be able to give, to be able to receive, and yet to
understand that there is no giver and no receiver is a different state of understanding. When you talk about giving
or receiving, you're talking about two things, and inherent
in the act of identifying those two things as separate is the
creation of life's suffering. Yet, the answer is not a simple
negation—not giving and not receiving. When we realize
that the ten thousand things are one reality, then how
could there possibly be a giver and a receiver? Where
would they stand in order to give or to receive? There is
no outside, nor is there an inside. To this, Yün-men offers,
"For the incurable disease, what is the treatment?"

And that leads us right into the main case, which actually details four kinds of sicknesses, not just two. Wan-sung has added notes to each line of the main koan, like a little whisper off-stage. To the first line, "*When the light doesn't penetrate completely, there are two kinds of sicknesses*," his note reads, "Do you feel your mouth dry up and your tongue shrivel?" He is saying that Yün-men's tongue should fall out of his mouth for talking like this. Of course, in a sense, he is also admiring Yün-men's teaching. But in order to talk about it, Yün-men has to wallow in the very same delusion that he is trying to heal. Sometimes the physician has to be exposed to the illness in order to get close enough to work with the patient.

When Yün-men says "*When the light doesn't penetrate completely, there are two kinds of sicknesses*," the light referred to is enlightenment. That enlightenment is your own light—it doesn't come from any place other than yourself and is inherent in the life of each one of us. The sicknesses being talked about in this koan occur as one advances in training, among people who have realized themselves. These are perhaps the most difficult sicknesses to heal. The ones you come into practice with, particularly when they are accompanied with a beginner's mind, are relatively easy to deal with. It's the after-realization sicknesses that become especially subtle and difficult to work with. Although there is enlightenment, it's still not thorough. There's a faint haze; what has been seen isn't quite clear and "the light doesn't penetrate completely."

When Yün-men presents, "*When wherever you are is not quite clear and there are things in front of you, that is one sickness*," Wan-sung responds, "When you see a ghost in the daylight, isn't that an illusion?" In that faint haze being illuminated by so-called enlightenment, there are dark spots remaining. The light is not reaching those spots, so what you see is a shadow in the haze, and that shadow looks like objects "*out* there." Of course, in true realization there is no inside or outside. That's what is realized. Yet despite that realization, somehow there is still this residual sense of something out there. It doesn't matter if it is a deep enlightenment or a shallow enlightenment, the realization is that oneness: no objects out there. We mention again and again, however, that to realize the absolute is not yet enlightenment, because our tendency is to create dualities with the Dharma in the same way we have always done with other things. All we do is replace our secular delusions with Dharma delusions based on separation and attachment.

In the next line Yün-men says, "*Even though you have thoroughly penetrated the emptiness of all Dharmas, there still somehow seems to be something. In this also, the light has not penetrated completely.*" Wan-sung's note says, "Already your chest is constricted. What does it matter if your throat is closed?" If you can't breathe because your chest won't take in the air, it doesn't matter that your throat is closed. Even though you have thoroughly penetrated the emptiness of all Dharmas, even in that, somehow, there seems to be something. This is what's called "person emptied and Dharmas emptied." When the person and Dharmas are both emptied, there doesn't seem to be anything remaining at all. But somehow, deeply hidden, something is still there. A single hair, and heaven and earth are separated. A hair's breadth, the least little thing that we place outside ourselves, by that much we separate ourselves from the ten thousand things.

Yün-men goes on to say, "*There are two kinds of sicknesses in the* dharmakāya." Dharmakāya is the absolute basis of all things, the basis of reality out of which the whole world of differentiation is manifested. Wan-sung comments, "Calamities don't happen alone." Thus, the first two calamities are followed by the second two calamities.

Then Yün-men says, "*Though you reach the* dharmakāya, *because dharma attachment is not forgotten and a view of the self still persists, you plummet into the* dharmakāya *side. That is one sickness.*" Wan-sung's note reads, "Not only are there false idols outside, there is also a false idol inside." This is called being stuck in emptiness or in the ghost cave. In order to attach to emptiness, a view of self must still exist.

Yün-men's main case continues: "*Though you penetrate through this, if you are negligent it is still no good.*" The note says, "Nursing sickness you lose your body." What will you do without a body? Yün-men's next line is, *Even after minute examination, when what inadequacy could there be, this is also a sickness.* And Wan-sung adds, "Before the doctor has gone out the door, already you're having another seizure."

When speaking of this koan, Yasutani Roshi commented, "Being able to penetrate through is thorough-going great enlightenment. It is entry into the *dharmakāya* world, and to discard this, too, is to be cured. For example, having had a thorough-going great enlightenment and having thrown it away and been cured, occasionally you'll fall into the *dharmakāya* side, or a view of the self arises and stays for awhile without being discarded." Sometimes this is referred to as developing a second self. You forget the self and the ten thousand things return to the self, and then you begin to intellectualize what you've seen. The minute you start defining it, categorizing it, analyzing it, fitting it into your reference system, you're creating this second self. The old self is forgotten and now you've created a new one, just as deluded as the one before. Yasutani said, "If with might and main, from moment to moment you go on paying close attention, you can't go wrong." This is called "however you look at it there is no inadequacy." And this too is a sickness. This is the sickness of having no sickness at all.

A monastic came to Chao-chou and asked him, "How can I deal with suffering?" and Chao-chou said, "Throw it away. Make yourself empty." And the monastic said, "I've made myself empty. Now what?" And Chao-chou said, "Get rid of that." When we say, "I've made myself empty," it is still an idea. "I've realized myself" is an idea; it's no different from the idea "I am deluded." It gets kind of sticky. In fact, the deeper you go, the stickier it gets. Wherever you stop, whatever you hold on to— right there, the sickness begins to show. If you don't attach, don't stop, don't hold on, it doesn't matter whether your practice is strong or weak, whether your enlightenment is bright or shallow; however you happen to be, you will naturally be in accord with the Way. Even a rank beginner can practice non-attachment, and by that practice of not holding on, be that much in accord with the Way of the Buddha. This is true not only for Buddhism but for all activity, for all practice.

These sicknesses are the subtle problems that are very hard to see in oneself. This is why if you are dealing with a sick teacher, what's transmitted is the sickness the teacher hasn't dealt with. Or you are creating your own sicknesses and they're not being seen, and that is what is transmitted. It is terribly important to handle these sicknesses. Yasutani calls Yün-men "King of the great doctors of Zen," and advises that "If those people who have one-piece enlightenment and come to realization after realization do not fully and freely perspire over sober-minded and honest koans such as this, their realization will not be authentic."

He just loves these delicate koans that comprise *The Book of Equanimity*.

In the appreciatory verse that accompanies this koan, Hung-chih very nicely develops its teaching:

> *Multitudes of shapes allowed to be as is—*
> *Boundless, thorough liberation still obstructs the eye.*
> *To sweep out this garden, who has the strength?*
> *Concealed in one's heart, it of itself gives rise to*
> *   feelings.*
> *Steeped in gathering autumn lies a boat upon blue.*
> *Illumined by snowy reed flowers stands a pole with*
> *   lights suffused.*
> *An old fisherman with a skewered perch thinks of*
> *   going to the market;*
> *Carefree, a leaf sails over the waves.*

Multitudes of shapes allowed to be as is. Having realized the nature of the *dharmakāya*, you allow things to be as they are. The mountain is high, the water is wet, the big one is a big Buddha, the small one is a small Buddha. Male is totally complete; female is totally complete. They don't lack anything; they don't need anything. The left hand is complete, and the right hand is complete. Absolute is complete, differentiation is complete. Allow each thing to be as it is: the blue heron has long legs, the duck has short legs. In that they're perfect. In that is their salvation. The duck's short legs are the salvation of the duck. The heron's long legs are the salvation of the heron. The maleness is the salvation of the male, and the femaleness is the salvation of the female. None lacks anything. Perfect and complete. And to see this is to have opened the Dharma eye.

Boundless, thorough liberation still obstructs the eye.

This boundless, thorough liberation is the exact opposite of the multitudes of shapes referred to in the previous line. It's looking at the other side and seeing that the ten thousand things are one. In this sickness, what obstructs the eye is the fact that the ten thousand things are one, that there is no difference or separation. If you are stuck in unity, where there is no differentiation, then you can't see this stick [holds up his stick] or hear this sound [bangs stick on the table]. Why? Because it fills the universe. It's not, however, functional.

To sweep out this garden, who has the strength? To sweep out the garden is to sweep out the rubbish in one's head, to sweep out the sickness of enlightenment. Wan-sung's note to this line is, "Wiping traces away makes marks. Trying to conceal makes more visible." This is like the sacred turtle who goes ashore and lays her eggs in the sand. Her footprints in the sand enable predators to find the eggs so she uses her tail to wipe them away as she goes back into the ocean. Of course, what's left behind is the little swish that her tail made.

When I first started practicing with a new teacher, because I was a senior practitioner from another monastery I thought that I needed to be serene. So I practiced serenity. Whenever I saw my teacher walking down the road, I would put this blissful look on my face, and with my eyes half closed I'd say, "Hi, Roshi." He would walk by and after I'd passed, he would call to me, "Daido!" I'd turn and he'd look at me and go, "Uhh!" letting me know that he saw the strain concealed under my serene face. Hard to conceal. Impossible!

This is further explored in the next line, *Concealed in one's heart, it of itself gives rise to feelings.* Just in the hiding, feelings arise, and the process results in all kinds of mental permutations and their expression in deluded actions. This is all part of Dharma attachment: Dharma this, Dharma that. It's like those who say, "Everybody should be a Buddhist. The world is so screwed up because everyone is not a Buddhist. If everyone became a Buddhist there would be peace on earth." That's the worst kind of delusion.

Steeped in gathering autumn lies a boat upon blue. Illumined by snowy reed flowers stands a pole with light suffused. The autumn is a metaphor for the absolute basis of things. The comment on this phrase is, "Submerged in stagnant water." It doesn't move—thus, sickness. The pole among the reeds is a much clearer state, free of stagnation.

Then my favorite line in the poem: *The old fisherman with the skewered perch thinks of going to market.* The note says, "Selling the merchandise he makes a profit." And finally, *Carefree, a leaf sails over the waves.* And the note says, "Finding the subtlety, following the stream."

The leaf is the boat. The leaf is free. And just the way a leaf is carried by the wind and the current, this small boat squeaks and groans as the waves move it and the fisherman sits in it. It's taking him is where he's going to sell the fish. Sometimes it's here and sometimes it's on the other side of the river. Wherever and whenever time, causes, and conditions manifest the need by letting this boat freely arrive there, that's where he's going to take the skewered fish—which is what he's realized, his Dharma—and put it up for sale. This too is an illusion, because we already have the fish. It's like taking a bucket of water, calling it wine, and selling it beside the river. Somehow, if there is a price on it and it's in a nice bucket, everybody buys it even though they are ten feet from the flowing river themselves, and can stick their head in the water and get the same thing.

This appreciatory verse gets clearer and clearer as it

dispenses with the sicknesses. Finally we reach this old fisherman with no further intentions—he's not caught up with teaching or success—and he's wondering if he should take the fish to the market. The fisherman is the old grandpa who is going to sell this fish, the Dharma. He's going to say, "Buy here. Come on, buy this fish. It's fresh. Can I interest you in this fish?" And no discounts, pay the full price.

Discounts are what make it easy. Pay your thirty-five bucks and you're a student. Of what? Going for the discount is how you can get ripped off. It's thinking that you can somehow skip over the barriers of asking the vital questions of life and death. "You can come here for thirty-five bucks. You don't need to have the question of life and death—it's okay." That's a discount. We don't offer discounts at this Monastery. It's full price only—and you pay through the nose. That's what the five barrier gates are. That's what this kindly old fisherman is saying, "Eat this fish. It's good for you. But no discounts!"

This old fisherman reminds me of a time when I was a kid. There were very few cars in the early 1930s. The garbageman, the policeman, the milkman, the baker—all had horses and wagons, and one of the highlights of Saturday mornings was when these peddlers came by. The horses were trained so the garbageman would throw the contents of a pail into the wagon and when the horse heard it land, he'd start walking on to the next house and stop at the next garbage pail. One very old man would come along selling fresh fish packed in ice. He didn't speak English, so he would yell his pitch in Italian. My grandmother would open the window and yell down in Italian, "How good is it?" And he would say, "It's the best!" She'd say, "Five cents a pound sounds too much. It can't be that good. It's packed on ice, it's not alive." He would say something back, and they'd go back and forth. Finally, he would get her down from the second floor and out of the house to where the wagon was; then the debate would continue, and they would shake their fists at each other. In the end, if the fish was really good, and worth it, my grandmother would buy it—but no discounts!

That old fisherman is the eye of wisdom; the leaf and his boat are the eye of compassion. One is the eye of Manjushri and the other is the eye of Samantabhadra Bodhisattva, manifesting according to the circumstances and conditions. All Buddhas have these two eyes, as do all sentient beings, as does each one of you.

> *Born in a single instant, the life of ten thousand*
> *Buddhas.*
> *Timeless and alone between heaven and earth, the*
> *honored one.*
> *How many years now have I enjoyed the ancient win*
> *of Kapila?*

Kapila is the Indian state where Shakyamuni Buddha was born. That wine of Kapila has been nourishing us in this sangha for years. How many years have I personally enjoyed the wine, the ancient wine of Kapila? In awe and gratitude my eyes fill with tears.

TWELVE

YÜN-YEN'S GREAT COMPASSION

The Book of Equanimity, Case 54

PROLOGUE

> *Crystal clear on all sides, open and unobstructed in all directions, emanating light and making the earth tremble in all places, subtly exercising spiritual powers at all times—tell me, how is this manifested?*

THE MAIN CASE

> *Yün-yen asked Tao-wu, "What does the Bodhisattva of Great Compassion do with so many hands and eyes?" Tao-wu said, "It's like someone reaching back for a pillow in the middle of the night." Yün-yen said, "I understand." Tao-wu said, "How do you understand?" Yün-yen said, "All over the body there are hands and eyes." Tao-wu said, "You've said a lot there, but you got only*

eighty percent." Yün-yen said, "What about you, elder brother?" Tao-wu said, "Throughout the body are hands and eyes."

The Capping Verse

One hole, emptiness pervading:
Crystal clear on all sides.
Formlessly, selflessly, spring enters the pipes:
Unstopped, unhindered, the moon traverses the sky.
Pure jewel eyes, arms of virtues:
All over the body—how does it compare to throughout the body being it?
The present hands and eyes reveal the whole works:
The great function works in all ways—what is taboo?

We are living at a time in the life of this planet when the ten thousand hands and eyes of Great Compassion are needed more than ever before. There are influential politicians throughout the world who intend to employ doomsday weapons when "it is appropriate." There are Congressional leaders in our country who have said, "The United States is not ruling out the use of biological warfare, gas, and nuclear bombs as a response to a similar attack." Amid such threats and confusion, where is the Bodhisattva of Great Compassion?

It seems you can never find a bodhisattva when you need one. The fact is you'll never find a bodhisattva, because "bodhisattva" is intimacy itself, and in intimacy there is no separation and no finding. The bodhisattva of compassion reaches everywhere, so there is no way of knowing her. On the other hand, where there is no inti-

162

macy, there can be no bodhisattva; there is only this and that. You hit me, I hit you. Biological warfare, gas warfare, nuclear warfare—who is the hitter and who is it that gets hit? Whose pain is it? What is the pain?

Yasutani Roshi often used the analogy of two hands to help people appreciate how compassion works. If you were to create egos, ideas of separate selves, and give one to each of your hands, then you would have two hands feeling very distinct from each other, one being right and the other left. They would not be superimposable. One could move while the other held still. There would be undeniable differences between them.

If you put money into the left hand, the right hand might get suspicious, "Why does the left hand always get the money? Why doesn't anybody give money to me?" Jealousy could arise from the idea that each hand is an entirely separate thing. Left hand throws a log into the fire. The sleeve gets hooked and it can't get out. It starts burning and crying out for help. The right hand wants to help, but hesitates because it doesn't want to get hurt. We can easily appreciate that hesitancy.

When we enlighten these hands, they realize that they are two parts of the same reality—Daido. The two are the same thing. They can act differently without obstructing each other, but they are still the same reality. Now, if we put money into the left hand, the right hand doesn't mind. Left hand has it, right hand has it. That does not make sense unless you know that they're the same thing. Left hand has it, right hand has it. You have it, I have it; you're happy, I'm happy; you drink, I get drunk. Unless you *know* that they're the same thing, that doesn't happen. When the left hand gets caught in a fire and is burning, the right hand responds immediately—there is no hesitation. If the left hand is burning, the right hand *is* burning. That doesn't make sense unless you have realized that unity, that oneness. The realization itself is wisdom. The action, responding to the hand burning in the fire, is compassion.

There are infinite ways that compassion works. Many years ago, when my first teacher, Soen Nakagawa, was still a young monastic, he was called upon by a friend of the temple where he was training. The man had a daughter, a young woman only seventeen years old, who was studying ballet with the hope of becoming a professional dancer. She was very good and had undeniable potential. One day she was in a car accident and became paralyzed from the waist down, putting an abrupt end to her dancing aspirations. Her parents were very wealthy and took her to every reputable hospital, East and West, to every neurosurgeon who offered the slightest hope, but nothing could be done about the paralysis. The girl became increasingly depressed and despondent. The family tried a number of therapists in an effort to help with her anguish and lethargy, but the situation seemed hopeless. Over several years she just got more and more withdrawn. She was still in the spring of her life, but she was completely filled with apathy. She just sat in her room. She wouldn't read, she wouldn't talk, she wouldn't do anything. She barely ate.

The father asked Soen if he would come over and offer help. Soen said, "I'm not a doctor or a psychologist; I have none of those skills. But I'll come and just see what I can do." He came and talked with the woman for a while. Then he pulled out a small piece of rice paper and a brush. He made some ink with his inkstone and painted for her a picture of Jizo Bodhisattva, the bodhisattva of the helpless beings—children, animals, and anyone else who is hurt and helpless. Jizo is always portrayed with hands held in gassho. He responds when needed. Soen wrote a short poem next to the drawing and gave it to her. She was very thankful. Then he said, "You try it." He gave her the brush, she painted one on a piece of rice paper, and he made a big fuss over it. Soen was always very dramatic and charismatic, and had a way of slipping inside your soul and heart. He asked her to do another one and was even happier about it. At the end of his visit, he left a pile of paper with her and said, "Do one each day. I'll come back next week and see how you're doing. Number them to keep track of each one that you do."

He came back a week later and she had done seven of them. He said, "Wonderful!" He gave her another stack of papers and said, "Do two a day and I'll come back in a month." A month later she had done them and he had her do even more. He kept coming back, and she kept doing the paintings. After about two years, the depression was gone; she was feeling very much alive again. This woman has now become one of the great *sumi-e* painters of Japan. Several years ago I saw the two-millionth Jizo Bodhisattva she had painted. It was about ten feet by six feet. I photographed it for an illustration in a book. At that time the woman was in her eighties, totally healed, well-established, happy, and living a full life.

Is that the ten thousand hands and eyes of compassion and the manifestation of Avalokiteshvara Bodhisattva? What is Avalokiteshvara Bodhisattva? What are the ten thousand hands and eyes? What is it that makes it "crystal clear on all sides and unobstructed in all directions"? Where does the light that makes the earth tremble emanate from?

Compassion is manifesting form in accord with beings, acting in accord with imperative, doing what's necessary in that particular moment. It is not always "doing good" as we would normally conceive of it with our discriminative consciousness. It may even look like "doing bad." Its essential characteristic is that it is activity for the benefit of all beings—there is no self in it. Every time someone responds to an accident, every time a fireman enters a fire, every time a mother turns towards her crying child, Avalokiteshvara Bodhisattva comes to life. She is manifest in the form of the motorist who stops to help another motorist. That motorist is nothing other than the manifestation of the virtue of compassion and its eighty-four thousand hands and eyes.

One of the characteristics of Avalokiteshvara Bodhisattva, aside from the multiple hands and eyes she uses to respond to the world's needs, is her ability to manifest herself in whatever form is appropriate to the circumstance when the need arises. She doesn't appear in a female form with a halo over her head, and hands and eyes all over the body, but rather as something fitting to the situation. Sometimes she is a saint, sometimes a general, sometimes a derelict.

The introduction to the koan asks, *Crystal clear on all sides, open and unobstructed in all directions, emanating light and making the earth tremble in all places, subtly exercising spiritual powers at all times—tell me, how is this manifested?* In response, the koan shows it.

Yün-yen asked Tao-wu, "What does the Bodhisattva of Great Compassion do with so many hands and eyes?" In this koan, what, indeed, are the ten thousand hands and eyes of Avalokiteshvara Bodhisattva? Avalokiteshvara Bodhisattva is the bodhisattva who hears the cries of the world. There are many bodhisattvas, beings who put aside their realization, their own enlightenment, for the benefit of others. Not until every single sentient being on the face of this earth is enlightened do the bodhisattvas take care of their own enlightenment. There are bodhisattvas in all religions and in each one we find this great compassionate heart at work. But what is that great compassionate heart? Who are the bodhisattvas?

Tao-wu and Yün-yen both received the transmission from Yüeh-shan. Yün-yen transmitted to Tung-shan, and that marked the beginning of the Soto School, which is why this is an important koan in Soto School teachings. The bodhisattva functions in the world of this and that, and yet the statement is made: *Crystal clear on all sides, open and unobstructed in all directions....* This indicates a life of no hindrance which reaches everywhere. It points to the absolute manifestation of Buddha in the world, among the myriad things.

This is precisely the way the Buddhist Precepts function. Wisdom is the realization of no separation. Compassion is the actualization of wisdom and its activity in the world of separation. I*t's like someone reaching back for a pillow in the middle of the night.* There is no thought moving there. In compassion there is no sense of an active agent or the activity that the agent performs. It happens. Someone falls, you pick them up. There's a fire, you put it out. There's a cry, you respond.

Yün-yen said, "All over the body there are hands and eyes." Tao-wu said, "You said a lot there, but you got only eighty percent." Yün-yen said, "What about you, elder brother?" Tao-wu said "Throughout the body there are hands and eyes." Is there a difference? All over the body hands and eyes—eighty percent; throughout the body hands and eyes—is that one hundred percent? Why eighty percent? Why not fifty percent? What's the magic of eighty percent?

There once was a hermit who was blind. After a rain, on a muddy road, he would wear pure white shoes and go to the market. Someone once asked him, "You're blind. How come there's no mud on your shoes?" The mountain man raised his staff and said, "There's an eye on this staff." (He knows where to step!) Wan-sung comments, "The mountain man is proof that when reaching for a pillow at night, there is an eye in the hand. When eating, there is an eye on the tongue. When recognizing people on hearing them speak, there is an eye in the ears."

Another master was conversing with a deaf man, writing notes in order to communicate. Suddenly, he started laughing, "He and I are both strange people. I use my hand for a mouth and he uses his eyes for an ear." The Buddha spoke of the interchanging functions of the six senses and of "the whole-body-and-mind hands and eyes."

There are thirty-two responses of Avalokiteshvara Bodhisattva referred to in the *Lotus Sutra*, but there are millions of manifestations of those responses. A master said, "A thousand hands illustrate the many-sidedness of the guidance of the deluded in the salvation of beings. A thousand eyes illustrate the breadth of emanating light to illuminate the darkness. If there were no sentient beings and no mundane turmoil, then not even a finger would remain, much less thousands or tens of thousands of arms. Not even an eyelid would be there, much less thousands or tens of thousands of eyes." It's *because* of delusion that there's enlightenment. It's *because* of enlightenment that there's delusion.

Was Yün-yen wrong in saying, "All over the body there are hands and eyes"? Is that why Tao-wu said, "You've said a lot there, but you got only eighty percent"? Yün-yen asked, "What about you?" Tao-wu responded, "Throughout the body are hands and eyes." Is there a difference between "throughout the body" and "all over the body" and, if so, what is it?

In the verse, the last line, *What is taboo?* asks us to consider "What is not allowed?" Or, as Wan-sung says,

"What is right? What is wrong?" Is there a right and wrong? If so, what is it? *Emptiness pervading* is all directions becoming crystal clear. It's like a willow-grown river bank on a warm day in a gentle breeze—where is the spring? What shape is the spring? We can't really say. Nevertheless, it is able to accord with things and to come in its time, unstoppable, unhindered. There is no stopping spring. When it arrives, it truly arrives. Spring is the great heart of compassion. What shape is it? Where is it? Whose is it?

As long as we conceal ourselves in this bag of skin, there is no hope for compassion to unfold. All we have is a bunch of skin bags poking at each other, creating karma. We're continously creating a cause and an effect. There is individual karma and there is group karma. There is also a karma of a family, of a country, and of a planet. All of these are one reality, and that reality is each one of us. It is your reality, your planet, your life. Those are all one thing, not three.

There are notes added by Master Wan-sung to each line of the koan and the verse. *Yün-yen asked Tao-wu, "What does the Bodhisattva of Great Compassion do with so many hands and eyes?"* The note says, "What's your aim in asking such a question?"

Tao-wu said, "It's like someone reaching back for a pillow in the middle of night." The note says, "A miraculous power. It's not the same as the little kind." There is something wonderful and profound about that gesture. And about this gesture [holds up the stick], and this one [adjusts his eyeglasses].

Yün-yen said, "I understand." The note says, "Don't pretend to be enlightened."

Tao-wu said, "How do you understand?" The note says, "After all, he doesn't let him go."

Yün-yen said, "All over the body there are hands and eyes." The note says, "There's no gap."

Tao-wu said, "You've said a lot there, but you got only eighty percent." The note says, "My tongue is short." Because he has a short tongue he can only say eighty percent.

Yün-yen said, "What about you, elder brother?" The note says, "When the reason is superior, then adhere to it."

Tao-wu said, "Throughout the body there are hands and eyes." The note says, "No obstruction."

When Yün-yen said, *All over the body there are hands and eyes,* the note states that there are no gaps, no spaces. When Tao-wu said, *Throughout the body there are hands and eyes,* Wan-sung's note indicates that this reveals no obstruction, nothing in the way. Is there a difference? No gap, no obstruction. Are these two ancients saying the same thing or are they saying something different? If they're saying something different, which one is right? If they're saying the same thing, why does Tao-wu say it's only eighty percent? Of course, perhaps Tao-wu is also saying only eighty percent.

Addressing the verse, *One hole, emptiness pervading,* the note says, "Vertically extending through past, present, and future."

Crystal clear on all sides. The note says, "Horizontally covering the ten directions." The whole thing is covered, vertically and horizontally. One of them is talking about three-dimensional space: the x, y, and z axes. The other one's talking about the axis of time: past, present, future. Always right here, right now. Avalokiteshvara Bodhisattva is not a being living 2,500 years ago. She is not an entity of the future or a creation emerging out of the *Lotus Sutra.* She is the life of each one of us. The great heart of

Avalokiteshvara Bodhisattva beats in each one of us. But unless you discover it, you can't give it life. Our giving life to it manifests it in the world, allowing it to heal and nourish, to respond to the cries.

Formlessly, selflessly, spring enters the pipes. Master Wan-sung's note says, "Receiving blessings according to the season." This is the endless spring of enlightenment, the endless spring of intimacy with this whole great earth and everything it contains.

Unstopped, unhindered, the moon traverses the sky. The note says, "It falls naturally into the valley ahead."

Pure jewel eyes, arms of virtues. The note says, "Looking ahead and behind, picking up East and West."

All over the body—how does it compare to throughout the body being it? The note says, "Can't rationalize it." *I* say, someone asked me that question a long time ago and I still haven't figured it out.

The present hands and eyes reveal the whole works. The note says, "The thief's loot is already exposed."

The great function works in all ways—what is taboo? The note says, "No right or wrong." What does that mean? Does it mean that when our President pushes the button it is neither right nor wrong? That Hitler was neither right nor wrong? What does right and wrong have to do with Yün-yen and Tao-wu?

Is Yün-yen wrong and Tao-wu right? Or maybe they're both wrong. Or maybe they're both right. Or maybe it's neither right nor wrong. And what's the meaning of the eighty percent?

To study the Buddha Way is to study the self and to study the self is to forget the self. In fact, to forget the self is to be intimate with the self, and to be intimate with the self is the hands and eyes of Great Compassion. It is to really *be* yourself. You're not going to find compassion anywhere else.

The activity of Great Compassion, the ten thousand hands and eyes, has no formula. There are no rule books, no maps, no directions. Compassion arises out of wisdom. It is wisdom itself. The most important question is how will you do it? Well, you put your left foot in front of your right foot and then you put your right foot in front of your left foot. Do you understand? You do? That's not it. That's not walking. That's talking. See what walking itself is. And once you see clearly what walking itself is, understand that it's only eighty percent. You can't save all sentient beings until you're prepared to be saved yourself. You can't be saved yourself until you forget the self. To forget the self is your practice. It is zazen. And that's always right here, right now.

So what will you do? How will you do it? And, most importantly, when will you do it? Tomorrow? Keep in mind that tomorrow doesn't exist. Tomorrow is *always* tomorrow. Yesterday doesn't exist. It's already happened. There's only now. Your life is now. Your practice is right now.

THIRTEEN

ADVICE OF THE CATERPILLAR

Koans of the Way of Reality, Case 52

PROLOGUE

The very body and mind of all beings is as great and boundless as the universe itself. As for how small it is, it is finer than a single atom. We should understand that holding on and letting go are not another's doing. Rolling up and rolling out are both within one's own power. If you want to free what is stuck and loosen that which is bound, simply remove all traces of mental activity. At this very moment, if one's vision and hearing are clear, and color and sound are purely perceived, tell me, which side is the right side? "This side" doesn't reach it; "that side" doesn't reach it. "Neither this nor that" misses it. "Both this and that" are ten thousand miles from the truth. Avoid the slightest trace of right and wrong, and say a word.

The Main Case

The caterpillar said,[1] "One side[2] will make you grow bigger,[3] and the other side[4] will make you grow smaller."[5] "One side of what? The other side of what?" thought Alice to herself.[6] "Of the mushroom," said the caterpillar.[7] Alice looked at the mushroom,[8] trying to make out which were the two sides of it, as it was perfectly round.[9]

The Capping Verse

> *Rather than free the body, free the mind.*
> *When the mind is at peace, the body is at peace.*
> *When body and mind are both set free,*
> *The Way is clear and undisguised.*

This is a relatively modern koan that deals with a subject as old as Buddhism and humanity itself. The subject is dualism and its propensity to create all kinds of barriers in our lives. The following scenario is familiar to all of us. "I come to a fork in the road. Which way should I go? I have no idea where each path leads. If I choose the wrong way, I'm doomed. How will I make the right choice?"

The interesting thing is that many decisions that need to be made are really not decisions at all. Let's say you have two possibilities, A and B. You start with A. You assume that that's what you're going to do. You follow A to its logical conclusion. Then you do the same thing with B, following it through to its logical conclusion. If the results at the end of A and B are the same, then there was no question to begin with although, initially, there may have appeared to be a question.

But of course not all problems are like that; not all questions are like that. Some require a real and unique resolution. Yet, in the Zen teaching of the *Faith-Mind Poem*, Seng-ts'an, the Third Ancestor of China says, "The great Way is not difficult; only avoid picking and choosing. When love and hate are both absent, the true way is clear and undisguised."

I have always felt close to this poem. When I first started Zen training, I read and studied it over and over again. I didn't understand it, but that didn't surprise me— I had absolutely no comprehension of any of what I was reading and hearing about Zen in those days. Somehow I was being driven by an intuitive recognition and resonance. I knew in my heart that Zen was the right path for me and that, sooner or later, understanding and clarity would come.

In this poem, I had a particularly difficult time struggling with the line, "When love and hate are both absent." I could understand the absence of hate, but couldn't fathom what it meant for love to be absent. I didn't have any sense of the relationship between dualities; love on one side, hate on the other; good on one side, evil on the other; heaven, hell; male, female; holy, profane; sacred, secular. But slowly I had come to realize that these dualities were the source of conflict and tension not only in my life, but in the lives of most people around me. They were universal; yet nobody seemed to have any answers about how to deal with them. Then, the Third Ancestor comes along and says, "Avoid picking and choosing." But we have to make decisions. How do we avoid picking and choosing?

Confronted with this puzzle, great Master Chao-chou responded freely and appropriately: A monastic asked Chao-chou, "How do you avoid picking and choosing?" Chao-chou said, "Between heaven and earth, I alone am the honored one." The monastic said, "That's picking and choosing." And Chao-chou said, "Asshole! Where's the picking and choosing?"

The prologue to this koan says, *The very body and mind of all beings is as great and boundless as the universe itself.* It reaches everywhere. The problem is that we don't see it, we don't realize it. We may believe it or we may even understand it intellectually; we may find comfort in believing and understanding it, but by not seeing it, the self is confined to this bag of skin. The truth has to be realized. When it's realized, it reaches everywhere.

As for how small it is, it is finer than a single atom. It is smaller than a speck of dust. How can that be? If it's so great that it reaches everywhere, that there's no place to put it, how is it that it's finer than a single atom? "Reaches everywhere" *means* reaches everywhere. No place is excluded. Not just the body and mind, *this* body and mind. This bag of skin. This deluded, profane mind, or this enlightened, holy mind.

The next line says, *We should understand that holding on and letting go are not another's doing.* "Holding on" refers to a teaching device. The teacher holds back, takes away, and negates. By not being supportive, he throws you back on yourself. "Letting go" refers to the teacher's being nourishing, positive, supportive, and encouraging. But sooner or later, the teacher must disappear. Zen practice has to do with empowerment, and empowerment cannot take place when a teacher is hanging around your neck. Not only must you "kill the Buddha when you meet the Buddha," but at some point you must also kill the teacher. And the teacher helps that along by appearing and disappearing. Sometimes appearing in a grain of sand, sometimes appearing as the vast universe itself. Ultimately, we recognize that appearing and disappearing is a characteristic not just of teachers, but of all beings. It's not another's doing. *Rolling up and rolling out are both within one's own power.* We have the freedom to become indiscernible, leaving no trace, or to manifest ourselves everywhere.

I experienced this many times with my teacher, Maezumi Roshi. There were times when Roshi was like a 100,000-foot high mountain—fierce, relentless, unmoving. Butting my head up against it was useless; his presence was overpowering. Other times he would disappear. He would become so insignificant as to be nothing, absolutely nothing. Once, on a tour with several Japanese tea ceremony teachers, we were in a tea house and I suddenly forgot he was there. We all ignored him as he was off in a corner by himself, non-existent. There's a time to be present, and there's a time to disappear. We should be able to move and live either way. That's real freedom.

One day, the Tibetan teacher Trungpa Rinpoche and his entourage of bodyguards and assistants came to Roshi's house for a visit. Trungpa walked into the living room and sat on a chair to take his shoes off, observing the Japanese custom of entering a household barefoot. Trungpa was paralyzed on one side and had some difficulty moving. As his attendant went to help him, Roshi pushed the attendant aside and started taking off Trungpa Rinpoche's shoes. Boy, was I pissed! Afterwards I said, "Roshi, what is this? You don't have to take his shoes off! You're just as great a master as he is. In fact, you're a greater master than he is!" (Students tend to identify with their teachers and idolize them. They want their teacher to be the best teacher in the whole universe.) Roshi shook his head and said, "His practice is to be king. My practice is to be servant." And I crawled back into my shell to think about that a little bit. All of one's actions are within one's own power. If you give that power up, you create a nose-ring that allows anyone who takes hold of it to manipulate you.

If you want to free what is stuck, loosen that which is bound, simply remove all traces of mental activity. When the mind is empty, it's not grasping at anything. It's not holding on to anything. This doesn't mean not thinking; it means not attaching to thought. It doesn't mean not loving; it means not attaching to love. It doesn't mean not caring; it means not attaching, not sticking, not holding, not grasping. Everything is in a constant state of change, of becoming. The moment you grab it and say, "I've got it!" it's changed, and you've changed.

At this very moment, if one's vision and hearing are clear, and color and sound are purely perceived, tell me, which side is the right side? Before the mind takes hold of things, before it starts comparing them, analyzing them, evaluating them, categorizing them, liking them and disliking them, there is pure cognition. Before the mind starts moving, there's just seeing, just hearing, just touching, just tasting. There's no evaluation.

When my hand reaches down and touches a cup, long before it is a cup, there is a simple touch. That moment of contact is pure cognition. Within microseconds, my brain starts processing the information. I feel its texture, temperature, shape; whether it is smooth or rough, warm or cold, hard-edged or round. With enough information, I will identify it. The interesting and troubling development that comes out of this process is that once identified, I don't see it anymore. I say, "Oh, that's a cup," and it becomes one of the million cups, its uniqueness lost.

Seeing occurs before the wheels of processing start. At that moment, when one's vision and hearing are clear, and color and sound are purely received, which side is the right side? In pure cognition, how do you make a decision? How do you know whether it's this or that, good or bad? How do you differentiate? How do you get across the street?

"This side" doesn't reach it; "that side" doesn't reach it. "Neither this nor that" misses it. "Both this and that" are ten thousand miles from the truth. This adds further complications to the question "Which side is the right side?" You can use any of the dualities in this framework—good or evil, holy or profane, enlightened or deluded, monastic or lay practitioner, male or female. It's not one and it's not the other. It's not neither and it's not both. How do you respond?

Avoid the slightest trace of right and wrong, and say a word. This final line tells us how to do it. It was this the type of imperative that brought the monastic Ming to a deep enlightenment in his encounter with the Sixth Ancestor. Ming was chasing after Hui-neng, determined to retrieve the bowl and robe of bodhidharma from him. Finally, when he caught up to Hui-neng, the Sixth Ancestor put down the robe and bowl and said, "This robe was given to me on faith. How can it be fought for by force? I leave it for you to take it." Ming tried to pick up the robe and bowl but couldn't—they were as heavy as a mountain. He fell to his knees, trembling, and said, "I come for the teachings, not the robe. Please teach me, oh lay brother." Completely open, completely receptive, completely ready, he was a man teetering on the brink of realization. Immediately, the Sixth Ancestor struck.

"Think neither good nor evil," he said. "At that very moment, what is the true self of monastic Ming?" Ming saw it instantly. Avoid the slightest trace of right and wrong. At that instant, which is the right side?

The main case: *The caterpillar said, "One side will make you grow bigger, and the other side will make you grow smaller." "One side of what? The other side of what?" thought Alice to herself. "Of the mushroom," said the caterpillar. Alice looked at the mushroom, trying to make out which were the two sides of it, as it was perfectly round.*

This koan is adapted from *Alice's Adventures in Wonderland*. During her journey down the rabbit hole, Alice encountered the wise caterpillar. At the time of the meeting, she was about three inches tall, or the same size as the caterpillar. The caterpillar, sitting on a mushroom, smoking a pipe, said, "Who are you?" Alice responded, "I hardly know, sir, just at the present. At least, I know who I was when I got up in the morning, but I think I must have changed several times since then." We all do that. How many faces do we wear in the course of one day? "What do you mean by that?" said the caterpillar sternly. "Explain yourself." "I can't explain myself, I'm afraid sir," answered Alice, "I'm not myself, you see."

What is yourself? Are you the grumpy, angry one that got up in the morning? The pleasant employee of the afternoon? The romantic lover of the evening? Which one are you? Who are you, really? "I don't see!" exclaimed the caterpillar. "I'm afraid I can't put it more clearly," said Alice, "for I can't understand it myself, to begin with. And being so many different sizes in a day is very confusing."

Being many different things in a day *is* very confusing. As much as possible, I work very hard to add to the ones that you've already got. That was my teacher's gift to me. When I was certain that I couldn't be split in any more directions, he added ten more tasks for me to do. I wasn't sure whether he was trying to get me to go in ten thousand directions at once, or trying to get me to see that the ten thousand directions are one thing.

"It's very confusing," continued Alice. "It isn't," countered the caterpillar. "Well, perhaps you haven't found it so yet," said Alice. "But when you turn into a chrysalis—you will someday, you know—and then after that into a butterfly, I should think you'll feel a little queer, won't you?" "Not a bit," said the caterpillar. "Well, perhaps your feeling may be different," mused Alice, "all I know is that it would feel very queer to me." "You!" shouted the caterpillar contemptuously. "Who are you?"

Indeed, that's the question we constantly come back to. Who are you? No matter where you stand, you must be free to appear in a speck of dust or in vast space, to manifest the ten thousand hands and eyes of Avalokiteshvara Bodhisattva or to just simply disappear.

As the dialogue went on, Alice eventually got enraged with the caterpillar's attitude. After all, the caterpillar wasn't exactly polite. He wasn't a kind zendo monitor, saying, "Please sit still. If you don't sit still, you'll annoy your neighbor; every time you move, you'll create more distractions for yourself, and the more you move, the more sitting hurts. Besides which, it's not really zazen...." The caterpillar was screaming, "Don't move!" The message was very clear and direct. Alice, annoyed and flustered, stomped out. The caterpillar shouted after her, "Come back! I have something important to say." Alice turned and came back again.

This is a standard device in Zen teachings. There is a saying, "What good is a monastic who turns her head when called?" Sometime monastics will turn their backs on their teacher, flourish their sleeves, and walk out. The teacher will call. If they stop, or even hesitate, doubt is present. A hook is embedded in them. The teacher has the other end of the line in his hand and is reeling it back in.

Alice stopped, turned around, and came back. Obviously, her question wasn't resolved. If she had had no question, if the great doubt had been settled, she would have kept going. He could have told her nothing. But she was still dissatisfied and turned back. The caterpillar said, "Keep your temper!" "Is that all?" asked Alice, swallowing her anger as well as she could. "No," said the caterpillar.

Being a pretty sharp caterpillar, he didn't just come out and reveal the secrets. For a few minutes he puffed away without speaking, then unfolded his arms, took the hookah out of his mouth, and said, "So you think you've changed, do you?" "I'm afraid I have, sir," said Alice. "I can't remember things as I used to, and I don't keep the same size for ten minutes together." "Can't remember what things?" demanded the caterpillar, returning to his harsh cross-examination. After further exchanges, Alice finally came to the critical point. She wanted to return to her normal size. But she wasn't clear what that was. "What size do you want to be?" asked the caterpillar. "Oh, I'm not particular as to size, only I don't like changing so often, you know." "I *don't* know," snapped the caterpillar. Alice remained silent. She had never been contradicted so much in all her life, and she thought she was losing her temper again. "Are you contented now?" inquired the caterpillar. "Well, I should like to be a little larger, if you wouldn't mind," said Alice. "Three inches is such a wretched height to be." The caterpillar, all three inches of him, straightened up in his chair and said, "It's a very good height indeed!"

Alice waited patiently until he chose to speak again. In a minute or two the caterpillar yawned, shook himself, got down off the mushroom, and crawled away into the grass, remarking as he went, "One side will make you grow taller, the other side will make you grow shorter." "One side of what, the other side of what?" thought Alice to herself. "Of the mushroom," said the caterpillar, just as if she had asked it aloud, and in another moment he was out of sight.

Alice in Wonderland is a modern Western fairy tale. Here we are not taking it up as a fairy tale, but as a koan. Everything in it, everything I said so far is real, as real as this moment, as you and I. Or as unreal as this moment. The tale is as much a dream as this is a dream.

To clarify the points of the koan, I have added the following footnotes. *The caterpillar said....* The footnote says, "What's he saying? Caterpillars don't talk. They must be traveling the same road for this conversation to take place. Complications are sure to follow." Traveling the same road means speaking the same language, coming from the same source, being on the same path. Sometimes the questions and the answers can't be heard because the person isn't ready to hear them. Walking on the same path is where they can be heard, where they can be seen. That's why commitment in Zen practice is so important, why entry into training is not to be taken lightly. Until there is deep reckoning with one's questions, there's no receptivity.

A similar process operates when students contemplate receiving the Precepts. Why don't we give them to everybody? Why doesn't receiving the Precepts happen at the outset of training? Because you can't hear the Precepts until a certain point in time. You can't hear certain koans until you've heard the ones before. To introduce them too early would be like trying to give sex education to a five-year-old. When kids ask, "Where do babies come from, Daddy?" you don't start explaining all the details of male and female reproductive organs. Kids don't want to know that. They can't deal with it, having no framework or vocabulary to absorb it. A lot depends on where the question is coming from.

The caterpillar said, "One side…." The footnote says, "If there is one side, there must be another side." The minute you create one, you've created two along with the multiplicity of three, four, five—endless dualities. *"… will make you grow bigger."* The footnote says, "I'm large, and contain the multitudes. KA! Reaching everywhere. How big am I?" That's what Alice was worried about. Maybe I'll become bigger and bigger and bigger. How big is big? How vast is boundless? How big is infinity? I remember when I studied physical sciences in college, I was confronted with the question of infinity. I would sit there, trying to grasp it with my mind. What does it mean? What's at the edge of it? I would punch myself in the head, thinking that I would understand it if I hit myself hard enough. Entertaining infinity is like division by a smaller and smaller number. When you finally divide by zero—infinity. How big is it?

And the other side … continued the caterpillar. The footnote says, "Why does he speak only in halves?" Why doesn't he speak of the whole thing? … *will make you grow smaller.* The footnote says, "Ten thousand universes in a single speck of dust. Is it bigger or smaller; the same or different? Does reaching everywhere include them both?"

"One side of what? The other side of what?" thought Alice to herself. The footnote says, "Concern is born. The whole phenomenal universe is born." The minute the mind starts moving, heaven and earth are separated. Self and other are separated. Concern, fear, anger, ignorance, love, hate, holiness and profanity arise.

"Of the mushroom," said the caterpillar. The footnote says, "Although he's not a member of the household, there's a fragrant air about this one," speaking highly of this caterpillar's understanding of things.

Alice looked at the mushroom. The footnote says, "Is this seeing, or is it just looking?" Return to the prologue and the concept of pure cognition: in pure cognition, which side is the right side? Right side and wrong side don't exist. Sides don't exist. Pure cognition knows only one reality.

Then the final line, ... *trying to make out which were the two sides of it, as it was perfectly round.* The footnote says, "The mushroom is perfect and complete. No upside or downside, no inside or outside, no one side or other side, from beginning to end. Difficult to understand." I will go even further and say this is impossible to understand. So don't try to understand it. And believing it isn't going to do you any good either.

Alice tried all sorts of things. She got herself into a lot of trouble. Now she reached around the mushroom as far as she could and broke off two pieces and bit into one of them. Suddenly something hit her under the chin. She realized it was her feet. She had shrunk and she couldn't open her mouth to eat the other chunk. Finally she got a little bit into her mouth, and her neck started to grow all the way into outer space. Her hands couldn't reach her mouth anymore. She looked down and all she could see were tree-tops and the wide landscape. She had no idea where her body was, where the hand holding the mushroom was. She was in this very complicated situation. She was still caught in the realm of left and right, big and small.

No matter how wonderful your decision-making is, how precise and scientific your picking and choosing, so long as it continues to be picking and choosing, there are endless hells to be experienced. The question persists: how do you avoid picking and choosing? "Between heaven and earth, I alone am the honored one." That's fine for Chao-chou, but how about you?

THE CAPPING VERSE

Rather than free the body, free the mind.
When the mind is at peace, the body is at peace.
When body and mind are both set free,
The Way is clear and undisguised.

Alice was totally involved in trying to free her body from this weird state she found herself in; one moment big, next moment small, one moment so tiny she was going to be eaten, next moment so big everything moved out of her reach. She couldn't find the middle way.

The caterpillar tried to help her, but she really didn't get it. Not then, anyway. All the while she was working on the body. But to free the body, you must free the mind. How do you free the mind? Empty the mind. If the mind is at peace, the body is at peace. You can see it in your breathing. When your mind is agitated, your breath is agitated. When your mind is quiet, the breath is deep, easy, almost without effort, barely perceptible. Mind and body are not two things. When body and mind are both set free, the Way is clear and undisguised.

That's how we repay the debt we owe to the ancestors who have conveyed this truth mind-to-mind, generation-to-generation, for 2,500 years. There's no other way to do it. A student came to dokusan recently, filled with gratitude. I knew the feeling, because I've felt it hundreds of times with my own teacher. I used to wonder, "Why is this guy doing this for me? I don't count. I'm so unimportant and he's treating me like I'm something special. Why? What did I ever do to deserve such good fortune?" This student was expressing something similar. "I want to DO something for you, I want to give you something, and I want it to be big and wonderful, and I want it to capture and express everything that I'm feeling."

I responded to him by saying that the greatest gift I could get from anybody is their realization. And I meant it. That lets me know that what I've been doing over these past fifteen years of teaching hasn't been wasted. What students do by way of their own realization is to confirm and actualize my realization. They confirm and actualize the realization of all Buddhas. They confirm and actualize the realization of Shakyamuni Buddha of the past, and of Maitreya Buddha who is yet to be born, and they confirm their own life.

It's no small thing that we're talking about, Alice and the caterpillar notwithstanding. What we're dealing with has to do with the great matter that is the life of each one of us, and it's not to be taken lightly. That's what this practice is about. To take care of it, throw yourself into it. Challenge yourself and take a risk. Take a chance. You've got nothing to lose but your life. When you die once, you can never die again.

FOURTEEN
THE STONE LION

*Koans of the
Way of Reality,
Case 103*

PROLOGUE

> *Confined in a cage, up against a wall, pressed
> against barriers—if you linger in thought, holding back
> your potential, you will remain mired in fear and
> frozen inaction. If, on the other hand, you advance fear-
> lessly and without hesitation, you manifest your power as
> a competent adept of the Way. Passing through entan-
> glements and barriers without hindrance, the time and
> season of great peace is attained. How do you advance
> fearlessly and without hesitation? Listen to the following.*

THE MAIN CASE

> *The National Teacher, Ta-cheng, and Emperor Su-
> tsung arrived at the front gate of the imperial palace.*

189

The National Teacher pointed to a stone lion and said,
"Your majesty, this lion is so very rare, can you give me
a single turning phrase about it?" The Emperor said, "I
cannot give a phrase;[1] please, will the Master give one?"[2]
The National Teacher replied, "Oh, this is the mountain
monastic's fault."[3] Later Chen-ying of Ta-yüan asked
the National Teacher,[4] "Did the Emperor understand?"[5]
The National Teacher said, "Let's put aside whether he
understood; how do you understand it?"[6]

THE CAPPING VERSE

Each crisis, an opportunity,
Yet if you fail to act, you miss it by a thousand miles.
The cave of the Blue Dragon is ominous.
Only the fearless dare to enter.
It is here that the forest of patterns is clearly revealed,
The myriad forms evident.
It is here that the one bright pearl is hidden.

Fear is one of the central themes we work with in our
practice. When we examine fear, we find that it is almost
always based in the past, in something we have carried
around for many years. It is part of the baggage we call
our "self." Through the process of zazen, through studying the self, that baggage becomes quite evident and
accessible.

Confined in a cage, up against the wall, pressed against
barriers—if you linger in thought, holding back your poten-
tial, you will remain mired in fear and frozen inaction.
Like the stone lion the National Teacher was pointing to,
you may look like a lion, but you can't move or do anything. Although each one of us has the potential of

Buddhahood, as soon as we start analyzing, we give rise not to freedom but to more things to analyze, more things to understand. As the inaction continues, the fear persists. We come up with all kinds of wonderful explanations for our fear, but somehow they don't seem to help. We define it, categorize it, analyze it, judge it, understand it—still it persists. What is this fear?

The dictionary says fear is "an agitation or dismay in the anticipation of danger or harm." Usually the dictionary is not very accurate, but in this case it does point out the key to what makes fear work—anticipation. Fear always has to do with what is going to happen next. It is always about the next corner, next day, next hour, next moment. What if...?

If, on the other hand, you advance fearlessly and without hesitation, you manifest your power as a competent adept of the Way. What is that power? Power is *ki*. *Ki* is uncovered in the process of zazen. Just the simple action of acknowledging a thought and letting it go and bringing your attention back to the breath builds power. Little by little, day by day, the practice of sitting, of watching the flow of thoughts without analyzing, judging, or understanding them, builds confidence almost imperceptibly.

Passing through entanglements and barriers without hindrance, the time and season of great peace is attained. The season of great peace is what we call the "endless spring." The endless spring is always present, just as spring is always present. In the frozen branches buried beneath three feet of snow, spring is present. Buried deep beneath years of conditioning lives a Buddha. But unless we realize and activate that potential, it remains dormant and doesn't impart any strength to our lives or to anyone else.

Fearlessness can be understood on many different levels. Sometimes being fearless is just being stupid. If, when everyone else panics, you remain calm, perhaps you don't understand the problem. That kind of dull-witted stupidity is not true fearlessness. There is also the fearlessness of the young, who still see themselves as invulnerable. That sense of invulnerability and willingness to take chances is what the military loves about young people. On the other hand, the kind of fearlessness I'm speaking of is a generous, compassionate fearlessness. It is not a matter of just exerting one's power. I'm speaking of spiritual fearlessness, one of the attributes of a spiritual warrior. We see this kind of fearlessness throughout history, manifested by all of the great teachers—Moses, Jesus, St. Teresa, Buddha, Bodhidharma. Their fearlessness was not self-centered. It was compassionate. That is why I stress repeatedly to be generous with your practice, with your zazen. Don't just practice for yourself, but for all sentient beings. Give your zazen to someone who needs it.

The experience of fearlessness is totally dependent upon the experience of fear. Fearlessness is not a matter of ignoring fear, but of really acknowledging it and being empowered by it. That is what keeps it from being stupid. The anticipation is still there, but the agitation is not. There is only readiness. If you are driving a car that has a spare tire, you don't fear having a flat. You have a way of taking care of it. If you have turned over a canoe several times and made it to shore, then white water doesn't pose a big threat to you. You still anticipate the danger, and respond to it, but there is a sense of preparedness and of ability to respond.

One of the first things taught in the martial arts is not how to fight but how to lose, how to fall down and get up. Falling down and getting up are not two separate things; they are one thing. The force of falling down, of failure, is part and parcel of the force of returning to one's feet, of recovery. We go through life fearing death. And we go through life fearing life. There we are, caught between two iron mountains. We're afraid we're going to die or we're afraid we're going to live. We wonder how to deal with all of the difficulties of life, creating fear of failure, as well as fear of success. It's amazing. I hear it all the time from people who are stuck on the edge of seeing the koan Mu. They become gripped by fear. They are afraid of seeing Mu and yet they don't want to fail. They want to do it and they don't want to do it. If they do it, they feel it may change them in some way that they don't like. They're afraid that they may suddenly become monastics and lose whatever possessions they have; yet at the same time they really want to see it. So there they sit, frozen in fear.

Usually, at the bottom of fear is a sense of inadequacy, a lack of confidence. It is like the victim syndrome— we keep waiting for something to happen. How do we deal with it? Ordinarily we do one of two things. We may panic, becoming overwhelmed and eventually closing down, pulling back in one way or another. Sometimes closing down becomes a matter of numbing ourselves— using entertainment, getting stoned, getting drunk, changing the subject. These are all different forms of denial. Or, we take the opposite stand and turn the fear into anger, becoming a raging bull and confronting it, horns lowered, head on. But somehow the fear doesn't go away, though it seems to have retreated for the moment.

I remember a student who worked in New York City. He was a film editor, a large but gentle man. One night, at two or three o'clock in the morning, he came out of the editing studios on a side street in a rough neighborhood. As he walked towards his car just a few blocks away, he heard footsteps behind him. He saw a reflection in the window: three guys were following him. He knew he was going to have to go around the corner into the dark, where he would probably be attacked. If he struggled, they probably would kill him. Very likely, he thought to himself, they have weapons. All these things were going through his mind. Within the course of a block and a half, his mind just kept running on and on and on. He reached a point where he was in such total frenzy that he turned into a raging bull. He decided that since he was going to die anyway, he would go out kicking. He whipped around, faced them, and yelled, "All right, let's do it!" But when he rushed toward them, they scattered in the ten directions. They just ran for their lives. He couldn't believe it. He was still shaking as he jumped into his car and drove off. I asked him, "How is the fear now?" He'd always had this fear of dark streets. He said it was still there. He hadn't resolved it with that encounter. That one success didn't do anything for him, except save him that one time. We have to go a little bit deeper than just turning fear into anger and confrontation. Fearlessness is not a matter of being without fear; it is a matter of transcending fear.

How does one advance fearlessly and without hesitation? Fearlessness is different from courage. In the dictionary, courage is defined as "a quality of mind or temperament that enables one to stand fast in the face of opposition, hardship, or danger." Fearlessness is having or showing no fear when faced with something dangerous, difficult, or unknown. Within courage there might be tremendous fear. Yet you stand fast. In fearlessness, on the other hand, the fear doesn't arrive; it has been transcended. There are all kinds of reasons for that kind of transcendence. There is the fearlessness of a mother. Mothers, especially among mammals, are very protective of their young. There is nothing more harmless than the big black bears that run around on this mountain. But confront a mother and her cub, and you've got something to deal with, because the mother has no sense of fear for herself. Her only concern is the welfare of that cub. Even when wounded, she will persist in protecting her cub.

In this koan about National Teacher Ta-cheng and Emperor Su-tsung, the teacher is testing the Emperor. Being a National Teacher must have been a pretty touchy job back in those days. The Emperors had no hesitation about ordering the beheading of people they didn't like. And they changed religions the way most people change socks. One day Taoists are in and Buddhists are out; a few years later, the Buddhists are in and the Taoists are out. When you challenged the Emperor you were taking your life in your hands.

"Your majesty, this lion is so very rare, can you give me a single turning phrase about it?" the National Teacher asks. He is demanding, "Show me your understanding of it, show me your Dharma." A turning phrase is one that is alive and jumping, vital, and capable of imparting strength. What can *you* say about the stone lion? Obviously, swords and arrows are not considerations when the imperative to teach goes into effect. What is the imperative? It is the Dharma, the teaching imperative. Every opportunity that presents itself is an opportunity to impart life.

The Emperor responds, *"I cannot give a phrase."* The note to this line says, "An honest person is hard to find. Still, there could be something here." Is he just being honest about his lack of understanding? Or is he presenting a reflection of his understanding? Is he saying that it is unspeakable, beyond words and ideas? The Emperor then says, *"Please, will the master give one?"* The note says, "As it turns out, he doesn't flinch when faced with danger.

Turning the spear around, he threatens the old man." He has taken the same question and turned it around and confronted the old man with it. *The National Teacher replied, "Oh, this is the mountain monastic's fault."* The note says, "Very intimate, indeed. All eighty-six ancestors have suffered this illness." Is he just trying to cover himself—It's my fault, my fault that you don't know, my fault for asking the question. Or is he showing him something? What is the illness common to all the ancestors, to all the teachers in the lineage? What does "very intimate, indeed" mean in reference to that question? We need to see clearly what the National Teacher really meant when he said that "it is the mountain monastic's fault." Mountain monastic is a reference to himself. But what is it that is his fault? The whole universe is his fault! The whole universe is his responsibility!

Later Chen-ying of Ta-yüan asked the National Teacher. . . . The note says, "A wounded tiger appears out of the weeds. What is this monastic really seeking?" Wounded by what? Obviously, this monastic is wounded by the questions constantly running through his head. Weeds symbolize delusion; he steps out of the weeds when he asks for the teaching. But, there is asking and then there is asking. The monastic inquires, "Did the Emperor understand?" The note says, "Yesterday has already happened. Tomorrow has not yet happened. How about now?" What does the monastic *really* want to know? What does it matter whether the Emperor understood or not? The old teacher immediately sees that and says, "*Let's put aside whether he understood; how do you understand it?*" The note says, "Seeing a cage, he builds a cage. This kind of kindness is hard to repay. Successive generations only transmitted this."

Taking responsibility is the other side of denial or

blame. Our tendency in dealing with the barriers in our lives is to push them out of the way, to deny them. We do this in all sorts of ways. One of the common "new age" ways is to adopt catch words. Catch words have a ring to them. We begin to define ourselves according to the catchy new category we fit in. We pick from all the different syndromes, or definitions, that we can chose from, and we make a nice nest for ourselves. Somehow we feel that when we can name it, or find a category for it, we can set it aside. I'm a _____. Fill in the space yourself. Take, for instance, any minority: implicit is a lack of access to power. That is very frustrating. There can be a real sense of hopelessness and helplessness, even of fear, depending upon the context. Yet frequently, these catch words create such a false sense of comfort that we begin to feel we don't have to do anything about the situation. There's a sense of, "Now that we know what it is, it's settled." That is just another way of avoiding responsibility, another form of denial.

Our government has mastered that kind of denial. Years ago, at the dawn of Madison Avenue, I remember the research done by advertising firms on how colors and shapes could be used to control people. One could become a vice-president by coming up with just the right word or catch phrase. A product would start selling like crazy; people would respond to it. Certain words, colors, shapes, and contexts are almost hypnotic. Madison Avenue has become expert in manipulation. I was in the advertising business for a time, and I went to many courses the advertising institutes offered. It didn't take long for that technology to travel from advertising to government and the military, to be used to control people in other ways. More than just a way of getting people to buy something they don't want to buy, the technology of advertising has become a very dangerous kind of mass programming.

Many veterans are aware of how the government has come up with a series of terms, war after war, for something the bureaucracy has needed to deny. During the Civil War they called it "nostalgia"—that was the term used to describe the mind of someone who spent time on a battlefield and was shot at every day, who killed other human beings in his daily work. In World War I it was called "shell shock." They figured some soldiers got "weird" because bombs were exploding too close to them. Then in World War II it was called "battle fatigue." Each war that followed has had different definitions, including the Korean and Vietnam Wars. All the names are basically ways of denying the real problem. This phenomenon isn't a matter of being wounded physically; it isn't something physical like losing an arm or a leg. If you took these people out of combat, their symptoms would largely go away. And no one worried too much about the problem because it had always had a name. In every war they've changed the name. But each name is another form of denial.

We do the same thing; we make our nests in words and phrases. There is a whole system of koans dealing specifically with how we get caught in the entanglements of language. You can't move forward and you can't move backward, so you just make a nest. Maybe the problem will go away. That won't work in koan study, just as it doesn't work in the rest of our lives.

We need to look carefully at the statement, "It's my fault." What does it mean to take responsibility? Responsibility is very empowering. Blaming takes away your power. And the value of blaming is very short-lived, because the pain persists, the fear persists, the anxiety persists. When we take responsibility, there is no denial, no blaming. There is just trusting. Trusting means giving yourself permission to be yourself. It means giving yourself permission to either fail or succeed, because you are prepared for either. You know how to fail. When you fall, you use the force of the fall, transforming it into the thrust of recovery. And you do it again and again. When there is no illusion, then failure and success are not so powerful. There is only the action, the doing. In that same taking of responsibility we give birth to fearlessness. There is no fear in the anticipation or in the presence of danger. There is only the readiness for action.

The capping verse of this koan says:

> *Each crisis, an opportunity.*
> *Yet if you fail to act, you miss it by a thousand miles.*
> *The cave of the Blue Dragon is ominous.*
> *Only the fearless dare to enter.*

It is sad that most of the advances people make in practice come from the crises they face. When things are going smoothly and life is easy, sitting usually loses vitality and becomes sluggish. When a crisis appears, an opportunity appears—an opportunity to enter a new territory, to penetrate a barrier, to overcome a difficulty. If you fail to act when that opportunity presents itself, you miss something very special and important in your life. Many times we just let the crisis pass, instead of seeing it as a wonderful Dharma meal with which to nourish ourselves. We shy away from it, hoping that it will go away. And chances are, if you deny it long enough, it will somehow disappear into the cobwebs of your unconscious. It is still there and functioning, but we don't have to deal with it. But it is always there. That is why I get very touchy about people working on the koan Mu prematurely. I've seen too many people use Mu and their zazen as another kind of suppression, as another hiding place. It works quite well as a way to keep you from dealing with something you don't want to deal with: just Mu it out of your mind. That is nothing more than suppression. The problem just lies there and festers, waiting for an opportunity to present itself. It doesn't go away until you've dealt with it, until you've empowered yourself with it.

I remember vividly at age eleven, after I had been playing the clarinet for about a year, I had to perform a solo in a school play. I was shy, and during rehearsal the teacher kept saying, "Hold your head up, John. You know, hold the clarinet up and really play." When the time came to actually do the performance, with everybody in the audience—all the students, the teachers, my parents and their friends—my teacher, standing offstage, said, "Heads up!" I threw my head back and let out this god-awful squeak. Well, everybody laughed. And that was it. I crumbled. I didn't realize until many years later how this event had affected my whole life, and especially my ability to speak in public.

I was still feeling the effects in my thirties. I had done some scientific work that resulted in a paper to be present-ed at an international conference. I had somehow envi-sioned myself delivering the paper to 30 or 40 other scien-tists. When I got to the conference, I realized that I was billed for the big auditorium, the "Golden Room," which meant that hundreds of people would be there for my morning talk. So the night before the talk, I got very drunk. I convinced a friend of mine from the same labora-tory to present the talk for me. He agreed; he would have no trouble confronting 2,000 people. Every time I'd run into somebody in an elevator, and they'd look at my name tag and say, "Oh, I'm looking forward to your talk, Dr.

Loori," I would get even sicker. I knew that all these people were experts, and they were going to find all these things wrong with my paper. They were all going to laugh. I was the same eleven-year-old with the squeaky clarinet. I remember that morning when the talk was announced, I heard my name, and I started getting nauseous. (I was also very hung over.) I was sitting way in the back of the auditorium. At one point during the presentation the slide machine jammed. The presenter called my name out from the stage and asked if I could fix the machine. I threw up and left.

It took years of practice after that to be able to talk to a group of people and not feel worried about failure; to be stupid, if being stupid is what comes out, and to be smart, if being smart is what comes out. To allow it to be the way it is. That is what fearlessness is really about. You can't defeat someone who is fearless in this way.

So where does all of this take place? How does all of this take place? The poem says, *The cave of the Blue Dragon is ominous.* The cave of the Blue Dragon is ourselves. The cave of the Blue Dragon is that place within each one of us where we store all the psychological bilge we don't want to deal with. When you push something away, when you deny or suppress something, where does it go? The cave of the Blue Dragon. The cave of the Blue Dragon is, indeed, ominous. We don't want to deal with it. The process of descending into the cave of the Blue Dragon turns you into a child in some ways. *Only the fearless dare to enter.* This is where fearlessness really pays off. In the cave of the Blue Dragon ... *the forest of patterns is clearly revealed.* The way we function, what we're about, where we're sticking, what the buttons are—all the myriad forms of our routines and denials are evident. It is in the cave of the Blue Dragon that we find out about ourselves.

And it is in the cave of the Blue Dragon that the one bright pearl is hidden.

That one bright pearl is the intimacy the National Teacher points to. Its radiance fills the universe and is present whether we realize it or not. We can go through life like a stone lion, sitting in front of the public library in New York City, or we can be a real golden-haired lion. There is nothing sweeter and more gentle than a lioness with her cubs. And there is nothing more ferocious than a lioness when she is taking responsibility for those cubs. Both these qualities, fearlessness and gentleness, are part of the life of all Buddhas, all sentient beings. These qualities are part of your life and my life. We are born with them, but somehow along the way we lose sight of them. There are all kinds of logical, justifiable reasons for getting lost. Nothing happens without a cause; there is a karma to all of it. But I don't care what the cause is, or where it came from—the only one who can heal your illness is you. The only one that has the power to heal it is you. The rest of us, ultimately, are only bystanders. Each one of us can only nod to ourselves.

The National Teacher, the Emperor, the stone lion, the ten thousand things, all the barriers, all the peace and the joy of this world—all are nothing but the self. The question is how you understand it and how you use your mind. When the crises come up, don't turn away. Take action. The cave of the Blue Dragon—it's your Blue Dragon, and it's your one bright pearl.

FIFTEEN

THE THIRTEENTH
DAUGHTER'S DHARMA

Koans of the
Way of Reality,
Case 95

PROLOGUE

> *Stop! Stop talking and contriving and the iron tree*
> *will bloom, the stone woman will give birth to a child in*
> *the night. Even a nimble lass can lose her footing on a*
> *slippery floor. Like the god Achilles, though free in every*
> *way, still there was a stumbling point. But tell me, where*
> *is her error? If you say there is none, you miss it. If you say*
> *there is an error, you're ten thousand miles away from*
> *the truth. If you try to say that there's neither, I'll run*
> *you out of here with my stick. What do you say? Speak.*

THE MAIN CASE

> *When the thirteenth daughter of Cheng was twelve, she*
> *accompanied a monastic to Ta-wei mountain.*[1] *As the*

monastic was rising from making a bow before the Master, Kuei-shan asked, "Where do you live?"[2] The monastic replied, "I live beside the stream at Nan-tai."[3] Kuei-shan shouted for her to leave,[4] and then asked again, "Where does that old lady behind you live?"[5] The thirteenth daughter stepped forward and stood with her arms folded in front of her.[6] Kuei-shan asked the same question again.[7] The thirteenth daughter replied, "I've already presented it for Your Reverence."[8] Kuei-shan said, "Go."[9] As she was walking out from the Dharma hall, the monastic said, "The thirteenth daughter usually says that she knows Zen, and that her mouth is quick and sharp. But today she was questioned by the great Master Kuei-shan, and she didn't have a reply for him at all."[10] The thirteenth daughter answered, "My goodness. How can you talk like that? And you still say that you're on a pilgrimage. Take off your patched robe and give it to me."[11] Later the thirteenth daughter told the entire story to Lao-shan,[12] saying, "Visiting Kuei-shan I answered like that. Was my answer correct?"[13] Lao-shan said, "I won't say that there wasn't a mistake."[14] The thirteenth daughter asked, "Where was the mistake?"[15] Lao-shan scolded her.[16] The thirteenth daughter said, "Adding flowers to brocade."[17]

THE CAPPING VERSE

> Fangs bared, claws unsheathed,
> The lion cub hasn't learned fear.
> It's not a matter for hesitating over.
> The head and tail belong to the same lion.
> A cat barks, a dog purrs,
> The mother lode is every mountain.

Women do not figure prominently in the ancient

koans. The only one identified by name that appears in the standard collections is Iron Grindstone Lu, Dharma successor of Master Kuei-shan, who is one of the principals in this koan. The others are nameless nuns, roadside teachers, and vendors incidental to the central story lines. This koan is drawn from Master Dogen's *300 Koan Shobogenzo*, and its treatment of women is consistent with the cultural norm of the times. The Dharma coming to us from China and Japan reflects the characteristics of those respective cultures, with all of their deep-seated prejudices. In our American Zen practice, it is up to us to make the changes to redress those prejudices, and the collection of koans we are compiling at Zen Mountain Monastery entitled *Koans of the Way of Reality* will include as many cases involving women as I can gather. There aren't that many from the traditional sources. Aitken Roshi translated a handful. A few Kamakura koans also deal with women.

Just as women have difficulty identifying with many of the stories that are so exclusively male-oriented, lay practitioners run into a similar problem with koans about monastics. Traditional koans were directed to monastics and were about monastics. To make them more accessible, I frequently change the language and call the characters "adepts" or "practitioners," unless the word "monastic" is an intrinsic part of the meaning of the koan. I also remove specifically male language of the koans as much as is possible, if I can do so without the presentation getting clumsy. But it would be nice to have both lay people and monastics in the koans. It would be nice to have both men and women. It's okay to have separation—it's a very important aspect of reality—but we should also understand the unity that underlies it. And, oddly enough, that's what this koan is all about.

The prologue begins, *Stop! Stop talking and contriving*

*and the iron tree will bloom, the stone woman will give birth
to a child in the night.* "Iron tree blooming" and "stone
woman giving birth to a child in the night" are metaphors
used in Zen writings to express the occurrence of something inconceivable. An iron tree has no life in it. It is
dead, one-sided, like emptiness. Flowers blooming are
manifestations within the phenomenal world. What is the
relationship of those two things? A stone woman is barren,
lifeless—absolute. Giving birth to a child happens in the
world—relative. Emptiness and form—what is their relationship?

As Master Dogen points out, the birth is "giving birth
to a child in the night." The night referred to is the
absolute; night is one side, day is the other. Night is like
the darkness, and day is like the light we refer to in *The
Sutra of the Identity of Relative and Absolute*: "Light and
darkness are a pair, like the foot before and the foot
behind in walking. Within light there is darkness, within
darkness there is light." It is the night referred to when
Chao-chou asks T'ou-tzu, "When a person who has died
the Great Death returns to life, how is it?" and T'ou-tzu
responds, "They shouldn't go by night, they should go by
day." In other words, they should manifest coming back
to life in the world of phenomena, in the bright light of
day. The night of Dogen is emptiness; out of that emptiness comes this life, the "child" born of the stone woman.

*Even a nimble lass can lose her footing on a slippery
floor.* This twelve-year–old daughter of Cheng was obviously extraordinary. Can you imagine it? Most twelve-
year– olds these days want to watch television or hang out
at the mall. This one is doing pilgrimages all over China
with a fellow monastic. She goes to see Kuei-shan, living
on his mountain somewhere in a godforsaken part of the
country. It was an isolated region where the monastics

couldn't even beg and the community had to raise buf-
faloes and grow their own food to survive. The journey
must have been long and dangerous. Cheng's daughter
had to have a strong spiritual drive. Evidently she practiced and had some understanding. She reminds me of
Ling-chao, the daughter of Layman P'ang, one of the
more renowned lay practitioners in the history of Zen.
Ling-chao, from a very early age, was very clear in her
grasp of the Dharma. Although both her mother and
father were deeply enlightened, she was the clearest. The
three of them would do Dharma combat at the dinner
table or while working in the fields.

This thirteenth daughter, as nimble, quick, and sharp-
tongued as she is, sometime loses her balance and poise on
"the slippery floor." Of course, the slippery floor is old
Kuei-shan. Kuei-shan had three prominent disciples. One
was Hsiang-yen, who early in his training felt that he was
hopeless, gave up formal study, left his teacher and went
to take care of the graveyard of the National Teacher. One
day, while he was sweeping the paths, a small pebble hit a
bamboo stalk. Hearing the sound, Hsiang-yen came to
realization. Yang-shan was the second successor. He went
on to find the Igyo School of Zen which lasted for 300
years. He and Kuei-shan represent the ideal of the teacher-
student relationship. The third successor was Iron
Grindstone Lu, a very famous monastic who was respected
for her killer instinct and ability in Dharma encounters.
She settled somewhere on Kuei-shan Mountain, and very
likely had disciples. The records of her teachings are probably buried somewhere in Chinese literature. I hope that a
scholar specifically interested in finding out about this
woman will one day dig them out and translate them. I
figure if I keep mentioning it, sooner or later the right
person will hear, and the work will be done.

The prologue continues, *Like the god Achilles, though free in every way, still there was a stumbling point.* You may recall the story of Achilles. His flaw was his heel. He was perfect in every other way, immortal except for the one weak spot that brought about his downfall. This was a common device of Greek tragedy. All the gods and goddesses were perfect in every respect except for one tragic flaw. In the case of our heroine, tell me, ... *where is her error? If you say there is none, you miss it.* You fall into one side. *If you say there is an error, you're ten thousand miles away from the truth.* That's falling into the other side. *If you try to say that there's neither, I'll run you out of here with my stick.* That, too, misses it. So what do you say?

I've added notes to the main case. *When the thirteenth daughter of Cheng was twelve, she accompanied a monastic to Ta-wei Mountain.* The note says, "They plan to gang up on the old man. Why gather a crowd?" *As the monastic was rising from making a bow before the Master, Kuei-shan asked, "Where do you live?"* The note says, "Everyone in the world is the same. Still, he must ask. He has a vow to make trouble. She will inevitably understand it in the ordinary way." He is making trouble. Everyone in the world is the same—Buddhas pervade throughout space and time. The thrust of his question is to get her to present her understanding.

The monastic replied, "I live beside the stream at Nantai." The note says, "She may be misguided, but I will say she's truthful." Her answer could be understood in several ways. It's not necessarily wrong. *Kuei-shan shouted for her to leave.* The note says, "This is as it should be. Let her go on wearing out sandals." *Then again he asked, "Where does that old lady behind you live?"* The note says, "Let's see if they both fit on the same skewer." He is trying the same approach on the twelve-year old. *The thirteenth daughter*

208

stepped forward and stood with her arms folded in front of her. The note says, "This child walks right up and into the tiger's mouth. Check!" *Kuei-shan asked the same question again.* The note says, "Check it out, check it out. Even tiny ponds are sometimes as deep as the ocean." He has to probe a little bit further with this little one. How deep is she really? *The thirteenth daughter replied, "I've already presented it for Your Reverence."* The note says, "Ahh! Too much, too soon, too fast, too bad. Still, it amounts to something. I'll keep my binoculars on the horizon and watch." They used to say in China, "I'll hold my hand to my eyes and look off at the distant peaks." In other words, "You've got the stuff, and someday you'll realize it; I'll keep looking for you."

Kuei-shan said, "Go." The note says, "Indeed. Inevitably Kuei-shan diminishes people's worth." *As she was walking out from the Dharma hall, the monastic said, "The thirteenth daughter usually says that she knows Zen, and that her mouth is quick and sharp. But today she was questioned by the great Master Kuei-shan, and she didn't have a reply for him at all."* The note says, "Suddenly the little one doesn't seem so dull." *The thirteenth daughter answered, "My goodness. How can you talk like that? And you still say that you're on a pilgrimage. Take off your patched robe and give it to me."* The note says, "Indeed, get her. No, don't get her. Let her go on deceiving herself for the rest of her life." A pilgrimage was a big deal in those days, a matter of life and death. It was not like our modern spiritual journeys taken with the convenience of an airplane, a train, or a car. Pilgrimages in antiquity sometimes lasted for years. The travels took one over treacherous terrain and into dangerous country. One had to deal with thieves, wild animals, and lack of food. It took great determination to do it, and the process was likely to force one to clarify one's questions. So the twelve-year–old was doubtful about the monastic's aspirations, "How can you be so dull that you don't see what's going on. Take off your robe and give it to me," she said. Evidently the young one wasn't yet ordained, though the records show that she went on to become a successor of Chang Kung-an's Dharma.

Later the thirteenth daughter told the entire story to Lao-shan. The note says, "If you've lost your way, check the map and compass." The fact that she needs to ask somebody immediately shows that she's not clear. Somebody who knows where they're going goes. Nothing holds her back, nothing stops her. *"Visiting Kuei-shan I answered like that. Was my answer correct?"* The note says, "Wrong." Right there, she reveals herself. "But," it goes on to say, "I wonder, does this question have a barb in it?" Correct or incorrect? Can you see the barbs that existed all along here?

Her question *"Was my answer correct?"* seems to imply that there's a correct and an incorrect response. If Lao-shan had gone for the bait she would have nailed him. *Lao-shan said, "I won't say that there wasn't a mistake."* The note says, "A good hunter doesn't leave tracks." Predators, when tracking, usually place their hind leg into the footprints of their front leg, leaving as few traces as possible. Sometimes the overlap is exact. A house cat almost does it, and if it stays in the wild long enough, the footprints will eventually be one inside the other. Cats, wild and domesticated, are also meticulous about covering their own feces. At home they can be trained to use the toilet. It's very natural for them. If there's no place to scratch a hole and drop their feces into, they'll drop them into water. In the wild, they'll defecate into a stream when they're in a rocky terrain. The captive mountain lions in

210

the Catskill Game Preserve defecate into porcelain sinks a few feet off the ground because they don't want to leave their scat exposed on the concrete floor of their cages. Instinct tells them not to leave tracks or traces. That's what Lao-shan was doing in the way he answered.

The thirteenth daughter asked, "Where was the mistake?" The note says, "As it turns out, she has misunderstood. She's still young. The mother cat trains her kittens by playing with them." *Lao-shan scolded her.* The note says, "A nip on the rump is not quickly forgotten." A mother cat teaching her kittens will gently play with them, but every once in a while she really gives them a serious swat. It's a game, but a game of learning how to live and defend themselves.

During a recent camping trip, I hid in a pile of leaves and weeds beside a little bay, doing nature photography. Suddenly a mother duck appeared out of the reeds, going a mile a minute, quacking loudly and excitedly. She was throwing her head all over the place, drawing a lot of attention to herself, which in the wilderness is rather unusual. As she kept up the racket in the middle of this little cove, there was an explosion of feathers—baroom! seven ducks, clearly her children, came bursting out of the sky from the other side of the bay, landing in a perfect formation right next to her—plump! plump! plump! plump! plump! plump! plump! She just continued, sounding really angry. "Quack! Quack! Quack! Quack! Quack!" Then she started swimming away, and they all fell in line behind her. When she reached the next cove, she turned around and faced them, all the while quacking. They formed a tight arc near her and listened attentively. She kept on yelling at them for a minute longer, and then she finally stopped. When she took off, they all peeled off one at a time, right behind her. The lesson was complete.

Lao-shan scolded her. The thirteenth daughter said,
"Adding flowers to brocade." The note says, "She's still
showing her fangs, but the old thief has already left with
everything." Adding flowers to brocade refers to something extra. It's the same as "adding frost to snow." She's
saying that he's overdoing it, still feisty and ready for a
fight. But by this time the old man is long gone. As she is
showing her fangs, the thief has already left with everything. I have to keep reminding myself that she's twelve
years old. She may be bright, but she's still only a twelve-
year old.

The capping verse:

> *Fangs bared, claws unsheathed,*
> *The lion cub hasn't learned fear.*
> *It's not a matter for hesitating over.*
> *The head and tail belong to the same lion.*
> *A cat barks, a dog purrs,*
> *The mother lode is every mountain.*

The girl lost out in her hesitation. Her hesitation is,
first of all, "I've already presented it for you, Your
Reverence." Second of all, after being arrogant with the
monastic, she went to test herself with Lao-shan, spilling
more of her doubt. *It's not a matter for hesitating over.*
The minute you stop to ponder it, your mind is moving,
you've already separated heaven and hell, and it's too late.
The head and tail belong to the same lion. They're two parts
of the same reality, not one here and the other one there.
Mistake on one side, no mistake on the other side. *A cat
barks, a dog purrs, the mother lode is every mountain.* In
gold mining days, when you were searching for the source
of all the gold, you would follow the little veins of the precious metal that might lead you to the mother lode, where

the whole treasure was. Mother lode is Shobogenzo, the storehouse of the pure Dharma eye. And the mother lode *is* every mountain. It's not just this mountain or that mountain, but every one of them.

In the early history of Zen in China, there was no formalized, standardized training. It took several hundred years for the process to be organized. People usually traveled from place to place, asking questions of various masters. When they decided they'd had enough, they would start teaching, whether they were approved or not. People who studied with them had no idea what degree of understanding these self-proclaimed teachers had. Self-styled, *buji*, Zen was surfacing all over the place. Traditional Dharma combat exposed some of these people. Many koans deal with their shortcomings.

Things haven't really changed. The tendency to stop one's practice before it is completed and before one's realization has been sanctioned by a true teacher still persists. That's one of the reasons why we've taken precautions with groups affiliated with this Monastery. We've incorporated these sitting groups, and our intent is to let people know that when they go to one of the affiliates, they will not be dealing with some self-appointed guru, but with somebody trained to provide instructions and support. There will be reassurance that someone is taking care of things. It's very difficult for people brand-new to practice to be critical, particularly if they're seeking help with some sort of trauma. A person just reaching out for help sees a center offering something called "Zen" and assumes that the training is authentic. Sometimes that can be misleading, disappointing, and eventually very painful. When the blind lead the blind, everybody crashes into walls.

When this problem was recognized in China, attempts were made to assure continuity of genuine transmission by standardizing the training. Pai-chang was responsible for forming early versions of the monastic code. Monastics began living and practicing together under the supervision of and in close contact with a teacher. Dharma combat became a regular aspect of the training. Koans were collected and used in systems by different masters. Through time, this process kept on evolving and stayed vital. Yet the very organization of the teachings tended to make the Dharma stale. The only reason why Zen practice has stayed alive all these years is because of the clarity of the teachers. That clarity is what has been transmitted generation to generation.

We're in a very wonderful position in the twentieth century, with the Dharma new in this country. We have 2,500 years of history to learn from. Retrospectively, it's very clear where things went astray. It's very clear where the difficulties were, and what needs to be done to maintain the integrity of the teachings. If methods are too heavy-handed, the whole process gets smothered. If it is too loose, it drifts toward *buji* Zen. Somewhere there is a point where the two extremes meet in perfect harmony. That's what we're accomplishing in this generation, so that the generations to come will be able to practice diligently, easily, and with confidence in the form that they will receive.

In the meantime, there is still today to take care of. Please do it well. Take advantage of this time. More and more I feel a deep obligation to those of you who want to accomplish yourselves. More and more I feel a deep obligation to stay with you, and to see that you succeed. That's the iron yoke of the teacher. If there is a single student struggling to realize herself or himself, the teacher's imperative is to assist in every way, in a way equal to the student's own practice and determination. That is essential.

214

SIXTEEN

TAO-WU TENDS THE SICK

The Book of Equanimity, Case 83

PROLOGUE

The whole body being sickness, Vimalakirti is hard to cure. The grass being usable for medicine, Manjushri uses it well. How can that compare to calling on a transcendent person and gaining peace and well being?

THE MAIN CASE

Kuei-shan asked Tao-wu, "Where are you coming from?" Tao-wu said, "I've come from tending the sick." Kuei-shan said, "How many people were sick?" Tao-wu said, "There were the sick and the not sick." Kuei-shan said, "Isn't the one not sick you?" Tao-wu said, "Being sick and not being sick have nothing to do with him at all. Speak quickly, speak quickly." Kuei-shan said, *"Even if I could say anything, it would have no relation."*

THE CAPPING VERSE

> *When has the wonderful medicine ever passed his*
> *   mouth?*
> *Even the miraculous physician can't hold his wrist.*
> *As though existent, he is basically not non-existent.*
> *Utterly empty, he is basically not existent.*
> *Not perishing yet born. Alive without dying.*
> *Completely transcending the four prehistoric Buddhas.*
> *Walking alone after the empty eon.*
> *Subsisting peacefully—sky covers, earth supports.*
> *Moving on—the sun flies, the moon runs.*

In some koans, spiritual practice is presented in terms of sickness and medicine. Sicknesses, or afflictions, are basically ordinary human delusions and problems. One koan lists four afflictions, another enumerates six. The four are: the idea of the self, self-delusion, self-conceit, and self-love. The six are: greed, anger, ignorance, pride, opinion, and doubt. All of the afflictions cited in Buddhist teachings originate from the same place, and that place is the notion of the existence of a self, or even the idea of existence as such. You can't have greed, anger, and ignorance unless the illusion of a self exists.

It is interesting and important to note that the way Buddhism sometimes speaks of the self—in terms of "really be yourself," "trust yourself," "realize yourself"—has been adopted and bastardized by some New Age philosophies in such a way as to result in ideologies of self-centeredness. When Buddhism speaks of the self in these terms, it is the transcendent self, where there is no ego and no separation between the bag of skin and the ten thousand things.

When the illusion of a self finally disappears, what is manifested are compassion, wisdom, and enlightenment, the other sides of the three sicknesses of greed, anger, and ignorance. The question is, "What is the medicine?" Sickness being delusion and health being enlightenment, in a sense we can say that the medicine is the Dharma.

Several koans in different collections deal with the issue of sickness and medicine. Besides the koan of Vimalakirti's sickness discussed in this chapter, there is a *The Blue Cliff Record* koan, "The Great Master Ma-tsu is Unwell," dealing with Ma-tsu's illness. There is the koan of Tung-shan's illness; there is Yün-men's "Two Sicknesses," and Yün-men's "Medicine and sickness heal each other; all the world is medicine. Where do you find yourself?"

The prologue of this koan begins with, *The whole body being sickness, Vimalakirti is hard to cure.* Vimalakirti was an enlightened lay practitioner who lived at the time of the Buddha and was considered by many people to have a realization equivalent to that of the Buddha. One day, the Buddha said to his assembly of monastics, "Vimalakirti is ill, please visit him." The monastics resisted at first because they knew something unusual was up. Meetings with Vimalakirti always turned into powerful Dharma combats. With Buddha's encouragement, they finally went. According to the sutra that tells the story, thousands of monastics fit into the little house of Vimalakirti. Their visit was an occasion for some very profound teachings.

Vimalakirti was sick because human beings are sick, because the whole world is sick. His sickness was of the whole body and mind; that's why it was hard to cure.

When you're sick with the whole body and mind, there is nothing outside that. In a sense, it is the same as saying that there is no-sickness. Just as when you are the pain, and the pain fills the whole universe, then we can say there is no pain. You need a reference system to talk about pain, and when the reference system is consumed by the pain, there is no longer any perception of it.

The prologue goes on to say, *The grass being usable for medicine, Manjushri uses it well.* In one of the sutras, Manjushri said to Sudana, "Please find me something that is not medicine." Sudana searched everywhere and returned saying, "I can't find anything that is not medicine." Manjushri said, "Then gather me something that is medicine." Sudana reached down and picked up a blade of grass and handed it to him. Manjushri held it up and showed it to the assembly, saying, "This medicine can kill people, and it can also bring people to life."

Manjushri can use medicine to kill or he can use it to give life. Of course, this killing is the killing of the ego, of the idea of a self. Giving life is the nourishment, the compassion, the manifestation of the Great Death in the ten thousand things. Be that as it may, *How can that compare to calling on a transcendent person and gaining peace and well being?*

In the main case, *Kuei-shan asked Tao-wu, "Where are you coming from?"* The teacher is putting out the probing pole. What is your understanding? How clear are you? The question can be answered in a very ordinary way, as it was when Tung-shan visited Yün-men. Yün-men asked, "Where are you coming from?" and Tung-shan replied, "From such-and-such monastery, Master." Yün-men then asked, "When did you leave there?" "About two months ago." Yün-men kept trying, "*When* did you leave there?" "On such-and-such a day." Suddenly Yün-men shouted,

"I give you thirty blows of my stick!" Tung-shan had no idea what he had done wrong. There was an innocence there, but Yün-men was trying to get him to see what he was doing with his life. The next morning, after Tung-shan had been sitting all night with that exchange, he went back to Yün-men and said, "Last night you gave me thirty blows of your stick. I don't know where my fault is." He wanted to know. He reached out and asked. Many of us don't ask. The reason we don't ask is because the cup is filled; we figure we already know, and we are satisfied with our ideas. When the cup is full there is no place to put the tea. "Where was I at fault?" Yün-men immediately struck again, "You rice bag, wandering from monastery to monastery. Where will you ever have today?" pointing out to Tung-shan that he was spending his life looking for the truth outside himself. This time Tung-shan saw it. When the same question is put to Tao-wu, he answers very differently. *"I've come from tending the sick."*

Tao-wu was a successor of Yüeh-shan, and Dharma brother to Yün-yen, Tung-shan's teacher, the founder of the Soto lineage. Kuei-shan was the successor to Pai-chang and the founder of the Igyo lineage. The time was about 800 A.D. Kuei-shan and Tao-wu were the tenth generation from the Sixth Ancestor, Hui-neng. Both were about the same age, each a successor to a different lineage, and each from different parts of China. What we have here are two adepts testing and probing each other, clarifying and polishing their understanding.

In a sense, all of the koans—all of the skillful means we use in training—are tending the sick. The medicine is the teaching. The practices are given to cure our spiritual ills. The question: *"Where are you coming from?"* Tao-wu said, *"I've come from tending the sick."* This is a good answer; it's the work of a Bodhisattva of Compassion manifesting her life through ten thousand hands and eyes, nourishing and healing. But Kuei-shan doesn't let it go at that. He goes a little further: *"How many people were sick?"* *Tao-wu said, "There were the sick and the not sick."*

The question is a trap Kuei-shan sets up, but Tao-wu doesn't fall into it. In a sense, "sick and not sick" is separating it. We call it "two moons," or "creating a second moon," another reality, an illusion. We refer to the second moon as an additional reality because absolute and relative are one thing. When we split it we produce two realities where there is only one. So, "sick and not sick" doesn't quite do it and Kuei-shan continues: *"Isn't the one not sick you?"*

Again, another trap. Tao-wu immediately comes back: *"Being sick and not being sick have nothing to do with him at all. Speak quickly, speak quickly."* What do you have to say? Kuei-shan responds: *"Even if I could say anything, it would have no relation."* It would have no relation to that place that is neither sick nor not sick, neither absolute nor relative, neither good nor bad.

In *The Book of Equanimity* collection of koans, Wan-sung has added notes to each of the lines of the main case and the verse. For the first line, when Kuei-shan asks Tao-wu, *"Where are you coming from?"* Wan-sung adds, "Where he is coming from needs clarification." Tao-wu says, *"I've come from tending the sick,"* and Wan-sung writes, "As it turns out, you've produced the second moon." Kuei-shan asks, *"Isn't the one not sick you?"* Wan-sung calls this a "pitfall for a tiger." You don't catch little frogs with this kind of a question. When Tao-wu replies, *"Being sick and not being sick have nothing to do with him at all. Speak quickly, speak quickly,"* Wan-sung's comment is, "He's been wrapped head to foot with vines by the gourd." And when Kuei-shan says, *"Even if I could say anything, it would have no relation,"* the note reads, "Calamity does not enter the door of the careful." Wan-sung is praising Kuei-shan for his handling of this.

When has the wonderful medicine ever passed his mouth? Even the miraculous physician can't hold his wrist. In this verse, the first two lines refer to the disappearance of both medicine and sickness. When taking medicine, the mouth is forgotten. When taking the pulse, the wrist is forgotten. This is what Wan-sung calls an incurable disease. You say it exists, yet throughout the body there is not a shadow or a reflection. You say it doesn't exist, yet the whole world is never hidden. We should understand that existence and non-existence, like all the other dualities, are not two separate things. That's the key to appreciating this koan. On one side we have sickness, and on the other side we have no sickness. On one side we have medicine, on the other side we have sickness. It's the relationship between these dualities that causes us the greatest problems, and it's in those very relationships that the solutions to the problems appear.

Somehow we have a tendency to fall into one side or the other, and get stuck in extremes. The Middle Way, the beautiful place of balance that falls into neither side, seems so incredibly difficult to be attained and sustained. It's not a fifty-fifty mixture of both sides, but the truth of the Buddha Way. The Buddha Way *is* the Middle Way. There are times when a koan may reveal one side or the other for the purpose of expedience, and the teacher risks being a "foul-smelling one," reeking with holiness or the stink of Zen. This is done for the benefit of all sentient beings and, knowingly, the teacher offends. Ultimately, the koan always comes down on neither one side nor the other. But in koans when the student points to the absolute, the teacher will point to the relative. When the student points

221

to the relative, the teacher will point to the absolute. When the student points to neither absolute nor relative, the lotus blooms in the fire.

As though existent, he is basically not non-existent. Utterly empty, he is basically not existent. Not perishing yet born. Alive without dying. There's an account in Chinese legends of an old priest who had a ten-volume scripture on immortality. He ran into a Buddhist master and asked him, "In Buddhist teachings, is there a method of eternal life without death that surpasses the methods of the wizards of China?" That master said, "Pfft! How can this country have a method of eternal life? Even if you could extend your years, once the reward is ended you fall." Or, to rephrase: even if you could extend your life, sooner or later the extension wears out and that's the end of it. Then he took a copy of the scripture on the contemplation of the Buddha of Infinite Life and gave it to the old priest saying, "This is the method of the Great Wizard to eternally realize liberation and forever leave birth and death." Of course, the question of birth and death is fundamental to our practice. The question of birth and death, of life and death, is the question that started the spiritual search of the Buddha.

Throughout history, in Buddhism and other religions, sages and teachers have all had the question of life and death as the central theme, the cutting edge of their practice. The question of life and death is the question of all the dualities—good and bad, heaven and earth, self and other, enlightenment and delusion. When you resolve the question of life and death, you resolve the question of duality. It's not a matter of postponing death, but a matter of understanding death. That's why everyone who enters Zen Mountain Monastery as a student presents a petition saying that they've come here realizing that the question of life and death is a Great Matter. If it's not the question of life and death that's brought someone to this practice, being here is a waste of time. There are very few things that I would say are a waste of time in terms of practice, but that's one of them. If you don't have the question, you haven't entered the Way. The search hasn't begun. If there's no question and you're not searching, there's no answer.

Putting the question to rest requires that the student has what we call the three pillars of practice, the first of which is great faith. This is faith not only in oneself but also in the process that is being engaged. Great faith means boundless faith, vast without edges. Great doubt is the second pillar, and it functions in dynamic tension with one's faith; they work against each other. That's the life of the practice. Great determination is the cutting edge. If any one of the three components is missing, the tripod doesn't stand but wobbles around. Practice wobbles around and doesn't go anywhere.

The great doubt is to deeply ask the questions: Who am I? What is life? What is truth? What is reality? What is God? All of those questions address the absolute nature of reality, the ground of being. Though it may take many different forms, basically it's always the same question, the question of life and death. This is what distinguishes a ground-of-being practice from a well-being practice, a transformational practice from a band-aid practice. The question is where to start. The search is where it begins.

Completely transcending the four prehistoric Buddhas. Wan-sung means before the heavens are formed, yet already complete. *Walking alone after the empty eon.* The empty eon is the period of time following the annihilation of the universe. After the heavens are already destroyed, and not yet destroyed. *Subsisting peacefully—sky covers, earth supports. Moving on—the sun flies, the moon runs.* In a sense, one side is the absolute basis, the other is the activity in creation that comes out of that stillness. When still, the root of heaven and earth and all things; when moving, harmonizing with the minds of the sages and Buddhas.

Wan-sung's notes to the verse are as follows. *When has the wonderful medicine ever passed his mouth?* The note says, "Can't be swallowed, can't be spit out." *Even the miraculous physician can't hold his wrist.* "There's no place to take hold of him." The miraculous physician could be the Buddha or Kuei-shan in this case. *As though existent, he's basically not non-existent.* "He's everywhere in the world, he reaches everywhere." *Utterly empty, he's basically not existent.* "You don't see so much as a hair." If he's everywhere, how can we speak of him as being existent, anyway? If you contain the whole universe, how can we differentiate you from it? Where will you put this gigantic body? *Not perishing yet born.* The note says, "Empty as the spirit of the valleys. Always undying." *Alive without dying.* "The Way grew of itself prior to the Emperor of images, before form." That's a reference to the Buddha's saying that life is the unborn and death is the unextinguished.

What is it that's born? When we speak of life and death, we're speaking of the idea of a self. What is the self? I ask this question constantly. And I either get an answer like "everything," which stinks to high heaven, or a list of aggregates: "my body, my mind, my thoughts," which can never be exhausted. What remains beyond the aggregates? What is self-ness itself? We always come up with answers that are collections of aggregates, but that misses the thing itself. What is the thing itself?

"Life is the unborn" means it never was born, it doesn't exist. "Death is the unextinguished" means it is never extinguished because it never existed to begin with. Then what is this? Who are you? What is life? Where do you find the self? Where do you find *your* self? People struggling with the koan Mu find themselves in their bag of skin with Mu outside—two separate things. "Be one with Mu," the teacher says. "I can't; it's out there." Who put it out there? Who put your self in the bag of skin? Isn't Mu all about how you use your mind? And isn't how you use your mind exactly how you live your life?

Completely transcending the four prehistoric Buddhas. Wan-sung comments, "Rolled out and it doesn't reach the beginning." *Walking alone after the empty eon.* "Rolled up and it doesn't reach the end." *Subsisting peacefully—sky covers, earth supports.* "Holding heaven and earth still." *Moving on—the sun flies, the moon runs.* "Action in creation." Sometimes medicine is poison. In fact, many medicines—probably all medicines—in certain quantities are poisons. Curare, which is used to treat neurological diseases, can actually kill you. South American Indians use it for poison darts. It paralyzes their prey and can cause a cardiac arrest. Yet, we use it for healing. Hiroshima and Nagasaki showed us how poisonous radiation is, but it also heals. Radiation therapy has saved thousands of lives. The sodium fluoride we use to keep our teeth from getting cavities is a rat poison. The safety of these things always has to do with the amount used, just the right amount— *oryoki.*

There are situations where we use sickness to heal sickness, and times when we use medicine to heal sickness. The medicine is the teachings. Isn't 2,500 years of giving medicine in accord with the disease the business of Buddhas and ancestors, passed on from generation to generation? There is a Dharma pharmacopoeia that contains all sorts of wonderful medicines. Sesshin is in that pharmacopoeia. Dharma combat, face-to-face teaching, liturgy, koan study, zazen, work practice, art practice, body practice, and academic study are all in that pharmacopoeia. Even little things like the monitors' encouragements during sesshin—"Don't look around," "Don't talk," "Be awake," "Go deeper"—are medicines, lighter medicines, but just as important. And as with any kind of medicine, if you don't take it, it doesn't help the disease.

What about the medicine for the sickness of looking around? Every time you look around you plug more data into your biocomputer and the wheels keep turning, analyzing, systematizing, judging, evaluating, tat tat tat tat tat tat tat tat. The internal dialogue goes on and on, ad nauseam, separating you further and further from your practice. "Don't look around" is the medicine. If you're not looking around, the opportunity for the mind to get quiet is increased a hundredfold, a thousandfold.

We may understand how sesshin, Dharma combat, face-to-face teaching, and zazen can function as medicines. But there are other medicines we may not readily appreciate. Pain is medicine. Suffering is medicine. Fear, deluded thoughts, self-centeredness, greed, anger, and ignorance are all medicines. Samsara itself is medicine. That's the lotus in the fire. The fire burns and the lotus blooms, and it's because the fire burns that the lotus can bloom. There would be no lotus if there were no fire.

Be all that as it may, I have a question for you. When the sickness is having no sickness at all, what's the medicine? That's the worst kind of disease to heal: the sickness of no sickness. Medicine and sickness heal each other. This is most difficult to see.

The beginning and the end have no starting point nor have they an ending point, and no communication whatsoever is possible. Why? Inexhaustible excellence reaches everywhere. Do you understand? If you don't understand, then find out. This is the place to do it. This is the time to do it. And you are the one to do it. So, please, take care of this Great Matter. The Great Matter is the matter of life and death. Your life. Your death.

SEVENTEEN

PAI-CHANG AND THE FOX

Gateless Gate, Case 2

THE MAIN CASE

Whenever Master Pai-chang gave teisho *on Zen, an old man sat with the monastics to listen, and always withdrew when they did. One day, however, he remained behind, and the Master asked, "Who are you standing here before me?" The old man replied, "I am not a human being. In the past, in the time of Kashyapa Buddha, I was the head of this monastery. Once a monastic asked me, 'Does an enlightened person also fall into causation or not?' I replied, 'An enlightened person does not.' Because of this I was made to live as a fox for 500 lives. Now I beg you, please say the turning words on my behalf and release me from the fox body." The old man then asked Pai-chang, "Does an enlightened person also fall into causation or not?" The Master said, "An enlightened person does not ignore causation." Hearing this, the old man was at once*

*enlightened. Making a bow to Pai-chang, he said, "I
have now been released from the fox body, which will be
found behind the mountain. I dare to make a request of
the Master. Please bury it as you would a deceased
monastic."*

*The Master had the ino strike the gavel and
announce to the monastics that there would be a funeral
for a deceased monastic after the mid-day meal. The
monastics wondered, saying "We're all in good health.
There's no sick monastic in the nirvana hall. What's it
all about?" After the meal, the Master led the monastics
to a rock behind the mountain, poked out a dead fox
with his staff, and cremated it.*

*In the evening, the Master ascended the rostrum in
the hall and told the monastics the whole story. Huang-
po thereupon asked, "The old man failed to give the correct turning words and was made to live as a fox for
500 lives, you say. If, however, his answer had not been
incorrect each time, what would he have become?" The
Master said, "Come closer to me, and I'll tell you."
Huang-po then stepped forward to Pai-chang and hit
him. The Master laughed aloud, clapping his hands, and
said, "I thought the foreigner had a red beard. Now I see
that it is a red-bearded foreigner."*

COMMENTARY

*Not falling into causation, why was he turned into
a fox? Not ignoring causation, why was he released from
the fox body? If you have an eye to see through this, then*

*you will know that the former head of the monastery did
enjoy his 500 happy, blessed lives as a fox.*

THE CAPPING VERSE

*Not falling, not ignoring,
Odd and even are on one die.
Not ignoring, not falling,
Hundreds and thousands of regrets.*

This is one of the finest koans in the *Gateless Gate* collection. It appears as the second case but, because of its
significance and subtlety, I have students skip over it until
they have completed all the other koans in the
Mumonkan. A student just beginning koan practice is not
mature enough in understanding or clarity to appreciate
the importance of the teachings in this koan. It is an
example of a *nanto* koan, *nanto* meaning "difficult to pass
though," according to the koan classification of Master
Hakuin. The reason it is difficult to pass through is that
the key point being made is a very elusive one, very easy to
miss or misinterpret.

Right from the beginning, the basic principle is
revealed. When the monastic asked the former head of
that monastery, "Does an enlightened person also fall into
causation or not?" and the abbot answered, "An enlightened person does not," he was immediately turned into a
fox. Wan-sung, in *The Book of Equanimity*, the other collection in which this koan appears, has added interesting
notes to these first lines. *Once a monastic asked me, "Does
an enlightened person also fall into causation or not?" I
replied, "An enlightened person does not."* The note: "A fitting statement is a stake to tie a donkey to for ten thou-

sand years." In other words, he's pointing out that this is exactly where this guy is stuck. The next line says, *Because of this I was made to live as a fox for 500 lives.* The note: "You just got through saying one doesn't fall into cause and effect." The abbot's answer immediately and inevitably resulted in cause and effect taking place.

There are many practitioners in this sangha who practice within prison walls. Many of them are incarcerated in the Green Haven Correctional Facility. Questions of cause and effect comes up frequently in my meetings with them. This is something that many of the prisoners deal with to a great extent. Because of the consequences of their actions, they've ended up living in prison. Some of them are in for murder, and have been sentenced for life. Many of them, since they began practicing Zen, have come to confront and question the implications of their actions for the first time in their lives. It's a very touchy situation. People tend to protect themselves. We deny, suppress, absorb ourselves in distractions, and in general avoid the difficult things in our lives. We create a protective coating around us that isolates us from life. When we begin Zen practice, we chip away at that shell. There is a phase when the student becomes very exposed and vulnerable. This is one of the reasons why it is critical for teachers to be responsible, to recognize and work with that vulnerability, and not to take self-centered advantage of it, as teachers have in the past, not only in our country, but in other countries as well. If the openness is used as a way of bringing a student to realization, that's one thing. If it's employed to the advantage of a narcissistically inclined teacher, it's a gross violation of the Precepts on the part of that teacher.

Some of the students at the prison who have significantly engaged this practice have become very vulnerable, which can be risky and dangerous, especially behind the prison walls. Part of their ability to survive there has to do with their invulnerable posture, the thick shell. The most advanced among them, practicing for eight or more years, have come to grips with causality in their lives, have taken responsibility for it, and have been able to move on. They have come out of that hiding place, and begun to manifest it in their lives. The practice actually turned their lives around, dramatically enough so that even the prison authorities and the correction officers have recognized the changes that have taken place. Some of the students have been put to work as counselors for other prisoners.

It is one thing to present the great principles of Dharma, or to sit and listen to them. It is quite another to confront the great principles with one's own life. That's why koan study, Dharma combat, and *mondo* exchanges are so vital to the life and continuity of this practice. They take the teachings out of the theoretical and abstract mode and thrust them into the present moment, giving them immediate, undeniable relevance.

In an attempt to do that at the prison during a Rohatsu sesshin, I presented the students there with a modern version of this koan. A very similar thing happened recently with a Dharma teacher here in America, who essentially made the statement that his realization, his enlightenment, enabled him to transcend cause and effect. As a result of that assumption, he is presently "living 500 lives as a fox." So this ancient koan surfaces in the twentieth century, right in our own front yard. People think that koans are archaic historical documents. With any sense of understanding, you will see that they pertain to you and me, in each and every day. They are the continuing process of this life itself.

Instead of asking the prisoners, "What would you have answered if you were Pai-chang?" or "How would you have handled it if you were Huang-po?" or "What would you say to the old man in order to save him from 500 lives as a fox?"—questions that seem ancient and far away, I reframed the story. I shared with them a very specific incident, where a teacher who had contracted HIV had sexual relationships with many of his students, thereby infecting many of them with the virus. He knew he had the virus, yet knowingly had relationships without protection and without informing his partners. When asked why he did that, he said that he was convinced that because of his realization he was able to transcend the cause and effect of having AIDS. In other words, his infection would not become an effect for someone else. The 500 lives of a fox have been the almost complete breakdown of the community of practitioners he was responsible to. In the immediate generation, there might be some hundred people infected. And who knows what the ripple effect of that will be as the infection spreads.

The teacher has now died. Some people he infected are slowly deteriorating and dying, suffering all the complications of AIDS. My question to the prisoners was, "What would you do? How would you have handled that situation as the teacher? How would you turn it around?" It was a real Dharma combat. People answered from the point of view of where their practice was. One guy said he'd throw himself off a cliff, and that's exactly the way he's practicing his life. He is tormented with regret and remorse for having killed many innocent people, not only in this country as a civilian, but as a licensed killer in Vietnam. And that's what we work on. Needless to say, I wouldn't accept his response. I told him it was a cop-out. How do you deal with it?

It's a good question for all of us to examine deeply. It's one thing to understand the principles of cause and effect, and quite another to see how they function in our lives. None of us is perfect. We're all going to err—no question about it. These are difficult and complicated times. There are no easy solutions. How do we deal with the problems we encounter? What's our understanding of who we are, what the universe is like? What is our moral responsibility? How can we practice our lives? What does it mean to be realized? What does it mean when Master Dogen says that practice and realization are one?

In appreciating this koan, the first thing we should look at is the old man. He says, "*I am not a human being. In the past, in the time of Kashyapa Buddha, I was the head of this monastery.*" Kashyapa Buddha is one of the legendary Buddhas who preceded Shakyamuni Buddha. Kashyapa Buddha is the Buddha who supposedly sat for 10,000 kalpas under the bodhi tree and never attained enlightenment. So this old man says that was the time when he was the head of the monastery. At that time a monastic asked him, "*Does an enlightened person also fall into causation or not?*" Because of his answer he was made to turn into a fox. What is this old man? What is the fox? To really chew up and digest this koan, you must understand its language. You have to grasp the essence of living the life of a fox. It is no small thing. To us, it's no big deal; in fact it may seem desirable. A fox can look beautiful wandering around the hillsides. For Chinese or Japanese people, however, to be called a fox is the worst thing imaginable. It was a vile curse to call someone a wild fox spirit. The positive associations we have in English to "being foxy"—shrewd, sharp, attractive—just did not apply when this koan appeared. It was derogatory through and through.

For saying that an enlightened person does not fall into causation the old teacher was turned into a fox. Why?

The sutras, again and again, say that enlightened beings don't fall into causation. In fact, one of them states, "An errant monastic does not fall into hell. This very place is the absolute place. There's no hell to fall into." It goes on to say, "A holy saint doesn't go to heaven. This very place is the absolute place. There's no heaven to ascend to." When the whole universe is causation itself, how can there be talk of falling or not falling? In one sense, you can correctly call it "falling" or you can correctly call it "not falling." But if there is even a single thought associated with either of those statements, heaven and earth are separated, and you turn into a fox and fall into hell.

When the old man asks Pai-chang how he would respond, Pai-chang says, "*An enlightened person does not ignore causation.*" How are these two statements—"Not falling into causation" and "Not ignoring causation"—different? Cause and effect is very clear. It's undeniable. There's nothing on earth that exists outside of the activity of cause and effect. Every moment, every existence, is causation itself. Outside it there is neither self nor other, neither I nor the world. There is no denying it. Master Dogen repeatedly focuses on this point in the *Shobogenzo*. For him, to deny cause and effect is to deny Buddha-Dharma. "Practice is enlightenment" reflects the same relationship. Practice (cause) and enlightenment (effect) are one. Cause and effect are one. It's a basic, quintessential teaching. And if you really understand "Cause and effect are one," you understand that cause doesn't precede effect, nor does effect follow cause.

Later in the koan Huang-po asks, "If he had answered correctly, what would he have turned into?" I ask you, "What would the correct answer be?" How could that old man have responded to the original question? How could our modern master have practiced his life in a way to avoid creating the pain and suffering in his own life and the lives of others? If the old man had answered correctly, what would he have become? Right in that becoming—old man becoming fox, fox turning back into old man—is the clue to the problem that he was dealing with, and the clue to the problem that we all deal with. When Huang-po challenges Pai-chang with "What would he have turned into if he answered correctly?" Pai-chang says, "*Come closer to me and I'll tell you.*" That's it! Come a little closer. Huang-po stepped up and hit Pai-chang. What was Huang-po communicating by striking his old teacher? And what was Pai-chang's response all about, clapping his hands and laughing? Was he approving of or responding to the hit? When Huang-po struck, was that Huang-po's answer as to what the old man would have become? Pai-chang concludes the exchange with the statement, *I thought the foreigner had a red beard. Now I see that it is a red-bearded foreigner.* What's the logic here? What's the communication? What is the old man? What is Pai-chang? What is the fox? None of them are man or fox.

The term "enlightened person" is intended to mean a person who has completed spiritual training, a person of *satori* who has accomplished emancipation and at last realized peace of mind. Such a person is not subject to retribution or transmigration. The whole point of practice is to free oneself of the chain of causation. That's the whole point of the teachings of Mahayana Buddhism. That's the definition of realization and freedom. In fact, it is such an obvious fact among Buddhists that it is not even discussed. It is a given. This is the position presented by the former head of the monastery, the old man, in his reply to: "*Does an enlightened person also fall into causation or not?*" So the question persists—why did he have to live 500 lives as a fox as a result of his answer? That's a central point of this koan. What does it really mean to be free from cause and effect, from retribution? This is where the truth of this koan, where the truth of Zen, is to be found. "An enlightened person does not fall into causation" will unequivocally turn one into a fox, unless one clearly knows what that truth really is.

Obviously, when he answered the monastic, the old man was uncertain. He became enlightened under Pai-chang's words, but at the time the monastic was questioning him, he wasn't clear. When he asked Pai-chang, "*Now I beg you, please say the turning words on my behalf and release me from the fox body,*" Pai-chang immediately replied, "*An enlightened person does not ignore causation.*" A turning word is something that is exactly the right statement for a person in a certain state of mind. It is an expression that brings realization. It can actually be anything. Sometimes a shout is a turning word. Sometimes a hit is a turning word. Sometimes just repeating the question becomes the turning word. Turning words are the words that turn one's mind to the truth. In that person's consciousness, it is the ultimate expression of truth.

In a literal way, we can say that Pai-chang's reply means that an enlightened person doesn't ignore the fact of cause and effect, but lives according to it. In a sense, this is diametrically opposed to "Unequivocally, he does not fall into causation." We could also say that what Pai-chang is saying is exactly the opposite of what the Mahayana sutras are saying. It's almost like stating that no matter how enlightened you become, you are still constantly subjected to perpetual rebirth and transmigration. That's a contradiction of the Mahayana definition of enlightenment. Is that Pai-chang's meaning and intention?

Hearing Pai-chang's words, the old man was at once enlightened. That's what the koan tells us. The old man was enlightened when he heard Pai-chang say, "The enlightened person does not ignore causation." If you think for a second that what the old man said, "not falling into causation," is an incorrect reply, and that Pai-chang's answer, "not ignoring causation," is the correct reply, then you're 10,000 miles away from it. Don't fall into that trap. That's what makes this a *nanto* koan. Immediately, we want to get logical. The old man said "not falling into causation," and he was turned into a fox. Pai-chang said "not ignoring causation," and he became a person again. Therefore Pai-chang must be right and the old man must be wrong. Wrong, wrong, wrong, wrong, wrong. It misses it. In fact, another old master said, "Not falling into causation, and he was turned into a fox. The first mistake. Not ignoring causation, and he was released from the fox body. The second mistake." Why does he call them both mistakes? If neither is correct, what is correct?

Also, don't get caught up in the story line. Pai-chang is a very shrewd teacher, and good teachers have a way of concocting complications. I'm sure Pai-chang was out for a walk on the mountain one day, and he found a dead fox, and he said, "Aha!" He took the fox, stuffed it in a cave, and came back to tell the monastics the story about the old man. "Have you noticed the old man that's been coming here?" When you are running a monastery with a thousand monastics, nobody notices if there is a stranger in the back. "Every time there's a *teisho*, he has been here. And after the last *teisho* he told me that he had once been the abbot of this monastery, thousands of years ago, and that he was made to live 500 lives as a fox simply because when a monastic asked him, 'Does an enlightened being fall into causation or not?' he answered 'An enlightened person does not,' quoting the sutra. And then he asked me, 'Does an enlightened being fall into causation or not?'

and I said to him, 'An enlightened person does not ignore causation.' Immediately, he was freed from the fox body. So come with me and let's bury that dead fox." All the monastics followed. Behind the mountain, Pai-chang poked out the dead fox, cremated it, and performed a funeral for a monastic. Huang-po, who was Pai-chang's main student, came up and did Dharma combat with the old man, making the truth even clearer. He was the only one among the thousand in the assembly who understood the teaching that Pai-chang was putting forth.

To get to another level of appreciation of this koan, we must understand that the fox body is a deluded body. It's that fox body that brings us to practice to begin with. All kinds of different reasons motivate us into practice. For some people it's just a matter of getting answers to questions. Even though these questions may lead us to realization, they usually come from a very deluded point of view. They're essentially life koans. Koans bring us into practice, and koans carry us all the way through practice. It doesn't matter whether we're doing koan study or sitting *shikan-taza*, our questions are in koans. Each time we clarify one, two or three others pop up in its place. Through the process of struggling with them we slowly, deliberately, hone our lives to perfection.

The "fox" that the old man was (and that the modern master I referred to was) represents a deluded point of view. The old man was already a fox before he answered the monastic's question, only he hadn't realized it. On hearing the words of Pai-chang, he was released from the fox body. Yet he was always free of the fox body, right from the very beginning, before he became a fox, after he became a fox, and after he returned from being a fox. He was always released from the fox body, only he didn't realize it either. That realization is the key. That realization was the basic difference between Pai-chang's statement and the old man's statement. But, if you think that when the old man said, "An enlightened being doesn't fall into causation," he was wrong, and that when Pai-chang said "An enlightened person doesn't ignore causation," he was correct, then you, too, are speaking from the fox body. Falling into, not falling into; being a fox, not being a fox; being a person, not being a person; correct and incorrect —all are part of the same duality that got this man into trouble in the first place.

"Falling and not falling" is a trap. That's why Dogen teaches that cause and effect are one, not one before and the other after. Effect doesn't follow cause. Cause doesn't precede effect. They're one in one instant. They are one moment that totally and completely consumes the whole universe. Realizing Pai-chang's words was the old man's atonement. His atonement was his realization, his at-one-ment. At one with what? At one with the fox body? At one with cause and effect? At one with the old man? The same thing can be asked regarding the modern master. What is his atonement? That was the question I put to the practitioners at Green Haven prison. What would you do to atone? How would you take responsibility for your life in that situation? How would you acknowledge the fact that what you do and what happens to you are the same thing? That's cause and effect. So, what is this modern master's atonement? How can it be realized and actualized? That's the only way to free oneself.

The practice of atonement is the practice of the Precepts. When we take the Precepts, we embrace a definition of the life of a Buddha. The Precepts are the process that a Buddha uses to actualize life within the world of phenomena. When we practice the Precepts, we practice atonement. The realization of atonement, or the realization of the Precepts, is enlightenment. It then becomes the manifestation of one's life.

Our tendency is always to hold onto one side or another. In that grasping and saying, "This is it," we begin to manifest the life of a fox. In the context of the koan, the questions that come up are: What was the old man if he wasn't a fox? If he wasn't an old man, then what was he? What's the fox? Why, when he said, "An enlightened being doesn't fall into causation," was he thrown into the life of a fox when that's a basic teaching of Buddhism? It's completely consistent with the sutras, the teachings of the Buddha himself. Why, when Pai-chang said, "He does not ignore causation," did the old man get enlightened? What is it that he saw? And why wasn't Pai-chang turned into a fox, since what he's saying is in opposition to what the sutras are saying?

You can see here that if you just accept what the sutras say from an academic perspective, you have reached a dead end. This is the outcome if you don't make the content of the sutras a vital part of your life. That's what the koans do. When I talk about koans, I'm talking about everybody's practice. Here at Zen Mountain Monastery, the people who are doing *shikantaza* also study and work, do art practice, body practice, and liturgy. They don't just sit. It's in all those other aspects of training that *shikantaza* begins to manifest itself. It's toward the *genjo-koans*, the koans of life, that the power of *shikantaza* is directed. If you just sit, it's very easy to become very passive, placid, and non-functional. It's like being dead, but not yet buried. With zazen alone, it's all compost but no seeds. Sometimes there are all seeds and no compost. That happens when there is plenty of reading, studying, and intellectualizing, but no zazen to nourish it, to allow it to grow, to help it to flower. And what is that flowering? That flowering is the realization of zazen, the actualization of the teachings. The sutras without zazen are just sutras. They're not yet the enlightenment of the Buddha. Liturgy without zazen is just liturgy. It's not yet the manifestation of the teachings of all Buddhas, past, present, and future.

And where does it show up? It shows up in every activity that we do. You can tell who is doing their zazen with the whole body and mind. I am not talking about people who are sitting cross–legged, assuming the form of zazen. That's not yet zazen. Let the mind sit along with the body. Unless that is happening, the same old stuff goes on. It can easily become a Dharma game. I was overhearing a number of conversations the other day at the Chinese restaurant in town. There was a table with six people who were evidently Buddhist practitioners. They were involved in an entertaining round of Buddhist gossip. There were three guys sitting next to me talking about the stock market, and across the room there were a couple of people talking about hunting. All the conversations were exactly the same. A waste. I heard the practitioners talking about what the teachers do when nobody's around, what secrets they know that the rest of the sangha does not. It was all words.

That's all nice. That's cocktail Zen. That's *buji* Zen, *buji* Buddhism. That's the Buddhism of the 1950s, when people sat around and talked about practice. That's not the flower that blooms out of zazen. That's talking about the flower. That's what this old monastic was doing, talking about cause and effect, quoting the sutra, not having yet realized it. That's what got the modern master in trouble, intellectualizing it, not having realized it. Realization makes all the difference in the world. It directly impacts on how you propagate your life, and how you relate to other people. The Vietnamese master Thich Nhat Hanh, addressing a group of people in San Francisco, encouraged them to start a Buddhist community; not a monastery, not a center, but a Buddhist community. It's very common in Asia. He was suggesting that they all practice and let their children practice. He said, "We need people to work in that place. We don't need monastics. We don't need enlightened people. We need happy people, because angry people can't do it. An angry person has nothing to offer a community that's trying to get started. But a happy person, even if stupid, even if deluded, a happy person nourishes, heals, and benefits all those who come in contact with him or her. An angry person poisons, obstructs, and puts out seeds of anger to every one that comes close. We need happy people."

I agree with him. The problem is that most people are unhappy, and that usually what we see as happiness is a facade of happiness. It's imitation. Imitation works for awhile, but in the long run it falters. We walk around with the big smile, and then when we're alone, the agony appears. That smile doesn't need to be fabricated. This life is a wonderful gift. It can be lived without difficulty in a way that is in peace and harmony with everything around us. Even if one is condemned to live the life of a fox. When you live the life of a fox through and through, with the whole body and mind, it's a wonderful, happy, and blessed life. It's only when we deny, separate ourselves, move away from, that we create the pain.

In the commentary on this koan, Wu-men says, *Not falling into causation, why was he turned into a fox? Not ignoring causation, why was he released from the fox body? If you have an eye to see through this, then you will know that the former head of the monastery did enjoy his 500 happy, blessed lives as a fox.* This is a wonderful summation of both parts of this koan. First of all, Wu-men is pointing out that the head of the monastery was turned into a fox as a result of his reply. Then he asks, why was he released as a result of Pai-chang's answer? This becomes a particularly burning question when you realize that his answer wasn't wrong, nor Pai-chang's answer right. So what is going on? The clue is, *If you have an eye to see through this, then you will know that the former head of the monastery did enjoy his 500 happy, blessed lives as a fox.*

Actually, there's no falling and no releasing. If you can see this from the absolute point of view, what does it really mean to be released from the fox body? What does it really mean to live a life as a fox? Wu-men is asking us to throw away all of the complications—turning into a fox, being released from the fox body. Then the way is clear.

Why is it so vital and important to know how to live 500 happy, blessed lives as a fox? Not to appreciate the pressing nature of that question is to miss the essence of how the koans function in our lives. To know how to live a happy, blessed life as a fox means to be able, under whatever circumstance, to be present with the whole body and mind, through and through. If you're a fox, be a fox with the whole body and mind. There is nothing but fox. There is no longer a reference system. When you cry, just cry, with the whole body and mind. Be crying. Then there is no crying. When you're happy, be happy with the whole body and mind, and then there is no happiness. What does it mean to be "it" with the whole body and mind, to be Mu with the whole body and mind, to be yourself with the whole body and mind? There is no crack in the Dharma eye. It is whole, continuous, from the past to the future with no gaps. Seamless.

Wu-men says, "If you have an eye"—that is, the spiritual eye—"to see that fundamentally Buddhas and ignorant beings are one, if you have an eye to see that purity and defilement are one, then you free yourself." The eye he's talking about is the third eye. If you have that eye, the Zen eye of *satori*, then you will know that the 500 fox lives were happy and blessed. When the old man is truly an old man, that life is a happy and blessed life. When the fox has transcended falling and releasing, and is truly a fox through and through, that life is a happy and blessed life. The happiness goes beyond the 500 lives. It is eternal happiness, penetrating all places and all ages.

How does one live 500 blessed lives as a prisoner? How does one live 500 blessed lives as a world leader? I've seen happy and clear prisoners, and sad, confused, and angry world leaders. So there is obviously more to what peace of mind and joy are about than how much money you have or don't have; than what position, authority, or power you have over others. This doesn't mean that being meek makes you happy, or that being strong makes you happy. It has nothing to do with conditions. It's got to do with really knowing yourself—who you are, what your life is—to realize it, and to live it out of what you've realized.

In the poem, Wu-men says,

> *Not falling, not ignoring,*
> *Odd and even are on one die.*
> *Not ignoring, not falling,*
> *Hundreds and thousands of regrets.*

Whether we say "not falling" or "not ignoring," all of it, in and of itself, is the essence of truth; not falling with the whole body and mind, not ignoring with the whole body and mind. And yet nothing is ever outside causation. Those relationships always exist—cause and effect, good and bad, enlightenment and delusion—but their elements are not different from each other. Form is exactly emptiness, emptiness exactly form. Cause is exactly effect, effect is exactly cause. It doesn't make logical sense. Heads is exactly tails, tails is exactly heads. Male is exactly female, female is exactly male. Buddhas are exactly creatures, creatures are exactly Buddhas. Enlightenment is exactly delusion, delusion is exactly enlightenment. It doesn't mean that it's a mixture, and it doesn't mean one or the other. It doesn't mean, "Well, if delusion is enlightenment, then I'll do whatever I want. It doesn't matter anyway." That's *buji* Zen. That's the result of understanding Zen intellectually. It's not form, and it's not emptiness. Yet form is exactly emptiness and emptiness exactly form. So where is that place of truth? It's not heads, it's not tails. It's not one, it's not two. It's neither one nor two.

The whole problem of the old man, the whole problem of anger, the whole problem of separation, is born of the idea of a self. Attachment is an illusion based on separation. Falling and not falling, form and emptiness, are all based on the illusion of the existence of a self. Attachment to the self is what separates body and mind, what creates fear and anxiety, what creates anger. It also creates attachments to ideas, to words, phrases, slogans, positions, power, authority, and control. It doesn't matter whether we have a big ego or a little ego. An ego trip is an ego trip. "Big deal self" is an ego trip. "The insignificant self" is an ego trip. "I can't do it" is an even bigger ego trip. "I'm no good. Everyone is better than I am" is the biggest ego trip of all. It's all got to do with self-preservation. There is no self to preserve. What are you holding on to? What are you protecting?

What is the self? What is it that's born? What is it that will die? It all has to do with right now. The past is right now. The future is right now. See what's right here, right now. That's where your life is. That's where your practice is. Buddha is right now. Pai-chang is right now. The old man and the fox are right now. Huang-po is right now.

Wu-men comments, "Whatever it may be, whenever it may be, it is always causation itself. Nothing can ever be outside of causation. Odd and even are on one and the same die. They are, after all, two faces of the same coin. If I say that they are one and the same, people may attach to this oneness and be caught in a net of sameness. Not ignoring or not falling, whatever one may say it is, hundreds and thousands of regrets." And then he asks, "What kind of life is it, this life of hundreds and thousands of regrets?" Then he adds that the essence of the entirety of this koan is in the last line—hundreds and thousands of regrets. The key to happy, blessed lives is hidden right there.

Whatever you think Mu is, forget it. It has no meaning whatsoever. If you're looking for meaning, you're wasting your time. This practice has nothing to do with meaning. Meaning is the words and ideas that describe reality. We're not talking about that here. Practice is directly experiencing that reality. That's why we do zazen. If we were looking for meanings, we'd be reading about it, not sitting and making ourselves empty. Make yourself empty. The only way to see Mu is to be Mu, and the only way to do that is to let go of the self that separates you from Mu. The only way through a barrier is to be the barrier. The only way that can happen is to forget the self which separates us from the barrier.

That's what the old man at first didn't understand, and later came to understand. Pai-chang could just as easily have answered, "An enlightened person does not fall into causation." But that's what the old man said, and he became a fox. Wouldn't Pai-chang become a fox? Right and wrong is what makes foxes. Good and evil is what makes foxes. Cause and effect is what makes foxes. How is it when there is neither absolute nor relative, cause nor effect, good nor bad, up nor down, fox nor person, teacher nor student, heaven nor hell?

The biggest barrier that most people face is the absolute, unequivocal conviction that they can't do it, that they'll never do it. And they're right. They can't, and they never will—not until they're convinced that they will. And, then again, they're right. You can only go as far as you allow yourself to go. Don't hold back. This life is too precious to waste. It's boundless. Whether we realize it or not, it's boundless, and when we do realize it, we free ourselves, each and every one of us, from that fox body. And not only do you free yourself from that fox body—you simultaneously free all sentient beings.

EIGHTEEN

TEACHINGS OF THE INSENTIENT

Transmission of the Light, Case 39

PROLOGUE

> *Followers of the Way, we should clearly understand that it cannot be given nor can it be received. Yet everywhere we go it is encountered, endlessly teaching and preaching. It is at once me and I am not it. To see in this way is to realize being just as it is.*

THE MAIN CASE

> *Tung-shan called on Master Yün-yen and asked, "Who can hear the teaching of insentient beings?" Yün-yen said, "It can be heard by the insentient." Tung-shan asked, "Do you hear it?" Yün-yen said, "If I heard it, you wouldn't hear my teaching." Tung-shan said, "If so, then I don't hear your teaching." Yün-yen said, "If you don't even hear my teaching, how could you hear the*

teaching of the insentient?" Tung-shan was greatly
enlightened at this. He spoke a verse to Yün-yen:

Wondrous, marvelous.
The teaching of the insentient is inconceivable.
If you listen with the ears, you won't understand.
When you hear the sound with your eyes, then you'll
know.

THE CAPPING VERSE

Extremely subtle,
Mystic consciousness is not mental attachment.
All the time it causes "that" to teach in great
profusion.

We are in a unique period of human history. For the
first time the major threats to our existence are not the
natural disasters that were the main fears for our predecessors a thousand years ago, but human-created dangers.
This places us at a critical time in evolution, a time that
could decide the fate of both the human race and the
planet we all share. The most compelling paradox we are
encountering is that, on the one hand, we possess a degree
of knowledge and technological capability hardly dreamed
of only decades ago. We understand complex data about
the furthest reaches of space and the most subtle workings
of minute fragments of atoms. On the other hand, millions of us starve. Our environment is polluted. The earth's
natural resources are being plundered at an alarming rate,
and the specter of nuclear war raises the possibility of the
extinction of our species and all life. In spite of our understanding so much about the universe and its functioning,

we've barely begun to scratch the surface of understanding who we are, what our life is, and what our relationship is with the ten thousand things that comprise phenomenal existence.

Our way of perceiving ourselves and the universe has remained dualistic and virtually static throughout the development of human history. It is a perspective that assumes separation of self and other. As a result of that assumption of duality, we've created forms of philosophy, art, science, medicine, ecology, theology, psychology, politics, sociology, ethics, and morality that are basically permutations and combinations derived from that initial premise of separation. The emerging consequences create the kind of world we now live in. The issues of nuclear war; pollution of natural resources; the AIDS epidemic; the national drug problems; poverty; starvation; immorality in religion, politics, and business—all share the common bottom line of how we understand the self. How we understand the self is how we understand the universe, and how we understand the universe determines how we relate to it, what we do about it, and how we combust our lives within it.

Very recently in the West, we've become aware of the existence of an entirely different way of understanding reality. Its origins go back to a piece of writing once known only to Buddhists. In *The Flower Garland Sutra*, composed in seventh-century China, a universe is described in which everything interpenetrates with everything else in identity and interdependence, in which everything needs everything else and there's not a single speck of dust that does not affect the whole. In the sutra's most resounding metaphor, the "Diamond Net of Indra," all existence is seen as a vast net of gems that extends throughout the universe, not only in the three dimensions of space but in the fourth dimension of time as well. Each point of this huge net contains a multi-faceted diamond which reflects every other diamond, and as such, essentially "contains" every other diamond in the net. The diamonds represent the entire universe of the past, present, and future. In a sense, what the metaphor depicts is how each and every thing in the universe contains every other thing throughout all time.

The Diamond Net of Indra is not just a philosophical postulation; it's a description of realized reality. It's the direct experience of thousands of Buddhist men and women for more than two thousand years. Predictably, no one took this teaching very seriously until the twentieth century, when the discovery of one of the unique uses of laser light demonstrated the relevance of this ancient image. Using laser light you can make a photographic image on a photographic plate; when laser light is transmitted through the plate, a three-dimensional image is projected. This in itself is pretty remarkable—a holographic image you can walk into, that allows you to actually sit among the objects in the picture. Even more remarkable (and what is radically changing our basic way of seeing things) is the fact that you can cut that photographic plate in half and project laser light through only half of it and still project the whole image. You can cut the half in half and project through it and still project the whole image, cut the quarter in half, cut the eighth in half and so on, down to the smallest piece of that photographic plate; when you project light through it, you project the whole image. Nothing is missing. This can indicate only one thing: each part of the plate contains all the information of the whole, just like the diamonds in the Diamond Net.

As a result of that discovery, biologists have begun to examine biology in terms of the holographic model. New brain theory also uses a holographic model, and physicists have begun to look at the universe through the "eyes" of a holographic paradigm. I think by the time we reach the twenty-first century we will definitely have experimental verification of the experience transmitted as the Diamond Net for 2,500 years among Buddhists.

Realizing the holographic universe is what I like to call "Twenty-first Century Mind," because it's only by coming to understand the nature of the universe as a whole that there is any possibility for doing something about the problems we face. Twenty-first century mind is the mind of ancient Buddhas; it's the Buddha mind, the mind of all sentient beings. We already have it, but we've buried it under a lifetime of conditioning—conditioning by our parents, teachers, culture, nation, and education. When we realize the holographic universe, there's no way to avoid responsibility for it, because it becomes unavoidably clear that what we do and what happens to us are the same thing. When you realize that deeply, it's no longer possible to postpone, blame, or be a victim. We create our universe—that's what is realized. That is the empowerment that comes from realization. When we listen to the problems of the world, it's easy to be overwhelmed by a feeling of despair. What can we do? The situation seems hopeless. Out of that despair and hopelessness can come a true empowerment, but that will only become real for us when we understand who we really are—beyond the bag of skin, beyond the words and ideas that describe ourselves. What is the truth, the reality of our existence? What is "beingness" itself?

At a very young age, Master Tung-shan was asking such probing questions. Upon hearing the line in the *Heart Sutra*, "No eye, ear, nose, tongue, body, mind," he touched his face and said, "I have eyes, ears, and nose.

Why does the scripture say they don't exist?" We've been chanting *Heart Sutra* here at the Monastery for years, and thousands of different people have stood in the zendo and intoned "No eye, ear, nose, tongue, body, mind. No color, sound, smell, taste, touch, phenomena. No world of sight, no world of consciousness." Yet I can count on one hand the number of students who asked the question this ten-year-old child asked his teacher. "Why does it say that? I have them." Tung-shan's teacher couldn't answer and directed him to a Zen master under whom he became ordained as a monastic when he was twenty-one years old.

Once, near the beginning of his study, Tung-shan was at the monastery of the great Master Nan-ch'üan on the anniversary of the death of Ma-tsu, who had been Nan-ch'üan's teacher. As they were preparing a memorial service, Nan-ch'üan asked the group of students, "We're having a memorial service for Ma-tsu tomorrow. Do you think he'll come?" At first nobody answered. Then the young monastic Tung-shan came forward and said, "He'll come when he has a companion." Nan-ch'üan said, "Although this is a young man, he is suitable for cutting and polishing." Tung-shan said, "Don't demean the good," and walked away.

Next, he called on Master Kuei-shan, and asked, "Recently I heard that the National Teacher had a saying about the teaching of insentient beings. I don't understand the subtle meaning." Kuei-shan said, "Do you remember it?" Tung-shan said, "Yes." Kuei-shan said, "Say it." Tung-shan said, "A monastic asked, 'What is the mind of the ancient Buddhas?' The teacher said, 'Fences, walls, tiles, pebbles.' The monastic said, 'Aren't those inanimate things?' The teacher said, 'Yes.' The monastic said, 'Can they teach?' The teacher said, 'They're always teaching clearly and unceasingly.' The monastic said, 'Why can't I hear them?' The teacher said, 'You yourself don't hear but you shouldn't hinder that which does hear.' The monastic said, 'Who can hear it?' The teacher said, 'The sages can.' The monastic said, 'Do you hear it?' The teacher said, 'No.' The monastic said, 'If you don't hear it, how do you know insentient things can teach?' The teacher said, 'It's luck that I don't hear it, for if I did I'd be equal to the sages and you wouldn't hear my teaching.' The monastic said, 'Then living beings have no part in it?' The teacher said, 'I teach for the sake of living beings, not for the saints and sages.' The monastic said, 'After sentient beings hear it, then what?' The teacher said, 'Then they're not sentient beings.' The monastic said, 'What scripture is the teaching of the inanimate based on?' The teacher said, 'Obviously words that do not accord with the classics are not the talk of a scholar. Haven't you read the *Flower Garland Scripture*? It says that lands teach, beings teach, all things and all times teach.'"

After Tung-shan had recited this story, Kuei-shan said, "I also have it here, but I hardly ever meet anyone suitable for it." Tung-shan said, "I don't understand. Please teach me." Kuei-shan held up the whisk and asked, "Understand?" Tung-shan said, "I don't." Kuei-shan said, "Words will never explain it to you." Tung-shan asked, "Is there anyone who can help me?" Kuei-shan directed him to Master Yün-yen.

Tung-shan left Kuei-shan and went to Master Yün-yen. Bringing up the preceding question, he asked: "Who can hear the teaching of the insentient?" Yün-yen responded, "The insentients can hear it." Tung-shan said, "Why don't I hear it?" Yün-yen held up the fly whisk and said, "Do you hear?" Tung-shan said, "No." Yün-yen said, "If you don't even hear my teaching, how could you hear the teaching of the insentient?" Tung-shan said, "What scripture contains the teaching of the insentient?" Yün-yen said, "Haven't you read in the *Amitabha Sutra* where it says that rivers, birds, trees, and groves all invoke the Buddha and the teachings?" At this, Tung-shan had an awakening.

What is it that Tung-shan realized? Two different teachers, two different lineages; same point, same teaching. What is the holding up of the whisk? The whisk referred to is a fly whisk, a small stick with horsehair on the end of it used to brush flies away without killing them. It became a symbol of the teaching, one of the items transmitted generation to generation. But it didn't matter that the whisk was something involved in the transmission; it was the holding up that revealed the teaching of the insentient. Raising the whisk, blinking the eyes, holding up the flower, calling and answering—all are concerned with intimacy. Intimacy is "Seeing form with the whole body and mind, hearing sound with the whole body and mind." When you do that, you understand things intimately. That's what Tung-shan was experiencing, the teaching that can be derived from the ten thousand things themselves. The very problems and barriers we face are the doorway to realization of the nature of the universe and the nature of the self.

How many ways can we say "intimacy"? We say that "no separation, no attachment" is intimacy. "No gain and no loss" is intimacy. "Cause and effect are one" is intimacy. "Responsibility" is intimacy. "Forget the self" is intimacy. "Really be yourself" is intimacy. All these are simply different ways of saying the same thing: be intimate. Yet so long as we lock ourselves into this bag of skin, we lock out the rest of the universe and there is no intimacy.

After expressing his understanding, Tung-shan said to Yün-yen, "I still have residual habits which have not yet been exhausted." Yün-yen said, "What have you done?" Tung-shan said, "I don't even practice the holy truths." In other words, no effort, no action, the action of non-action. Yün-yen said, "Are you happy?" Tung-shan said, "Yes. It's as though I've found a jewel in a trash heap." Then Tung-shan asked, "What should I do when I want to see my true being?" Yün-yen said, "Ask the messenger within." Tung-shan said, "I'm asking now." Yün-yen said, "What does he tell you?" The old man was trying to tell him: really trust yourself, have faith in yourself. The ten thousand things reduce to the self. The whole thing happens right here, in this very moment. As Tung-shan took leave of Yün-yen, he asked, "After your death, if someone asks me if I can describe your picture, how should I answer?" "Your picture" means "your teaching." In those days evidence of having received the transmission was having a picture of your teacher. The picture had a double meaning: it also meant the teacher's reality, his teaching. Yün-yen remained silent for a while and then said, "It's just this." Tung-shan sank into thought. Yün-yen said, "You should be most thoroughgoing in your understanding of this matter."

Tung-shan still had some doubts but later, upon seeing his reflection in the water while crossing a river, he was greatly enlightened to the meaning of what had transpired before. He said in verse:

> Don't seek it from others or you'll estrange from
> yourself.
> I now go out alone,
> Everywhere I encounter it.
> It now is me, I now am not it.
> One must understand it in this way to merge with
> being as it is.

Tung-shan's saying, "It now is me, I now am not it," has the same point as, "You and I are the same thing, yet I am not you and you are not me." Both sides of the statement exist simultaneously; it's not half of one side and half of the other, fifty-fifty. It's not a mixture. There is a unity beyond both that is neither absolute nor relative, neither up nor down, neither existing nor not existing. There is a reality that transcends all dualities, and the truth of this practice is to realize that. One of the difficulties with Zen practice is that people often put all of the attention on realizing the absolute basis of reality, and never complete the process. On the one hand we have the absolute basis in which there is "no eye, ear, nose, tongue, body, and mind." That is to be experienced. On the other hand we have the whole phenomenal universe. The truth is to be found in neither extreme. Sentient on one hand, insentient on the other. Secular on one hand, sacred on the other. Holy on one hand, profane on the other. Good, bad; man, woman; heaven, earth; up, down: all the dualities miss it. What is the truth that transcends them?

One of Tung-shan's great contributions is his formulation of the teaching called "The Five Ranks," depicting the integration of dualities. The first rank is "the relative within the absolute." This is emptiness—no eye, ear, nose, tongue, body, or mind. But there is no knowing it until we move to the next rank. The second rank is the realization of that emptiness, and is referred to as "the absolute within the relative." This is where the enlightenment experience, or *kensho* happens. But still there is separation: there is still absolute and relative; they are still dualistic. The third rank is "coming from within the absolute." When you realize the whole universe as nothing but yourself, you have to take care of it. You have to be very selfish because that self *is* the ten thousand things, existing in the past, present, and future. Every action you take affects the totality of that universe. But understanding that doesn't impart much strength, because in understanding there is still separation between the knower and the thing the knower knows. Believing also doesn't impart much strength—a belief system is usually dependent upon something else, and thus is vulnerable. But when you realize it you transform your life, and that transformation is empowering. No longer in the abstract, the whole matter becomes your very life itself and, inevitably, compassion begins to happen. You put your life on the line. There is just no way to avoid it when you realize that actually your life is already on the line.

Tung-shan's fourth rank is "arriving at mutual integration," the coming from both absolute and relative. At this stage they are still two things; like a mixture of salt and pepper. There's integration, but in integration there are still two things. This is expressed with the image of the bodhisattva, who, face covered with dirt, descends the mountain and re-enters the marketplace. In the fifth rank, "unity attained," there is no longer a mixture. It is one thing—neither absolute nor relative, up nor down, profane nor holy, good nor bad, male nor female. What is it?

This is the same as when Master Dogen writes about the teachings of mountains and rivers in the *Mountain and River Sutra:* "*He who doubts that mountains walk does not yet understand his own walking. It's not that he doesn't walk, but that he doesn't yet understand, has not made clear his walking. They who would understand their own walking must also understand the walking of the blue mountains. The blue mountains are neither sentient nor insentient. The self is neither sentient nor insentient.*"

Master Keizan, commenting on this koan, said, "*So good people, observing carefully, you have become fully aware*

*of this mystic consciousness. This is called insentient or inani-
mate. It is called inanimate because there is no running
after sound and form, no bondage of emotion or discrimination. The National Teacher really explained this principle in
detail, so when you hear talk of the insentient, don't make
the mistake of understanding it as fences or walls. As long as
your feelings and thoughts are not deluded and attached to
your perception, and your perception is not scattered here
and there at random, then that mystic consciousness will be
bright and unclouded, clearly aware. If you try to grasp this,
you cannot get it; it has no form, so it is not existent. If you
try to get rid of it, you cannot separate from it because it is
forever with you; it's not non-existent. It is not cognition, it
is not thought, it is not tied to any of the psycho-physical elements. Then what is it?"*

When Keizan says there is "no bondage of emotion or
discrimination" he does not mean lack of feeling or caring.
He means no *bondage*, no attachment. What is no
bondage to emotion? When you cry, just cry. When you
feel, just feel with the whole body and mind. Don't separate yourself; separation causes bondage, separation
inhibits and restricts our freedom.

This mystic teaching is always manifest and teaching
clearly. It is what causes us to raise the eyebrows and blink
the eyes. It is involved in our walking, standing, sitting,
reclining, washing, hurrying, dying, being born, eating
when hungry, and sleeping when tired. All this is teaching,
everything down to the chirping of insects. Nothing is
hidden. Therefore, everything is always teaching us clearly
and unceasingly.

We should see and we should hear these teachings.
We should see and hear the voice of these mountains and
rivers, and of the endangered and extinct species. We
should see and hear the voice of the atom, the homeless,

the children; the voice of the teachings of countless generations past, present, and future. If you try to see with the eye and hear with the ear, you'll never get it. Only if you see with the ear and hear with the eye will you truly be able to see "it" clearly. How do you see with the ear and hear with the eye? Zazen. Zazen is the dragon entering the water, the lion entering the mountain. Zazen is the Bodhi seat of the Buddha, the true transmission of the mind of the twenty-first century, the voice of the ten thousand things.

NINETEEN

BORN AS THE EARTH

*Koans of the
Way of Reality,
Case 88*

PROLOGUE

*Being born as the earth is not the same as being
born, or birth, or born into the world. It is not a matter
of simply occupying space on this great planet. Being
born as the earth is to realize the world, to realize the
mountains, the rivers, and the great earth as the body
and mind of the Tathagata, as one's own body and
mind. Dew on the pine trees, the thousand grasses, are
the real form of truth, the limitless life of endless spring.
The question is, where do you find yourself?*

THE MAIN CASE

*A visiting student began to say,[1] "The truths of the
earth continually wait.[2] They are not so concealed*

265

either.³ They are calm, subtle, untransmissable by print.³⁴
The master yelled, "Stop, stop!⁵ Is that Whitman's
poem?"⁶ The student said, "Yes."⁷ The master said,
"Those are the words that described this reality. What is
the reality itself?⁸ Show me."⁹ The student was unable to
respond.¹⁰

THE CAPPING VERSE

> *Listen!*
> *Mountain streams and bird songs*
> *All recite the sutras.*
> *Look!*
> *Mountain form, trees and forest,*
> *The body of suchness.*
> *Don't you see?*
> *It's not a matter of words—*
> *It contains the whole universe.*

Over the last few years we have been conducting at
the Monastery a series of workshops called *Born as the
Earth*. We are attempting to show the teachings of the
Buddha-Dharma in their relationship to the natural environment. The teachings, in this respect, are far ahead of
the world's understanding. In general, our ecology is
based on separation. The teachings, on the other hand, are
about intimacy. The way we view ourselves and the way
we view the ten thousand things is the fundamental matter
that makes all the difference in how we live our lives and
how we relate to all of the so called "externals."

In the context of the different retreats, we ask the

question, "Where does the earth end and where do I begin?" We study the practice of survival: survival in and of the mountains, the forest, the rivers, the cities; survival of the individual and of the human species, of the community and the family; and, indeed, survival of this great earth itself. It's a very important teaching, the teaching of the insentient. Given technological developments and the fragile state of affairs on earth, a lot of wisdom and compassion are needed.

The prologue points out that being born as the earth is not the same as being born. It is not about birth. It is not about coming into the world. It is not a matter of occupying time or space. It is beyond time and space. Being born as the earth is to realize the world, period. To realize the mountains, the rivers, and the great earth as the body and mind of the Tathagata—Tathagata is at once the name of the Buddha and the word that's used to describe suchness, this very moment, this right here and now — to realize it as one's own body and mind.

Dew on the pine, the grasses, and trees are the real form of truth. They are the limitless life of the endless spring. *Endless spring* is used in Buddhist texts to refer to enlightenment or realization. The question is, Where do you find yourself?

The incident reconstructed in the main case is told pretty much as it took place. A student started reciting one of Whitman's poems, and I knew a question was coming, so I interrupted him and asked if the verse was Whitman's. He said, "Yes, it is." And so the dialogue ensued.

As far as I know, Whitman was not a Buddhist. He probably never even read anything about Buddhism. But there is no question in my mind that he was realized. Once in a while any poet will walk on water, but Whitman was on water all the time. Even his inconsistencies are consistent. The poem that the student was quoting is:

> *The earth does not withhold, it is generous enough.*
> *The truths of the earth continually wait, they are not so*
>   *conceal'd either,*
> *They are calm, subtle, untransmissable by print,*
> *They are imbued through all things, conveying*
>   *themselves willingly....*
> *The earth does not argue,*
> *Is not pathetic, has no arrangements,*
> *Does not scream, haste, persuade, threaten, promise,*
> *Makes no discriminations, has no conceivable failures,*
> *Closes nothing, refuses nothing, shuts none out.*
> *Of all the powers, objects, states, it notifies, shuts none*
>   *out.*

What a wonderful way of being—and it is the potential of all sentient beings, every one of us, not just of the earth itself.

Whitman begins this poem, called "The Song of the Rolling Earth," by saying:

> *A song of the rolling earth, and of words according,*
> *Were you thinking that those were the words, those*
>   *upright lines those curves, angles, dots?*
> *No, those are not the words, the substantial words are*
>   *in the ground and sea,*
> *They are in the air, they are in you.*
> *Were you thinking that those were the words, those*
>   *delicious sounds out of your friends' mouths?*
> *No, the real words are more delicious than they.*
>
> *Human bodies are words, myriads of words,*

(In the best poems re-appears the body, man's or
   woman's, well-shaped, natural, gay,
Every part able, active, receptive, without shame or
   the need of shame.)

Air, soil, water, fire—those are words,
I myself am a word with them—my qualities inter-
   penetrate with theirs. . . .

It seems he understood that the words and ideas that describe reality are not the same as the reality itself, and that each one of us needs to realize it for ourselves. No one can do it for us. He says:

Whoever you are! motion and reflection are especially
   for you,
The divine ship sails the divine sea, for you.
Whoever you are! you are he or she for whom the earth
   is solid and liquid,
You are he or she for whom the sun and moon hang in
   the sky,
For none more than you are the present and the past,
For none more than you is immortality.

Each man to himself and each woman to herself, is the
   word of the past and the present, and the true word
   of immortality;
No one can acquire it for another—not one.
No one can grow for another—not one.

These could have been the words of the Buddha, Dogen, Han-shan, Tung-shan. We've heard them so many times—not nearly so eloquently, but of course this was written in our language; the others were translated, sometimes two or three times. But isn't it remarkable? I don't know if Whitman knew anything about formal zazen. I can find nothing in his biographies or his writings that indicates any *kensho* experience, but I am certain he has seen it. You can't fake something like this. There are poets who, because of a particular experience at one moment in time, can write something extraordinary. But then you see in other parts of their work that the clarity is not consistently there. It was just a momentary insight. But Whitman's vision is continual. You can go to almost any page of *Leaves of Grass*, let your eyes fall on any line, and there it is, again and again.

What a shame to take this beautiful insight and tie it up, frame it, with words and ideas. But that's what this koan is about. I've added notes to bring out the points being made, line by line.

A visiting student began to say.... and the note says, "There are many people with doubts. After all, if you don't ask, how will you understand?"

The next line: "*The truths of the earth continually wait.*" "True enough, but what are they? Where are they? Waiting for what?" "*They are not so concealed either.*" The note says, "Neither concealed nor revealed. Reaching everywhere." It is because they reach everywhere that there is no place to hide them and no place to reveal them. To reveal requires subject and object. To conceal requires subject and object. How is it when subject and object merge?

"*They are calm, subtle, untransmissable by print.*" Note says, "Aaaagh! When will it end? Gasping for breath, he goes on and on and on." *The master yelled, "Stop, stop!"* The note says, "Have mercy!" "*Is that Whitman's poem?*" "Careful here, he's after your nostrils." Getting hold of somebody's nostrils is a term used frequently in Zen literature. You can control a very massive animal, even a bull, by putting a nose ring in its nostril. You put a rope through that ring, tie the rope to a little fence post, and there is no way the bull can come loose because it hurts so much to struggle. He doesn't have the strength in his nose. He could knock the fence down, but he hasn't figured that out. Having your nostrils in someone else's hands is being controlled by them. That is what is going on here. The teacher is after the student's nostrils: "*Is that Whitman's poem?*"

The student said, "Yes." Note says: "Wrong! He sees the sword and proceeds to impale himself on it." Very cooperative. He is impaling himself on the sword of Manjushri, the sword that kills. He doesn't even wait for the teacher to use it. He just cheerfully jumps on it.

The master said, "Those are the words that described this reality. What is the reality itself?" Note says: "In the ten directions there are no barriers. On the four sides, no gates. North, east, south, west, above and below, no gaps. How do you see it?" No separation. The student was separating himself by quoting these words, by being caught up in the words. Indeed, by quoting Whitman's poem, he immediately revealed that he was ten thousand miles separated from the truth.

The next line simply says, "*Show me.*" "He steals his tongue and blocks off his throat. Where will you go to settle your body and establish your life? Take away the words, what remains?" *The student was unable to respond.* Note says: "Mouth agape, tongue hanging out, thirty blows of the stick is not enough to bring this one to life." Our tendency is to think that when we can name something, fit it into our system, describe it, then we understand it. That is largely how our academic education functions. That is how we make it through college and, quite often, it is how we attempt to get through life. We regurgitate what we've swallowed. That rote playback is too frequently regarded as an actual test of understanding. How do you go beyond that? How do we go beyond the words and ideas that describe reality and directly experience the reality itself? We spend a lifetime honing and perfecting the aspect of consciousness that is linear and sequential. Overpowered by words, ideas, positions, and understanding, the intuitive aspect of human consciousness is all but forgotten. But when the mind settles down and we stop talking to ourselves, this aspect of consciousness begins to open up. And nature is a wonderful place for that to happen. Nature is not logical. It's not predictable. It's not really understandable. We can categorize and analyze it, but that is not what nature is really about. A description of nature is no more the thing itself than descriptions of ourselves are what the self is really about.

The whole point of the *Born as the Earth* series is to make us open and receptive to the insentient, to nature herself as the teacher. We are going to keep doing it until somebody gets it—not here in the zendo, but out there—on a river, in the mountains, in the forest, on the side of a cliff, in the whitewater. After spending a week in the wild, I am ashamed to open my stinking mouth and try to talk about this incredible Dharma that we're so completely surrounded and interpenetrated by.

Being born as the earth is about intimacy. It is about wholeness and completeness. We tend to fragment ourselves. We tend to be our own worst enemies, all of us. And it's got to do with that internalized program, the program of the bio-computer, our conditioning. The way we respond to circumstances, the way we see ourselves, is all learned behavior. It took training to put it there. That's why the process of zazen is so necessary. Layer by layer we need to deal with that conditioning. Layer by layer, we peel it back, examining it, understanding it clearly, throwing it away, and going deeper. Layer by layer until finally we reach the ground of being, and that too needs to be seen, and thrown away. We just keep going. Zen practice is an endless process. And what it is about is really seeing the wholeness. First we see it within ourselves, then we see it in accord with the ten thousand things. Again, Whitman:

> *I swear the earth shall surely be complete to him or her*
> *who shall be complete,*
> *The earth remains jagged and broken only to him or*
> *her who remains jagged and broken*
>
> *I swear, there is no greatness of power that does not*
> *emulate those of the earth,*
> *There can be no theory of any account unless it corrobo-*
> *rate the theory of the earth,*
> *No politics, song, religion, behavior, or what not, is of*
> *account unless it compare with the amplitude of the*
> *earth,*
> *Unless it face the exactness, vitality, impartiality,*
> *rectitude of the earth.*
>
> *I swear I begin to see love with sweeter spasms than that*
> *which responds love,*
> *It is that which contains itself, which never invites and*
> *never refuses.*
>
> *I swear, I begin to see little or nothing in audible*
> *words,*
> *All merges toward the presentation of the unspoken*
> *meanings of the earth,*

273

*Toward him who sings the songs of the body and of the
truths of the earth,
Toward him who makes the dictionaries of words that
print cannot touch.*

With the gift of life comes the possibility of pain and
anguish. Also with it comes the possibility of great peace
and harmony. How it turns out is up to you. It is clear
that we haven't really bought into the description of reality passed onto us by our program. Intuitively, we sense
that there must be something else. There must be more to
it than what we've been told. More to it than the philoso-
phers and the priests and the politicians tell us. Well, we're
right. There is. But there isn't a soul on the face of this
great earth who can give it to us or do it for us. It is also
true that once you have made up your mind to do it, and
really put yourself to it, you will do it. If your effort is sincere, if you are honest with yourself, you will do it. No
beings *ever* come short of their own completeness. No
beings ever fail to cover the ground upon which they
stand.

But it is not easy. The self is programmed not to be
forgotten. You sit there trying to forget the self—and just
the trying recreates, from moment to moment, the self.
All kinds of barriers come up. Every time you get to that
edge of "falling away of body and mind," something pulls
you back. That is the program. "I'm here, I'm here, I'm
here—you're there." In a sense, that strong ego, that
strong sense of self and separateness that has been part of
the process of evolution, is how we have survived as a
species. We are not as fast as the other animals, or as agile.
We can't fly. We're not as strong as they are. All we have is
our intellect, our wit. And Big Ego. That intellect has now
developed to the point where it threatens to extinguish

274

the species itself. We've created a world that puts us on the threshold of life and death as a species. When that kind of power is in the hands of leaders convinced that who they are is the bag of skin and everything else is the rest of the universe, we have a dangerous situation. On the other hand, if you realize the earth, and are intimate with the ten thousand things, then there is no need for an Environmental Protection Agency, or for any protective legislation whatsoever. If you realize the earth, then there is no need for the Precepts. There is no way, having once realized the earth, that we could live our lives in the old way.

But everybody is not going to realize it, at least not for many lifetimes. And those of us who are lucky enough to find our way into this incredible Dharma have a responsibility to use its wisdom and sense of intimacy in a way that nourishes the earth itself and all its inhabitants. In a sense it's a very selfish thing, in that what you do to the earth, you do to yourself. What you do to the smallest thing on this great earth, you do to all of it. Cause and effect are one reality. Whitman says:

When I undertake to tell the best I find I cannot,
My tongue is ineffectual on its pivots,
My breath will not be obedient to its organs,
I become a dumb man.

Before the student even answered the teacher's question, it was clear that it was Whitman's poem—why did the teacher bother to ask? When the student answered yes, it was clear that he was lost in the entanglements of words and ideas, and had not yet experienced the intimacy that

Whitman points to.

The teacher then demanded that the student show the reality that the words point to. Say a word for the student—what is the reality that the poet points to? The student was unable to respond. Is Whitman's "dumb man" and the student's mute dumbness the same or different? How do you respond?

The truths of the earth continually wait. They are not so concealed either. If they are not concealed, where are they? What are they? What does it mean to be *imbued through all things, conveying themselves willingly?* This is a single reality that is being described. What is it?

Of all the powers, objects, states, it notifies, shuts none out. Clearly there is no place to stand, nothing to shut out, nothing to bring in. The question is, Where do you find yourself?

> *The best of the earth cannot be told anyhow, all or any*
>   *is best*
> *It is not what you anticipated, it is cheaper, easier,*
>   *nearer,*
> *Things are not dismissed from the places they held*
>   *before,*
> *The earth is just as positive and direct as it was before,*
> *Facts, religions, improvements, politics, trades, are as*
>   *real as before,*
> *But the soul is also real, it too is positive and direct,*
> *No reasoning, no proof has established it,*
> *Undeniable growth has established it.*

THE CAPPING VERSE

> *Listen!*
> *Mountain streams and bird songs*
> *All recite the sutras.*

Look!
Mountain form, trees and forests,
The body of suchness.
Don't you see?
It's not a matter of words —
It contains the whole universe.

I have said it many times, but I need to say it again: it is no small thing to be born human. With it comes a tremendous responsibility. That responsibility is due to our intelligence, our awareness. We have the power, each of us, not only to change our own lives and bring them into harmony with the ten thousand things, but also to nourish others, to heal this planet. The harmony, nourishment, and healing are within the capabilities of the same science and technology that have created the destruction. We can do it. All it takes is the will to do it. You can realize yourself; all it takes is the determination to do it. In both cases, we're fully equipped. We have everything needed to realize ourselves and transform our lives, and to realize the earth and transform this planet. As always, it is up to you. What will you do with the opportunity? When will you do it? Please, don't waste this precious life.

TWENTY

SACRED WILDNESS

Koans of the
Way of Reality,
Case 108

PROLOGUE

*The river never speaks, yet it knows how to find its
way to the Great Ocean. The mountains have no words,
yet the ten thousand things are born here. Where the
river finds its way, you can perceive the essence. Where
the mountain gives birth to the ten thousand things, you
can realize the action. When the mind moves, images
appear. Even if the mind does not move, this is not yet
true freedom. You must first take off the blinders and set
down the pack if you are to enter the sacred space. When
you let go, even river rocks and brambles are radiant.
When you hold on, even the mani jewel loses its brilliance. When you neither let go nor hold on, you are free
to ride the clouds and follow the wind.*

THE MAIN CASE

Buddha has said, "All things are ultimately liberated.[1]
They have no abode."[2] Master Dogen says,[3] "We should realize
that although they are liberated, without any bonds,[4] all
things are abiding in their own Dharma state."[5]

THE CAPPING VERSE

> *In the multitude of forms and the myriad appearances*
> *There is not a single thing.*
> *Mountains and rivers are not seen in a mirror.*
> *These mountains are endless—I seem to have lost my*
> *   way.*
> *Looking up, I can see there's still some light remaining.*
> *Actually, this is just west of my campsite.*

Since our arrival on Tremper Mountain, we have
been creating a mandala, a mandala of mountains and
rivers. The phrase "mountains and rivers" has a multiplicity of meanings in Buddhism—it can mean mountains and
rivers just as they are, and it also can be a metaphor for
absolute and relative. Sometimes "in the mountains" indicates absolute reality and "in the world" indicates its relative aspect, differentiated existence. The phrase can also
refer simply to the ups and downs of life. One key characteristic of any mandala is that to enter it one proceeds
from its edges towards the center. The edges are both the
gateways and the obstructions we wrestle with in our lives.
Sometimes it's our work, sometimes it's where we live,
sometimes it's our relationship. Essentially, all manifestations of samsara are gates, entrances to the heart of the

mandala. As you work toward its center, what you find there is stillness, no-mind, Buddha-mind, emptiness, your-self. And you simultaneously find that the edge of the mandala and the center of the mandala are the same thing. They are not separate.

The prologue to this koan says, *The river never speaks, yet it knows how to find its way to the Great Ocean. The mountains have no words, yet the ten thousand things are born here. Where the river finds its way, you can perceive the essence. Where the mountain gives birth to the ten thousand things, you can realize the action.* You can also realize the essence in the place of birth, and you can also realize the action in the river finding its way to the Great Ocean. Our tendency is to see things from one side or the other, and to miss the profound teaching that is neither one side nor the other, that is the place of perfect merging of the two.

We know that *When the mind moves, images appear.* We talk to ourselves. We create ideas and concepts. And yet, even if the mind does not move, that's just another nesting place. It's not yet freedom. How do you go beyond those two extremes? *You must first take off the blinders and set down the pack*—this refers to the stuff we carry, the ideas we hold on to. It's only when you let go of the baggage that you can enter "the sacred space." And where is the sacred space? Right where you stand. But it can't be seen until the blinders are removed and the pack is set down. It is then that *even river rocks and brambles are radiant. When you hold on, even the mani jewel loses its brilliance.* The mani jewel is the teaching. The brilliance of the teaching can't be heard when you're holding on to anything—there's no room for it. You can't hear it, you can't feel it, you can't taste it.

Buddha has said, "All things are ultimately liberated. They have no abode." To say they have "no abode" means they have no resting place, no permanence. One of the characteristics of all things is that they are in a constant state of becoming. Nothing is fixed. Everything is empty of fixed characteristics. And "empty of fixed characteristics" in itself is freedom or liberation.

To say there is no fixed place is just another way of saying that all things are empty. How can that be? What does it mean to be "empty"? Usually when we use that word in our Western culture, it implies vacancy, the void. When the word is used in Buddhism it has a different connotation—it means empty of independent being. That is, to be *inter*dependent is precisely the same as to be "empty." To recognize one's body and mind as the body and mind of the whole universe, of the mountains and rivers themselves, is to realize the emptiness of all things. It is because things are empty that they can abide in their own Dharma state.

"Freedom" and "liberation" are interesting words. Freedom is defined in the dictionary as being "free from bondage or restraint." Liberation is understood in Buddhism as implying "no hindrances, a state of perfection and completion." Gary Snyder, in his book *The Practice of the Wild*, studies and plays with the word "wild," uncovering its many interesting dimensions and relationships. Drawing from the Oxford English Dictionary, he says that when the word "wild" is used in speaking of animals, it means "not tamed, undomesticated, or unruly"; of plants, "not cultivated"; of land, "uninhabited"; of food crops, "yielded without cultivation"; of societies, "uncivilized, resisting government"; of individuals, "unrestrained, loose"; of behavior, "destructive, cruel" or "artless, free, and spontaneous."

He suggests that if we look at "wildness" not from a negative point of view, what it's not, but rather from a positive point of view, we come up with a very different appreciation. In terms of plants, we have "self-propagating and self-maintaining"; of land, "a place where the original and potential vegetation and fauna are intact," or "pristine." In terms of food crops, the positive definition is "food supplies made available and sustainable by the natural excess and exuberance of wild plants in their growth." Of societies: "societies that grow from within and are maintained by a consensus and custom, rather than by explicit legislation." Of individuals: "following local customs, style, and etiquette." Of behavior: "fiercely resisting oppression, confinement, or exploitation. Unconditioned, expressive, physical, and open." When you begin to look at those definitions, you realize that the word "wild" and the word "free" have a great deal in common. In fact, you can even take it further and say that the words "wild," "free," and "nature" are very similar to what we call the "Tao," or "the Way," or the "Buddha-nature," or even "sacredness."

We have discovered over the past three years, during our explorations of the mountains and rivers, that the wilderness can be a tough teacher. A rabbit gets only one chance to run across an open field without first looking up. There is no second chance. That's the way the wilderness teaches. That's the way the insentients teach. Gary Snyder says, "For those who would seek directly by entering the primary temple [wilderness], the wilderness can be a ferocious teacher, rapidly stripping down the inexperienced or the careless. It's easy to make the mistakes that will bring one to an extremity. Practically speaking, a life that is vowed to simplicity, appropriate boldness, good humor, gratitude, unstinting work and play, and lots of walking brings us close to the actually existing world and its wholeness." The wilderness is at once a difficult teacher, and at the same time an open doorway to all in this great earth that we hold sacred. Snyder also says that people of the wild rarely seek out adventures. If they deliberately risk themselves, it is for a spiritual rather than economic reason, and definitely not for the purpose of just simply "getting a rush." The wilderness is filled with rushes; you don't have to create them.

We tend to think of the wild, the free, as being somehow far removed. We'll find it, we think, in the tundra, or deep in the forest, or high on the mountains. But in actual fact, we're surrounded and interpenetrated by wildness, regardless of where we live, whether in the city or the country. The mice in the pantry, the roaches in the wall, the deer on the turnpike—they each exist in the wilderness. The pigeons, the spiders, the bacteria on our skin, in our bodies—they are all free, wild, uncultivated, and unrestrained. The body itself is wild; certain aspects of us, our reflex actions, are manifestations of no mind, no effort. They just respond according to circumstances.

The mind is also free and wild. This free and wild mind includes two domains, though we tend to see only one side: the monkey mind that we sit with. The other side is very still, quiet, open, and receptive. It is not reflective, analyzing, or judging each thing. It simply sees with the whole body and mind, hears with the whole body and mind. Non-abiding mind is central to all of Zen practice, including the Zen arts, and to the practice of the wild. The minute you fix and reflect on something, you engage the bio–computer, and it takes you away from the moment. That's where we spend most of our time: preoccupied with the past, or preoccupied with the future, while the moment constantly in front of us is barely seen or heard or felt or tasted or touched.

"All things are ultimately liberated. They have no

abode." What kind of state is the state of no abode? How can the Buddha make the statement *have no abode* and not be contradicting Master Dogen when he says, "*We should realize that although they are liberated, without any bonds, all things are abiding in their own Dharma state.*" Isn't that referring to an "abode"? Abodes happen when you separate yourself from things. When you realize the whole phenomenal universe as this body and mind, how can there be an abode? It is because all things are ultimately liberated and have no abode that we can say they abide in their own Dharma state. In other words, each thing is just as it is.

I've added notes to each part of this koan: *Buddha has said, "All things are ultimately liberated."* The note says, "He opens up the trail for everyone. How can you miss it? Don't you see—it reaches everywhere?" The Way has no edges. Usually when we think of a path, we think of a clear-cut trail that's been etched out of the wilderness. But the Way that the Buddha opens encompasses the whole thing. It's not something etched out. There is no "this is on the trail and that is off the trail." The whole catastrophe is the trail, the mandala, the self. That's why the note says, "How can you miss it? Don't you see it reaches everywhere?" But tell me, if it reaches everywhere, how can we call it a Way or a path?

"They have no abode." The note says, "The abode of no abode. People will inevitably make a nest here." This is precisely what happens when we attach to non-attachment, when we cling to emptiness. We create two things: the thing being held on to and oneself. There's no intimacy there.

Master Dogen says.... The note comments, "Complications are sure to follow. What can possibly be said?" What can be further added to what the Buddha already said? "*We should realize that although they are liber-ated, without any bonds....*" The note says, "East mountain walks over water. The mountain flows, the river is still." Dogen is coming from this place of liberation when he says, "These mountains and rivers of the present are the actualization of the Way of ancient Buddhas.... Because the virtues of the mountains are high and broad, the power to ride the clouds is always penetrated from the mountains, and the ability to follow the wind is inevitably liberated from the mountains." Being free, without abode, the mountains can ride the clouds, follow the wind, walk, dance, and give birth to mountain children.

"*All things are abiding in their own Dharma state.*" The note says, "Mountains are mountains, rivers are rivers." Most people are familiar with the ancient saying, "In the beginning, mountains are mountains and rivers are rivers. Then after much study and reflection and going very deeply into oneself, one finds that mountains are many things, and rivers are many things, reaching every-where, encompassing the whole universe. And then, many years later, the mountains are mountains and rivers are rivers." We should understand that "mountains are moun-tains and rivers are rivers" as seen by the novice, and "mountains are mountains and rivers are rivers" as seen by the sage depict different ways of seeing. The novice does-n't see the sage's mountains and rivers, but the sage's view definitely includes the novice's mountains and rivers.

The *Mountains and Rivers Sutra* of Master Dogen is not a sutra about mountains and rivers, but the expression of the mountains and rivers themselves as the sutra, as the teaching, as the Buddha, as this very body and mind. "When people look at water, they see it only as flowing, without rest. This flow takes many forms and our way of seeing is just the one-sided human view. Water flows over the earth. It flows across the sky. It flows up, it flows down. It flows around bends, into deep abysses. It mounts up to form clouds, it descends to form pools."

The teachings of the insentient deal with intimacy, not with words. The teaching is not communicated by words, and yet it is intelligent. And how it communicates! Consider how impossible it is to walk through the forest without telegraphing your presence. Your movements are felt and relayed by all the birds and beasts. The crow tells it to the jay, and the jay expresses it to the kingfisher and the duck and the deer. Sitting in my camp, when neighboring campers walk back and forth, I am aware of their whereabouts, listening to the forest. As soon as they enter the woods on the far side, within seconds the message that they are on their way is passed through the little patch of woods. And all the animals understand it, even my very domesticated dog. Immediately he perks up and looks in the direction of the sounds. He waits for a visual sighting or a scent before starting his racket, barking and carrying on. Isn't that communication? Isn't that intelligence?

When you stop cultivation, even for a very short period of time, the wildness returns. That wildness is akin to the Buddha-nature. Civilization has a way of making wildness seem very negative. Yet, all things return to the wild: people, mountains, rivers, gardens, apples, the family cat. It doesn't take long. To be truly free, to be truly liberated and wild, is to be prepared to accept things as they are, abiding in their own Dharma state. Sometimes it's painful. And yet, it's also joyful and open. Always impermanent, never fixed. Unbounded, yet bountiful. Keep in mind that in a fixed universe, there can be no freedom. So, in a sense, we can say that mountains are the entire Dharma realm. In those words we include everything. Rivers are the entire Dharma realm. They permeate the ten directions. The self is the entire Dharma realm. When Master Dogen speaks of mountains and rivers, they're not the mountains and rivers of the poet or the naturalist. They're not the mountains and rivers of nirvana or samsara. They're the mountains and rivers of the true Dharma.

To realize the great river is to realize the Three Treasures: the Buddha, the Dharma, and the Sangha. It is to realize the Precepts. To realize these mountains and rivers is to realize Mu, to free oneself of birth and death. Not only to realize mountains and rivers, but to realize a single drop of water. In it are countless universes. Do you understand? In a single drop of water the entire Dharma realm, the whole phenomenal universe exists. Isn't it incredible? Mu is the entire Dharma realm. You are the entire Dharma realm: not just a drop of water, or mountains and rivers, or wise ones and sages. That being the case, what separates heaven from hell? What separates anger from wisdom, greed from compassion? The surface and the edge, inside and outside, flowing and not flowing, walking and not walking? What is the cause of that separation? A thought. A single thought and heaven and earth are a million miles apart. How can we avoid the thought? How can we avoid thinking? One great master said, "By thinking non-thinking." When there's not a single thought, then what? What do you do next? Get rid of it. "Not a single thought" is another thought; throw it away.

The capping verse says, *In the multitude of forms and the myriad appearances, there is not a single thing.* Unless you've separated yourself from the myriad things. When there is intimacy, when there is no separation, there is no thing. *Mountains and rivers are not seen in a mirror.* In other words, they are not seen through a reflection, but directly. How do you see directly? What happens when you see directly?

And then the last lines: *These mountains are endless—I seem to have lost my way. Looking up, I can see there's still some light remaining. Actually, this is just west of my campsite.* We spend a lot of time working in the zendo on that internal dialogue that separates us from things. We then take it and work on it in the midst of activity: in our work practice, in our body practice, in the arts of Zen. It's the same way we understand the functioning of the mind: on one side, stillness; on the other side, activity.

We start from the premise of original perfection. Each one of us is perfect and complete, lacking nothing. Then on top of that, through a lifetime of conditioning, we pile on all sorts of definitions and habitual behaviors. We pick up all kinds of baggage and create all kinds of blinders. What our Zen practice is about is simply returning to the ground of being. It's always been there. You're born with it, you'll die with it—whether you realize it or not. You can use it, if you realize it.

The process of realization is basically a process of clearing away the extra and getting to that place that's the heart, light, and spirit of each one of us. What you see at that point is the freedom that was always there, the nature that was always there, just wanting to come to the surface, just wanting to express itself.

> *The ancient wolf caves on Tremper Mountain*
> *Have long been empty.*
> *Yet wolf howls echo in the river valley with each*
> *   winter's full moon.*
> *Some say they are the sounds of the wind on the cliffs,*
> *   or coy-dogs.*
> *Others say, clearly this is the sound of the mountain*
> *   wolf.*
> *Have you heard them?*

If you want to hear them, you have to listen with the eye and see with the ear. Only then will you really understand. Only then will you really hear the teachings of the insentient. Only then will you hear the sermon of rock and water, the teachings of mountains and rivers.

TWENTY-ONE

THE LAST WORD

The Blue Cliff Record, Case 51

PROLOGUE

> As soon as there is affirmation and denial, you lose
> your mind in confusion. If you do not fall into grades
> and stages, then there is no seeking. But say, is letting go
> right or is holding fast right? At this point, if you have
> any trace of an interpretive route, you are still stuck in
> verbal explanations. If you are still involved with devices
> and objects, then all of this is haunting the fields and
> forests. Even if you arrive immediately at the point of
> solitary liberation, you have not avoided looking back to
> the village gate from ten thousand miles away. Can you
> reach it? If you cannot, just comprehend this perfectly
> obvious koan. Listen to the following.

THE MAIN CASE

> When Hsüeh-feng was living in a hut, there were

No monastics who came to pay their respects. Seeing *them* coming, he pushed open the door of the hut with his hand, popped out, and said, "What is it?" One of the monastics also said, "What is it?" Hsüeh-feng then lowered his head, went back inside the hut, and closed the door behind him.

Later the monastic came to Yen-t'ou. Yen-t'ou asked, "Where are you coming from?" The monastic replied, "I've come from Turtle Mountain." Yen-t'ou asked, "Did you get to see Hsüeh-feng?" The monastic said, "I went there." Yen-t'ou asked, "What did he have to say?" The monastic then told him of his encounter with Hsüeh-feng. When Yen-t'ou asked what Hsüeh-feng had said, the monastic replied, "He said nothing. He just lowered his head and went back inside the hut." Yen-t'ou said, "Ah, too bad I didn't tell old Hsüeh-feng the last word before. If I had told him, no one on earth could cope with him."

At the end of the summer the monastic again brought up the preceding story and asked for instruction. Yen-t'ou said, "Why didn't you ask earlier?" The monastic replied, "I didn't dare to be casual." Yen-t'ou said, "Though Hsüeh-feng is born in the same way as me, he doesn't die the same way as me. If you want to know the last word, just this is it."

THE CAPPING VERSE

The last word is spoken for you;
The time of light and dark pair by pair
Born of the same lineage they share the knowledge,
Dying of different lineages they're utterly separate.
Even Yellow Head and Blue Eyes have yet to discern.

292

South, North, East, West, let us return—
And in the depths of the night together
Look at the snow on thousand mountain peaks.

The last word of Zen. The first word of Zen. "In the beginning there was the Word." *Webster's Dictionary* says "word" is a spoken or written sign symbolizing an idea. Many times in Zen training we say that the words and ideas that describe reality miss it. Many times we say that we need to see the reality itself. Master Yün-men once said, "Painted cakes don't satisfy hunger," referring to the unsatisfactoriness of words and ideas to encompass reality. Master Dogen, however, said "Painted cakes satisfy hunger," pointing out that words and ideas *are* reality itself. Students work on the koan Mu. They sit—sometimes for years—with that koan, constantly asking themselves "What is Mu?" and I tell them again and again that Mu has no meaning whatsoever. Then what are they working on? How does one work on it? To see Mu is to *be* Mu.

A monastic once asked Master Lin-chi, "What is the truth of the teachings of the Buddha?" Lin-chi shouted, "KA!" Is that a word? What is the meaning of that shout? People sometimes ask, "What is the meaning of the *dharanis* we chant?" We don't translate the *dharanis* because they are not words; their meaning lies in the direct experience of chanting itself. They are not an abstraction of anything. The experience of chanting is similar to what is happening when you groan with pain or shout with joy. An incredible release comes with those sounds. They do something. But can you really say what the meaning of that groan or shout is?

Yen-t'ou and Hsüeh-feng had a very long relationship. Initially, they were both students of Master Te-shan who was known all over Tang Dynasty China as a tremendously powerful teacher. He used to say, "If you answer affirmatively, thirty blows of my stick. If you answer negatively, thirty blows of my stick. If you answer neither negatively nor affirmatively, thirty blows of my stick. If you speak, thirty blows. If you're silent, thirty blows. If there is neither speech nor silence, thirty blows!" Monastics were terrified to face him; there was no way out of getting a beating. To go face-to-face with him was to enter the lion's den. Yen-t'ou and Hsüeh-feng were two of his prime disciples. Yen-t'ou, though the younger of the two, was actually the more realized, having come to enlightenment long before Hsüeh-feng did.

In most of the koans that deal with their training at Te-shan's monastery, we meet them when Yen-t'ou was in his early thirties and Hsüeh-feng in his late forties. One day Te-shan, then a mature teacher in his eighties, came down to the dining hall carrying his bowls. Hsüeh-feng, the monastery cook, saw the old master and asked, "Where are you going with your bowls? The bell hasn't rung, the drum hasn't sounded—it's not time yet for dinner." At that rebuke, Te-shan quietly turned and went back to his room. Seeing Te-shan's seemingly meek response, Hsüeh-feng thought he had defeated the old man in Dharma combat. Because he thought he had really accomplished something, he was soon bragging about it to all the other monastics. Yen-t'ou, the head monastic, heard about the incident and came to Hsüeh-feng to hear the whole story first-hand. After listening to Hsüeh-feng's boasting, Yen-t'ou said, "Well, great master that he is, old Te-shan still hasn't realized the last word of Zen." Soon all the monastics were whispering among themselves, "The old man doesn't know the last word of Zen!"

Eventually, all this talk reached Te-shan's attention.

He sent for Yen-t'ou and asked, "Don't you approve of me?" Yen-t'ou leaned close and whispered something in Te-shan's ear that seemed to satisfy the old master. Later that day, Te-shan gave a talk, and for the first time in his years of teaching he was completely out of character, completely different from how he had ever been. When he concluded the talk, Yen-t'ou jumped up from his seat, applauded Te-shan heartily, and said, "At last! At last! The old man has realized the last word of Zen. No one can make fun of him from this point on." What incredible compassion Te-shan and Yen-t'ou showed throughout this drama, desperately trying to bring Hsüeh-feng to realization, trying to get him past the pride and self-centeredness that kept him separated from the truth. Old Te-shan was free, absolutely free. *When the wind blows from the East, the leaves collect in the West.* When Hsüeh-feng told him the dinner bell hadn't rung, Te-shan turned around and went to his room—as gently as a child.

Yen-t'ou later said to the old man, "Let me take Hsüeh-feng on a pilgrimage; maybe if we visit some of the other monasteries and see other teachers, something will happen and he will break through." Te-shan agreed to the trip and the two monastics went on their way. En route, Hsüeh-feng did come to realization, and Hsüeh-feng and Yen-t'ou returned to the monastery where they eventually became Dharma successors of Te-shan.

The koan in this chapter took place many years later, during one of the great purges in China, when all Buddhist monastics had been ordered to leave the monasteries and return to lay life. The monastic practice went underground, forcing monastics to continue practicing on their own. During this purge Hsüeh-feng lived as a hermit, while Yen-t'ou ran a ferry on the shores of a lake. When someone wanted to cross the lake, they would knock on a board Yen-t'ou had placed on the bank. From the woods he would hear the knock and ask, "Which side are you crossing to?" and wave his oar from among the weeds. Of course, taking people from one shore to another alludes to *prajna paramita*, the wisdom of the other shore, the idea of crossing over to enlightenment. When we chant the *Heart Sutra*, we say: "*Gate, gate, paragate, parasamgate bodhi svaha*" ("Go, go, hurry quickly, cross over to the other shore.") Yen-t'ou, of course, understood the truth of paramita: the truth of *that* shore and *this* shore being the *same* shore. That is what it means to cross over. Absolute and relative are not two separate things: form is exactly emptiness, and emptiness exactly form.

When the two wandering monastics in the koan came to pay their respects at Hsüeh-feng's hermitage, Hsüeh-feng pushed open the door of his hut, popped out, and said, "*What is it?*" And the monastic answered, "*What is it?*" Hsüeh-feng hung his head, turned around, went back into the hut, and closed the door. It is said that in so doing, Hsüeh-feng "hid his body but revealed his shadow." The monastics misinterpreted this, thinking that Hsüeh-feng returned to the hut because he was speechless, unable to respond. Little did they know that there was poison in his action, and that it was offered in order to kill them, to take away their egos, to help them die the Great Death.

Hsüeh-feng was showing one part of the truth, and in the prologue that prefaces the koan, Master Yüan-wu talks about this. He says: *As soon as there is affirmation and denial, you lose your mind in confusion.* That is one side. *If you do not fall into grades and stages, then there is no seeking.* That is the other side. One side is the relative: "eye, ear, nose, tongue, body, and mind." The other side is the absolute: "*no* eye, ear, nose, tongue, body, or mind." But what good is somebody with "no eye, ear, nose, tongue, body, or mind?" Such a person cannot even cross the street. That is certainly not what Zen practice is about.

Yüan-wu continues, *But say, is letting go right or is holding fast right?* Holding fast refers to the time when a teacher pulls back, denies, takes away, knocks out the pegs and nails, collapses the structure, pulls out the rug. That is the absolute: taking away everything we cherish, everything we hold most dearly. Holding fast is what Hsüeh-feng did when he dropped his head, turned around, and closed the door, leaving the monastics standing there. Letting go is the other side of that: it is giving, loving, nourishing, healing, supporting, approving.

Yüan-wu goes on to say, *At this point, if you have any trace of an interpretive route, you are still stuck in verbal explanations.* How do you transcend verbal explanations? How do you transcend speech or silence? You could just shut up and say nothing, but that is dead. Or you could run off at the mouth, but that misses the point, too. How do you avoid both extremes?

When these monastics went to visit Yen-t'ou he asked them, "*Where are you coming from?*" He was dangling the hook, trying to find out what their understanding was and what they were seeking. This is what happens whenever a student encounters a teacher—the teacher tests to find out what kind of clarity the student has. It is only then that the real teaching can start. The monastic said, "*I've come from Turtle Mountain.*" With this kind of answer, it could be that this monastic has seen something. (Turtle Mountain was the location of Hsüeh-feng's hermitage.) So, Yen-t'ou pursued it: "*Did you get to see Hsüeh-feng?*" The monastic said, "*I went there.*" Right then Yen-t'ou should have taken up his stick and driven the monastic

297

out. But he was as compassionate with the monastic as he had been with Hsüeh-feng all those years—acting like a doting old grandmother following a child around, protecting and helping him. Instead of taking the stick to the monastic, Yen-t'ou asked, "What did Hsüeh-feng have to say?" The monastic said, "Well, Hsüeh-feng came out and said, 'What *is* it?' and I responded, 'What is it?' Then Hsüeh-feng just lowered his head and went back into the hut."

That told Yen-t'ou a great deal about this monastic. Most importantly it told him that the monastic did not understand Hsüeh-feng at all, that he had completely missed Hsüeh-feng's teaching. Like the nice grandmother, Yen-t'ou said, "Too bad that when Hsüeh-feng was with me I didn't tell him the last word of Zen." Of course, he's referring back to that encounter with Te-shan carrying his bowls, when Te-shan didn't know the last word of Zen. *"If I had told him, no one on earth could cope with him."* The monastic said nothing, but just stayed on at the monastery for the remainder of the three-month training period. Finally, at the end of the summer, he went back to Yen-t'ou and asked for instruction. Yen-t'ou said, *"Why didn't you ask earlier?"*

We have the same problem here—nobody wants to ask, nobody wants to be a fool. When we don't ask, we're fools for not taking advantage of this incredible practice, this incredible Dharma. The monastic replied, *"I didn't dare to be casual."* A note to the koan says, "An imprisoned man increases in wisdom." The monastic was locked securely in his own cage. He had been carrying that cage around with him all his life, only he didn't recognize it as a cage. Hsüeh-feng showed it to him when he lowered his head and returned to the hut. He still didn't recognize it. He went to Yen-t'ou; Yen-t'ou showed it to him again, but he still didn't see that he was locked in.

Usually the way we deal with our cage is not by knocking it down and getting rid of the bars. Instead we redecorate it. We make it comfortable. We install wall-to-wall carpeting, get a television set, or get some good books. Yet it's still a cage, no matter how beautiful or comfortable we make it. We define the limits of our life with that cage. Finally, something happened with this monastic and he realized that he was locked in—so he asked. And Yen-t'ou said, *"Though Hsüeh-feng is born in the same way as I, he doesn't die the same way as I."*

When we talk about birth or about dying in terms of the Dharma, we usually refer to death as the Great Death, the absolute. We refer to birth as coming out of the absolute into the relative. In this case, however, the meanings are reversed. Being "born" means the realization of the absolute basis of reality, and "dying" means the functioning of our life in the world. *"Hsüeh-feng is born in the same way as I"* is Hsüeh-feng's and Yen-t'ou's realization of the absolute. *"He doesn't die the same way as I"* points to how Hsüeh-feng and Yen-t'ou manifest that realization differently in their daily lives and in their teachings.

Then Yen-t'ou said, *"If you want to know the last word, just this is it."* What is it? What is that last word of Zen? If you understand the first word of Zen, you'll know the last word of Zen. First word, last word—it is not a word. What is it? What is the truth that these two old masters have been pointing to? What is the truth that falls neither into absolute nor relative, neither into speech nor silence?

A monastic once asked another master, Feng-hsüeh, "How can we be free and non-transgressing? How can we avoid falling into neither speech nor silence?" Master Feng-hsüeh said, "How fondly I recall Chiang-nan in March; partridges calling, flowers in bloom." But those are words; how did he avoid falling into words? A monastic came to study with Master Yün-men; he had barely opened his mouth to begin quoting the poem of Chang-cho when Yün-men stopped him short and asked, "Isn't that the poem of Chang-cho?" The monastic said, "Yes, it is." Yün-men said, "You've missed it!" The monastic didn't even get two words out of his mouth; how did Yün-men know he had missed the point? What we are dealing with in each of these koans is intimacy. That is what Yen-t'ou was talking about and what Hsüeh-feng revealed. "Seeing forms with the whole body and mind, hearing sounds with the whole body and mind, one understands them intimately." In intimacy, there is no separation.

In his poem, Master Hsüeh-tou says:

> *The last word is spoken for you;*
> *The time of light and dark pair by pair*
> *Born of the same lineage they share the knowledge,*
> *Dying of different lineages they're utterly separate.*
> *Even Yellow Head and Blue Eyes have yet to discern.*
> *South, North, East, West, let us return—*
> *And in the depths of the night together*
> *Look at the snow on a thousand mountain peaks.*

The time of light and dark pair by pair. Light and dark refer to the absolute and relative. Take away the light and there is no discerning, no distinction, no "this" and no "that." Darkness is the absolute. But we can't function that way. In the light there is distinction, there is this and that, up and down, heaven and hell. Where is the place that falls into neither of those two? On one side we have silence and on the other we have words. Where is the truth? It's not half-and-half, black on one side and white on the other side. And gray is not the answer either. So what is it? What does it mean to be born of the same lineage and die of different lineages? Old Hsüeh-tou opened his big mouth to tell us: *The time of light and dark, pair by pair.* We chant in the *Identity of Relative and Absolute Sutra:* "like two arrows meeting in mid-air." Speech and silence, absolute and relative—like two arrows meeting in mid-air. Where is that meeting point?

A monastic once asked his master, "When Yen-t'ou says, 'So and so, and not so and so,' what is his meaning?" The master replied, "Both light and dark." The monastic bowed and left. A few days later he came back again and said, "A few days ago I received your compassionate instruction; but I can't see through it. I just don't understand. What did you mean?" The master replied, "I've told you the whole thing already." The monastic insisted, "Please light the way." "What are you in doubt over?" the master asked. The monastic said, "What is both light and dark?" The master answered, "Born the same and dying the same." The monastic bowed and left. Later there was another monastic who asked, "How is it when being born the same and dying the same?" The master said, "Shut your dog-mouth." The monastic said, "You can't eat food with your mouth closed, Master." The monastic then went to another master and said, "How is it when being born the same and dying the same?" The master said, "Like an ox without horns." The monastic said, "How is it when being born the same, but not dying the same?" The master said, "Like a tiger with horns." Master Hsüeh-tou comments that, "The last word is precisely this truth."

"Born in the same way," as we've seen, is Hsüeh-feng and Yen-t'ou's realization of the absolute. "Don't die the same way" means that despite their realization of the absolute, Hsüeh-feng and Yen-t'ou are utterly separate, utterly alone in the way they manifest that realization: not even "Yellow Head" (Shakyamuni Buddha) or "Blue Eyes" (Bodhidharma) can find them. In our lineage, the merging of the absolute and the relative is a vital matter. What good is it to stay up on a mountain peak? The Dharma needs to be manifest in everything we do; in the way we think, live, eat, write, and create.

As for me, I don't believe Yen-t'ou. His tongue should fall out of his mouth for treating these monastics that way. Why is he misleading them? Why doesn't he just show them the last word of Zen?

Sometimes teachers create cages in order to free us from a cage. Sometimes they create complications in order to free us from complications. It is a difficult thing to do because we are already free. Buddha knew it, old blue-eyed Bodhidharma knew it, all the ancient masters knew it—and yet they made constant effort to help us see, because we don't recognize our own freedom. When you try to understand the universe from inside your cage, the universe is a cage. What you see is who you are. When you are free from cages, the whole universe and everyone in it is free and unhindered, perfect and complete. Do you understand? If you do understand, then get this, too: that's not it. Those are words. My words. Those are ideas. My ideas. Understanding is not yours until you realize it yourself, manifest it in your own life, in your own sitting, walking, bowing, eating, working, writing, and relating to other human beings.

This life is no small thing. It is serious business, to be taken care of right away as though it were a fire on top of your head.

What, then, is the first word? Don't tell me, *show me*.

What, then, is the last word of Zen? Don't tell me, *show me*.

NOTES

CHAPTER ONE

1. He comes on straight away. He wants to know. Rocky Mountains are high, Catskill Mountains are low.

2. It's an old, worn-out question known everywhere. But still, he wants to put it to the test.

3. He goes right up and takes him out. Why is he being so kind to this monastic?

4. Mountains are mountains, rivers are rivers.

5. Neither of them understands. He's making quite a fuss. He should just shut up.

6. It engulfs the myriad forms. Between heaven and earth, what more is there?

7. Among the dead, a live one. He's treading on the ground of reality. Where do you think he went when he left?

Chapter Two

1. When you look at it, you're blinded.

2. Where did he get the news?

3. If you don't know what it is, why do you think there is one?

4. Not two, yet when the fish swims, the water gets muddy. Not two, yet when the bird flies, feathers fall.

5. Good news. But say, what is it good for?

6. There are many who still have doubts about this.

7. He keeps making piles of bones on level ground. Just don't talk about it.

8. Give him the pearl. Hit him. It won't do to let him go.

9. The whole universe calls out.

10. The ten thousand Dharmas answer.

11. Don't explain it for him. Let him go wrong for the rest of his life.

12. Confined in prison, he increases in wisdom. Still, he will never attain it.

Chapter Three

1. A single mouth, no tongue.

2. Indeed, how is that? What succession are we speaking about?

3. All the Buddhas and ancestors since time immemorial doubt this also.

4. Diamond-thorned steel brambles, no ordinary monastic can leap clear of this.

5. He holds up the sky and supports the earth. He's found his way amid the brambles. Still, it's difficult not to leave tracks.

6. Neither difficult nor easy. The ancient teachings on the tips of a thousand grasses.

7. The good tracker will leave no traces.

8. When the fish swims, the water is muddied. When the bird flies, a feather falls.

9. Like what? Is there anything to impart or not? He could have gotten out if he had kept his mouth shut, but he persisted.

10. It takes a fool to recognize a fool. Who would be laughing at these answers?

11. It's all dirt from the same hole. What's the use of so much talk?

12. Again, he comes on directly. He wants everybody to know.

13. Deaf, dumb, and blind, he acts according to imperative.

14. This is as it should be. What end will there ever be to it all?

CHAPTER THIRTEEN

1. What's he saying? Caterpillars don't talk. They must be traveling the same road for this conversation to take place. Complications are sure to follow.

2. If there is one side, there must be another side.

3. I'm large and contain the multitudes. KA! Reaching everywhere. How big am I?

4. Why does he speak only in halves?

5. Ten thousand universes in a single speck of dust. Is it bigger or smaller; the same or different? Does reaching everywhere include them both?

6. Concern is born. The whole phenomenal universe is born.

7. Although he's not a member of the household, there's a fragrant air about this one.

8. Is this seeing, or is it just looking?

9. The mushroom is perfect and complete. No upside or downside, no inside or outside, no one side or other side, from beginning to end. Difficult to understand.

CHAPTER FOURTEEN

1. An honest person is hard to find. Still, there could be something here.

2. As it turns out, he doesn't flinch when faced with danger. Turning the spear around, he threatens the old man.

3. Very intimate, indeed. All eighty-six ancestors have suffered this illness.

4. A wounded tiger appears out of the weeds. What is this monastic really seeking?

5. Yesterday has already happened. Tomorrow has not yet happened. How about now?

6. Seeing a cage, he builds a cage. This kind of kindness is hard to repay. Successive generations only transmitted this.

CHAPTER FIFTEEN

1. They plan to gang up on the old man. Why gather a crowd?

2. Everyone in the world is the same. Still, he must ask. He has a vow to make trouble. She will inevitably understand it in the ordinary way.

3. She may be misguided, but I will say she's truthful.

4. This is as it should be. Let her go on wearing out sandals.

5. Let's see if they both fit on the same skewer.

6. This child walks right up and into the tiger's mouth.

7. Check it out, check it out. Even tiny ponds are sometimes as deep as the ocean.

8. Ahh! Too much, too soon, too fast, too bad. Still, it amounts to something. I'll keep my binoculars on the horizon and watch.

9. Indeed. Inevitably Kuei-shan diminishes people's worth.

10. Suddenly the little one doesn't seem so dull.

11. Indeed, get her. No, don't get her. Let her go on deceiving herself for the rest of her life.

12. If you've lost your way, check the map and compass.

13. Wrong. But, I wonder, does this question have a barb in it?

14. A good hunter doesn't leave tracks.

15. As it turns out, she has misunderstood. She's still young. The mother cat trains her kittens by playing with them.

16. A nip on the rump is not quickly forgotten.

17. She's still showing her fangs, but the old thief has already left with everything.

CHAPTER NINETEEN

1. There are many people with doubts. After all, if you don't ask, how will you understand?

2. True enough, but what are they? Where are they? Waiting for what?

3. Neither concealed nor revealed. Reaching everywhere.

4. Aaaagh! When will it end? Gasping for breath, he goes on and on and on.

5. Have mercy!

6. Careful here, he's after your nostrils.

7. Wrong! He sees the sword and proceeds to impale himself on it.

8. In the ten directions there are no barriers. On the four sides, no gates. North, east, south, west, above and below, no gaps. How do you see it?

9. He steals his tongue and blocks off his throat. Where will you go to settle your body and establish your life? Take away the words, what remains?

10. Mouth agape, tongue hanging out, thirty blows of the stick is not enough to bring this one to life.

CHAPTER TWENTY

1. He opens up the trail for everyone. How can you miss it? Don't you see—it reaches everywhere?

2. The abode of no abode. People will inevitably make a nest here.

3. Complications are sure to follow. What can possibly be said?

4. East mountain walks over water. The mountain flows, the river is still.

5. Mountains are mountains, rivers are rivers.

QUESTIONS AND ANSWERS

Q: Can you explain the relationship between seeing a koan clearly and having an enlightenment experience?

A: Koans can often trigger a *kensho* experience, and most realization experiences come from that kind of triggering. It can happen with a traditional koan or with a koan in one's life. When you're working on a koan, you're building a great deal of energy and power in relationship to it. When there's the release, the opening, or what Maslow calls peak experience, there is a discharge of that energy. When that quantum leap happens, you're suddenly seeing things very, very differently. In a sense everything is the same; nothing has changed. All the facts remain the same, but you've completely transformed your vision, your way of seeing. That's usually very sudden. That's an insight. Enlightenment is a very broad, general term. We'd use the term *kensho* for the first breakthrough. *Kensho* literally means seeing the nature of the self. *Kensho* is not yet enlightenment; in other words, not complete enlighten-

ment. The psychological release that happens after a prolonged tension is in itself exhilarating, even euphoric, and
it's that euphoria that people mistake for enlightenment.
There are books filled with such accounts. *The Three
Pillars of Zen,* for example, contains many of these stories.
What they're describing is the euphoria. Well, the euphoria has nothing to do with the insight.

People tend to think that if you don't have that kind
of euphoric experience, then you haven't experienced any
insight, or *kensho.* That's not true; they're not necessarily
related. Euphoria has many sources. I've seen the very
same euphoria in the faces of hostages when they were
released after having been held for several days in a TWA
airliner years ago, an airliner on which several people were
killed. All of the hostages thought they were going to die.
Suddenly it was all over. They were set free, and as they
were coming out the door, they described feelings as if
they'd been reborn, loving the whole world, and on and
on—you could have taken the words and put them directly into *The Three Pillars of Zen,* because the experience was
the same. But it doesn't mean that those people that came
out of the plane were enlightened. Nor does it mean that
those euphoric descriptions in *The Three Pillars of Zen*
were descriptions of enlightenment. But there is an association with euphoria because of the release of tension.

Q: In the story about the hostages, I'm hearing that
in order to work with anything, you need to be in touch
with your suffering or your pain, like the people on the
plane.

A: No, it's different from that. You need to have settled most of the issues of your suffering and pain, because
if they come up constantly while you're working on a
koan, they constantly separate you from the koan. In order

to see a koan, you need to be the koan. In order to be a koan, you need to forget the self. You can't forget the self if it's constantly hurting, if you're constantly in agony.

Q: If you've passed one koan, have you passed them all?

A: It depends on what "passing the koan" means. It's quite possible by virtue of completely exhausting a single koan to be clear on all of the other koans. But mostly, passing a koan doesn't mean that. Passing a koan means satisfying whatever the particular requirement is of that teacher at that particular time. The very same koan five years later will have a whole different feel to it and will require a different response.

Q: If you're doing *shikantaza*, just sitting, do you think the results are similar, but that practice just takes longer?

A: *Shikantaza* is usually referred to as a "gradual" method. I do *shikantaza* now, but that's at the end of koan study. However, I know a number of Soto monastics that have been sitting for years, and the impact that their zazen has had on their life is very obvious. The same characteristics are manifested that usually come through the process of koan study. Basically, those characteristics are wisdom and compassion. In *shikantaza* students there is more accent on compassion, and not so much on the expression of the wisdom. Their understanding is much more tactile than intellectual.

Q: Can you answer a koan with another koan?

A: No, but a koan can bring up more questions. A good koan, which starts off with a single question, will end up raising hundreds of questions before it's finally resolved. And each one of those hundreds of questions needs to be resolved in the process.

Q: I'm reading D.T. Suzuki and am troubled because the word "zazen" is not even in the index in his books.

A: That was the big problem back in the 1960s when we first got interested in Zen. There were books on Zen, but there wasn't one single book that told you how to sit. I had no idea how to sit. Some authors would say that it was important to sit but they never said how to do it. Alan Watts talked about it all the time. It wasn't until years later that teachers began to appear and one or two books were published that introduced us to zazen. D.T. Suzuki was primarily a scholar. He studied at a monastery the way a scholar studies at a monastery. He wasn't a monastic. His zazen wasn't pivotal. I am not sure how he worked with koans. Most of the books that appeared over a long period of time—indeed, most of the books that are out—are books by scholars that are translations of classic works. It's very rare that you get a book directly from a teacher such as Dogen. Most of what you read of Dogen in *Shobogenzo* he wrote himself. But it's very rare. Most of the things we read about teachers are transcriptions of what they said. Very few teachers were writers. The literature is not a dependable thing. Plus the fact that, by definition, that's not it.

Q: On the one hand, to work on the koan involves basically no-self. On the other hand, words like "work, perseverance, and faith" are used, words which have a dualistic connotation. Are you using these words in another sense, or is this just a limitation of language?

A: That's the limitation of language. But remember that the answer doesn't come in the words. It's in an experience. You can have an experience and then you can describe the experience. The description is a description of the reality. The reality is the thing itself. People have a hard time grasping the difference between the word and the reality. The way we first get in touch with the world as an infant is direct. Your first contact is usually with your mother, and an infant knows its mother by the smell, taste, touch, sound, and ultimately by the visual image of her. All of that is a direct experience. But sooner or later, you learn language, and "mother" becomes "m-o-t-h-e-r," an abstraction of that reality. They're not the same thing. If I use the word "shout," it creates an image in everybody's mind. Each person will have their image, similar or different. But when I say "HUUUGH!" I communicate the experience directly. You feel it. You hear it. It is very different from the word "shout," which is an abstraction of that. That's what we continually confuse on all sorts of levels. After a while, we think we understand something because we can name it. That's the way our education works. If you can give a definition of something or categorize it, you're thought to understand it. Well, understanding is not good enough for koans. Understanding doesn't impart any strength. Believing doesn't impart any strength. It gives you information, but it doesn't impart strength. It's not transformative. Realizing is transformative, and that's what enlightenment is about. It's about realizing. It's about one's own direct and intimate experience of the koan. Insight, not description.

Q: Is the response to a koan specifically related to that koan? Could you be looking for the same shift in insight and understanding of something that could happen in another koan?

A: The koan is usually a very specific question. There

are layers of insight that happen in the process of seeing a koan that are important in and of themselves, but do not yet necessarily satisfy the koan. When students start working on a koan, what they get out of it depends on how much that koan impacts their lives. It's not simply a series of questions and answers, like taking an examination. That's one of the reasons why the teacher-student relationship is so pivotal. It's human-to-human. Institutions don't transmit the Buddha-dharma. People do, from Buddha to Buddha. It happens in that merging of minds, in the process of working with a koan. The full range of human experience comes into play. There's laughing and crying. There's anger. There's greed, there's hate. All of the emotions come up, and they're all dealt with as part of the process.

Q: Is *kensho* at all common? Can it happen before one is working on a koan, in the practice of breath-counting, let's say?

A: It's happened. History's shows us that it's happened. The Sixth Ancestor is a good example. Hui-neng wasn't a Buddhist. He had never studied Buddhism. He was an illiterate peasant living in the southern part of China. A monastic came to town and was chanting the *Diamond Sutra,* and when he chanted a particular line, Hui-neng had a *daikensho* experience—a great *kensho* experience. He was acknowledged by the Fifth Ancestor as being greatly enlightened, and received the Dharma transmission almost immediately. So, it is possible. But the chances of its happening that way are very slim. The chances of its happening using the process that has evolved over 2,500 years are much higher.

Q: You said that the teacher can approve the student

to go onto the next koan, although that approval doesn't always mean that the student has seen it.

A: Right. What happens is that the student will have presented it perfectly, but will have no idea what they've presented. The teacher knows that the student has no idea what he or she has presented. Sometimes something gets blurted out. Sometimes a student will come in and make a presentation, and the teacher will say, "No. Make it clearer." The student will present again. The teacher will continue, "Not enough, make it clearer," and keep pressing the student, and suddenly the student will say something. Maybe even in anger, or in despair. And the teacher will say, "Go onto the next one," and ring the bell. The student may have no idea what happened. That becomes a koan in and of itself. The student goes back to his or her seat and wants to know why the answer was passed. The student doesn't just want an okay. Sometimes he or she will even come back again with the same question. In the process of persisting, the student finally gets it. There's a nice example of such a delayed reaction. Elder T'ing came to Lin-chi and asked, "What is the great meaning of the Buddha-dharma?" Lin-chi punched him right in the mouth! As T'ing was standing there in shock, the attendant next to him said, "Why don't you bow?" T'ing, stunned, followed the instructions and bowed, and as he bowed he realized it. Human consciousness is a weird thing. It's so strange what triggers these breakthroughs. A pebble hitting bamboo. A falling peach blossom. If you wanted to be logical about it, you could set the whole thing up: have a hundred monastics sit here and drop peach blossoms until they see it. Or keep throwing stones until one of them hits the bamboo. Or break your leg in the door. Or ask the teacher to punch you in the nose. But it's got nothing to do with any of that. It's very easy to get side-tracked and assume that the thing that triggers the enlightenment is what the whole thing is about. Most of it doesn't make sense to anybody else. Writings about koans describe what happened to some monastic when he or she was suddenly enlightened. Well, why wasn't I enlightened while I was sitting there reading it? That person was primed. That person was ready. That person was at the very crest of struggle.

Q: What you're saying is that this process triggers something that all human beings have, even if they're not Buddhists. It could happen completely outside this context. What is this universal insight?

A: It's definitely universal. Before being a Buddhist I was a scientist. For 17 years I made my living through scientific research. I would sit for months on end with molecular models, and just turn them. Then I would drop the problem, just walk away from it. For two weeks I wouldn't think about it, and suddenly, Bam! the whole thing would fall into place. An Englishman in a book called *The Art of Scientific Investigation* addressed how that works. What he claims is that when scientists are working on mathematical equations they can't solve, they work with it exhaustively, and then finally they let it alone. That letting it alone means that the problem has left their waking consciousness, but is still going on at another level, at a much deeper level. When the solution becomes apparent at that deeper level, its sheer aesthetic beauty brings it up to surface consciousness, and you see it. It may be that a similar process is going on in koan study.

Q: Is the transformative experience of the first koan repeated when you go onto the other koans?

A: The first koan is usually very powerful. The later ones bring little bits of insight into that first koan.

Q: We don't drop apple blossoms and break legs, but we do sit zazen in a very specific form. Why?

A: It has to do with what that form is, what it does. Why for 2,500 years have people been sitting this way? Why did the Buddha sit this way? Why does your teacher sit this way? That posture has to do with stability, stability of the body and of the mind. If you want to be able to sit perfectly still without moving your body and go into deep *samadhi* without being stiff and tight, the full-lotus is the best way to do it. Now, why is it that you don't want to move? Because every time that you move, you telegraph information to the brain. You reinforce the illusion "I exist. I am here." That's what we create moment to moment to moment.

Q: I was wondering whether a student literally does koans sequentially, or whether they are selected out of the collections by the teacher.

A: We go koan by koan through all the collections. I don't have the luxury of being able to do it the other way. If I had five students I might do it that way, but when you're dealing with several hundred students, it's hard to keep track of who's where and why.

Q: What happens when students are away from the monastery and see the koan, but can't get up to the monastery? What do the students do? Do they continue sitting with it?

A: A good way to work with it is to keep sitting with it, letting it get clearer and clearer. Usually the first insight is not the clearest. It continues to open up for the student if he or she just stays with that same koan. Even when the student goes to other koans, all that's being done is clarifying that very same koan. Once you see it, you're not going to lose it, so just keep sitting with it.

Q: When students come in to *dokusan*, do they recite the whole koan?

A: Those with good memories can do that. It is more usual that they'll present the main case first, and then once they've seen the main case, we go on to the verse. They'll memorize it a piece at a time. That was the most difficult part of koan study for me, memorizing the koans. I begged my teacher to let me read them, and he wouldn't let me. He told me I needed to memorize them, and I continue the cruelty. I realize now the virtue in that. When a student is reciting the koan and leaves a nice little juicy chunk out, I pick up on it right away. Memorizing the koans also helps you make them your own. When you're really working inside a koan, you can smell T'ang dynasty China. You feel the body of Chao-chou. The whole thing becomes incredibly real for you. You literally put yourself into it. Once you've done that, it's very personal. It's like an account of your own life.

Q: Can you talk about everyday koans, problems that come up in your life and how to work with them effectively in practice?

A: Everyday koans, *genjo-koans,* usually first come up during the process of quieting the mind, before you get to the formal koans. They keep intruding themselves into the tranquility of your zazen. They are an itch that you can't scratch. Sooner or later you'll find yourself talking to the teacher about them. If you've ever advised a friend who's having difficulties, you know that what seems to you to be the most obvious way of dealing with the problem is not at all apparent to the other person. When you're really immersed in something, it's difficult to see where you're stuck. An outside person can be very useful.

But even so, the teacher never intrudes, never takes away from the student that opportunity for discovery. What the teacher will do is push or point or suggest, but never really try to resolve the question for the student. The only way through the koan, no matter what koan, is to be the koan. The only way through a barrier is to be the barrier. If the barrier is fear, the only way to the other side of that barrier of fear is to be that fear. If the barrier is pain, the only way to the other side is to be the pain. When you are the pain, when you are the barrier, the barrier fills the whole universe. The whole relativistic system disappears. When the barrier fills the universe, there's nothing outside it. It includes everything. The world of differentiation disappears. Sometimes pain becomes the first breakthrough for a student. While just being the pain, body and mind fall away. Self is forgotten. The way to work with any koan, in answer to your question, is to be the koan, be the barrier. Don't separate yourself. The tendency is to want to pull back. The tendency is to want to deny, to separate, to move away from the barrier or the pain. That's exactly the opposite of what needs to happen. You need to do a 180-degree turn and merge with it. Give the pain permission to encompass your whole body and mind.

Q: How do you determine whether a student has passed a koan?

A: How does a carpenter know another carpenter? Or a diver another deep-sea diver? A master diver says to a novice, "Okay, go down 200 feet and explore around the bottom." She comes back and the master diver tests her, "What did it feel like down there? What was your gauge reading? What was the bottom like? Was it sandy? Was it rocky? Was there any seaweed?" Anybody who's been down there, who's seen it, knows the kind of questions to ask. Any expert in any field will know someone else experienced in that field. A first-class violinist will know another violinist—two strokes on the violin, just how he or she picks the instrument up tells the story. Throw a hammer to a carpenter—just the way the carpenter grabs it and holds it says lot about him or her. We reveal ourselves constantly. We reveal our hesitancies, the places where we block, and the places that we're free and easy. And if you've seen it, there's no way to hide it. Probably a good third of the koans deal with testing the depth and clarity of student's enlightenment. Most of the testing seems very casual. Tung-shan comes to Master Yün-men and Yün-men says, "Where are you from?" And he says, "Oh, such-and-such a monastery." "When did you leave there?" "Such-and-such a date." "Where did you spend the last training period?" "At the other monastery." "When did you leave there?" "Such-and-such a date." "Thirty blows of my stick!" In other words, he disapproves of him. What he was doing with the questions was testing him. Any one of those questions could have been answered by revealing the Dharma. Only Tung-shan didn't even know what was wrong. He had no idea why he was given thirty blows of the stick. He agonized over it all night long, and the next day went back to the teacher and said, "Why did you disapprove of me last night?" Yün-men said, "You ricebag! Is that what you've been doing, running from this monastery to that monastery? Where will you have today?" At those words Tung-shan was enlightened. A student's understanding is tested not only through explicit questions, but through casual conversation that is really a Dharma combat.

Q: You say, "Koan study leads to trace-free and never-ending enlightenment." Could you explain what you mean by never-ending enlightenment? Does an enlightened person who gets Alzheimer's disease continue to be enlightened?

A: Of course! Why wouldn't they? If somebody with gray hair got Alzheimer's disease, what would happen? They'd be gray-haired with Alzheimer's disease; likewise they'd be enlightened with Alzheimer's disease. What does enlightenment mean? Enlightenment means to have seen the nature of the universe. A person who has Alzheimer's might not be able to express it, but the fact is, if they've seen it, they've seen it.

Q: Are they essentially any different from what they were when they were infants who haven't yet realized enlightenment? Infants are also enlightened. I mean, everybody has Buddha-nature.

A: Even the most deluded among us have Buddha-nature, have that enlightenment. Some may realize it, some may not. That was the statement that the Buddha made—all sentient beings are enlightened. All sentient beings are perfect and complete. There's nothing added. There's only something taken away. In other words, what you do is get rid of the extra, get rid of the conditioning and discover that inherent perfection underneath. That inherent perfection doesn't come there, doesn't leave there. Whether you have Alzheimer's disease or anything else, it remains. You may not realize it any longer, you may not be able to express it any longer, but it is nonetheless there.

Q: How do you know that this whole process doesn't become another level of conditioning?

A: That's what I used to think. I remember somewhere in the middle of my training, I said to a senior monastic where I was training, "Oh, I understand. What we do is we decondition ourselves and then recondition ourselves as enlightenment." He practically swallowed me alive. That's not what's happening. What's happening is that all of the conditioning is stripped away, and you practice so as not to accumulate it, not to recreate it. Although, that does happen. There are references in the literature to a second self, reconstructed after the initial breakthrough. Usually that ends up being a very holy self, one that stinks of Zen, one that's "perfect and complete." There are many koans that deal with that.

Q: If a student doing koan study doesn't have an answer to the koan to present, is *dokusan* still useful?

A: Sure. You can't play tennis unless you hit the ball back and forth. So if I say, "Let's play tennis," and you say, "Okay," and we go out into the court, and you stand there holding the ball and racquet and you won't throw or hit the ball, there's no tennis game. That happens a lot in *dokusan*. I say, "Let's play Zen," and people come to *dokusan* and don't say anything. "How are you doing?" "Fine." "Everything all right?" "Yep." "How's your sitting?" "Good." There's no room to do anything, so I just ring the bell and they go back, and I wait. Aitken Roshi addresses that in his book. He said that as a schoolteacher, he always felt he could do a lot more with a student who would throw a blackboard eraser at him when his back was turned, than with a student who never asked a question, never said anything. You don't get an opportunity to teach. It's through mistakes that teaching happens.

Q: You speak of letting go of the self. What is it that keeps letting go of the self?

A: Well, that's the point. There is nothing there. There never was anything there. We create the self moment-to-moment. In a sense, it's not a matter of letting go. It's a matter of not creating the self. We create the universe by the way we use our minds, by the way we interact with things. The organ of perception, the object of perception, and consciousness together create the illusion of what we call existence. But the fact is there is no existence there, other than the one we create. That's what the *Diamond Sutra* basically is talking about, over and over and over again, in a hundred different ways. Each paragraph is saying the same thing concerning non-existence. But the truth is that reality is neither existent or non-existent. Sentient beings are neither being or non-being. The truth doesn't lie in either of those extremes. The truth is neither absolute nor relative. That's the meeting point of the arrows, that place that is neither.

Q: Would you agree that the participant, the observer, is the one that creates reality? If that's the case, all koans are delusions, illusions, because unless I choose to focus on it, it doesn't really exist in a physical sense?

A: Oh, for sure. The whole catastrophe is empty, you know. Buddhism is empty. You're empty. I'm empty. Enlightenment is empty. None of it exists except by the virtue of the way we create it. That's what you realize.

Q: Is it a dream of a dream within a dream?

A: Well, it's speaking of a dream within a dream. You're the master. You can have nice dreams or bad dreams.

Q: I'm concerned by the statement that acknowledging the koan is what creates its reality, and the implication that you can then just dream a more pleasant dream. One of the problems I find with the world is that we simply choose not to acknowledge there is a hole in the ozone layer, and that in the last five minutes a woman died from being battered.

A: I understand what you're saying, but as Gary Snyder said, you can fence off your garden without hating the vermin. You can acknowledge the hole in the ozone layer and do something about it, without hating the people who created the fluorocarbons. In other words, it doesn't mean sticking your head in the ground and dreaming away the unpleasant things. It means taking responsibility, taking action, but doing it without anger, doing it without hate. Because that anger is the thing that compounds and creates more of the very same problem. That is karma.

Q: There is also a level of work involved in that acknowledging, that sensing of the problem, which can be very unpleasant. We have the capacity in our culture to insulate ourselves in a safety and comfort net. In the formal situation, we are presented with koans as gifts. And in life, you almost have to actively invite them and say, "I want to see."

A: You have to actively invite them even in the formal koan study. The fact that the next koan in the book happens to be "Ch'ien and Her Soul" doesn't mean that that has any significance to you. You have to make it significant to you in order for it to function. Also, the process of working with classical koans prepares you for a way of using your mind and working with the paradoxical questions that you encounter in your life. It's a process that opens up for you, and it's a process that doesn't end at the conclusion of formal koan training. It's a process that continues constantly. The koans on the Precepts happen all the time. Every time we make a moral and ethical decision, the koans on the Precepts pop up. It's one thing to sit there and take those vows regarding the Precepts, but it's quite another when you're faced with a dilemma. It is like one physician who is a student who took the Precepts, and had to pull the plug on a brain-dead infant. He was traumatized by it. He had just recently received the Precepts, and now he was going to kill somebody. It immediately became a koan. He called me up for the answer, and I said, "Sorry, that's not my job. I don't give answers to koans. You're going to have to work this out yourself. You took the vows. You understand the Precepts. You've received the information on it. Now make your moral and ethical decision, and live with the karmic consequences of it." As a physician and an employee of the state, he had an obligation to pull the plug, because the parents were asking for that. As a Buddhist, he had an entirely different way of seeing it. He was tossed back and forth. It is in that way that we come to deal with our life. We begin to see that the way to resolve the questions of life is not from reading books or following some expert or guru or Zen master or priest or rabbi, but by going very deep into ourselves, because that's where the truth is. That's where the inherent perfection resides. It's out of there that the truth will arise and manifest itself.

Q: You have talked about how different people deal with koans in different ways, through the gentle approach or the angry approach, for example. Can you say more about that?

A: The volatile stories get to the news because they

make great stories. The gentle being that just sits there month after month doing "Muuuuuu," and then one day sees it in a very easy way doesn't make a great story, but it happens. You don't need to push hard on these koans. It's possible to be with a koan gently, easily. People tend to do koan study according to their personalities, no matter what you say. Very aggressive people tend to attack the koan aggressively, and people who are usually timid tend to be very light on it. But, over a period of time, the arrogant, aggressive person and the timid, gentle person reach the same place. And that place is a place of confidence in oneself, a sense of the real strength in oneself, where arrogance and shyness have been replaced by self-confidence. The reason arrogant people come off the way they do is because they have no confidence in themselves, and they cover it up with a lot of posturing. This was highlighted when we first started teaching at the prison. There, in order to survive you've got to do lots of muscle work, have tattoos all over, and strut around. If you're not doing that, people will take advantage of you. You'll become somebody's slave. When I started talking about the practice of gentleness, all these brothers worried that their defenses would be gone, and that they would end up being victimized. It took me a long time to convince them of the difference between arrogance and self-confidence. Underneath the arrogance there is fear. You can see it in the eyes. It took years but the arrogance is being replaced by confidence. With that confidence comes gentleness. People who are confident don't have to prove anything to anybody. They trust themselves. That's what the process of working on yourself, through introspection and koan study, is about.

Q: How do you work with a koan outside the zendo?

A: Outside the zendo you should be doing what you're doing while you're doing it. If you're chopping carrots, chop carrots. If you're operating a chain-saw and worrying about Mu, you're liable to cut yourself up. You really need to be present with what you're doing. In the zendo when you're sitting, you work with the koan. But the fact is, the koan is always there.

Q: As a new student, it sounds incredibly intimidating to hear of hundreds of koans. As a non-resident student, what hope can I have of ever being approved?

A: It's like scaling the great iron mountain. I remember working with my own teacher and worrying about this. I'd sit there and figure: I've been practicing seven years, and if in seven years I did 200 koans, in x number of years I'll complete so many. I would go in and tell the teacher, "I'm going to be 87 years old before I finish. I'll never get a chance to enjoy the whole thing." He'd say, "Stop calculating and thinking about it. Just do it." The study doesn't progress at all the way you think it's going to. The first koan may take a long time, the next group may move very quickly. Suddenly you get stuck on something for a while. You think that's the end, you're never going to get past that. Then you pass it and things move fast again. The average length of time for a student to complete koan study is around 15 years.

Q: Some students do koan study and some do *shikantaza*. What's the difference between them?

A: *Shikantaza* is "just sitting," but although some people do koans in *dokusan* and others don't, in a sense everybody is doing koan study. You can't be here without hearing a talk once a week on a koan. I'm bringing koans up all the time. Everybody hears them and it affects their sitting. The difference is actually much more theoretical than real.

Q: How do you make the decision about who does what kind of practice?

A: Usually it's got more to do with the student than it does with me. Many students don't like confrontations. They freeze up with questions. Being placed in the position of dealing with me as an adversary cannot be tolerated by them. Or they don't have those kinds of questions. They don't lose sleep over what the ultimate nature of the universe is. They just trust the process. They just enjoy sitting. *Shikantaza* fits their personality. Other people have got to know. They are the ones with whom I use koans as skillful means. It's specifically designed for intellectuals. It destroys the whole intellectual process. It's a beautiful thing to watch.

Q: Talking about the intellectual approach, I'm really confused about what to do with all the books available now. How much should one read?

A: We are definitely amid an information glut. People come into training and they've already read fifty books. They know more about Zen than I do. And it's pretty hard to tell them not to read any books. They want to know, and they do it. I let them saturate themselves until they sink with the information, and as they're breathing their last breath, I say to them, "That's not it."

Q: I want to hear more about the nature of great faith and great doubt, and how you reconcile that faith with losing the self.

A: Great faith, great doubt, and great determination really blossom fully during koan study. Before that you're working on forgetting the self. Forgetting the self is not something that you do by determination. You don't sit down and say, "I'm going to forget the self," because every time you give rise to that thought what you're doing is recreating the self. You can't achieve inactivity through activity. The way it happens is through the process of working with the breath. Every time a thought arises, you acknowledge it, you let it go. You come back again to the breath, and single-mindedly stay with the breath. Even reflecting on that, saying to yourself, "Oh now I'm staying with the breath," is a thought. You have to treat that as a thought. The witness needs to disappear, so that ultimately there is just the breath breathing itself. There is no observer, just the breath breathing. The mind is not moving. When the mind is not moving, because mind and self are co-dependent, there is no self.

Q: Being a lay student who doesn't get many chances to come up here, I wanted to ask you about the language of koans. When I listen to discourses or read a talk, I can intuit what you're saying to a certain degree, but I cannot articulate it.

A: The language is a tough one. The way I got into the language was to read koans the way people read novels. I really enjoyed them. They've always excited me. It's the same feeling that pulled me into research; the unknown, the mysteries. I wanted to know. Getting exposed to the koans, little by little you begin to build an understanding of that language. It's like any other language. It's through usage that you begin to learn the vernacular.

Q: How should someone working with the breath

deal with koans? I find them so inscrutable that I almost ignore them.

A: Ignore them.

Q: Ignore them?

A: If you're working with the breath, don't let yourself get side-tracked. During the discourse, listen to the koan with the whole body and mind, then let it go. I remember spending years, before I was doing koan study, or while I was working on Mu, listening to the talks and being totally confounded. I would sit in the zendo and think, "What the hell are these guys talking about? I'm an educated person. I went to school. I understand the English language. He's speaking English. Why don't I understand him? And why are all these other people sitting around with smirks on their faces? Do they really understand?" I used to get really angry with them. That went on for a number of years, but I just kept listening. I remember taking home a tape of one talk, and I must have played that tape a hundred times. All I did was go over the main case. I can still hear the speaker's accent. I'd listen and I'd listen and I'd listen. It wasn't until eight years later that the whole thing began to make sense. All the things that I had listened to suddenly started falling into place. All of those endless discourses and *teishos* that I had sat through in pain and half-asleep, that had just vaguely sunk into my primordial brain, started producing fruit. So don't worry about it. Just listen to it, throw it away, and go back to your breath. When the time comes, it will bear fruit. What you're doing is fertilizing the ground right now.

Q: You were talking earlier about how some people had a *kensho* experience when a plum blossom fell, or when a bamboo was struck by a pebble. Their senses triggered something, or something interacting with their senses did. I'm wondering if they were in a more open state of mind, if their senses were more vital or alive in some way?

A: The question is, if it's not the senses, what else would trigger it? What else is there?

Q: I guess I've paid more attention to the stories where it's the senses and not the words that tipped the scale, because I can relate better to them.

A: Remember that words and thoughts relate to the mind which, in Buddhism, is one of the sense organs, one of the six organs of perception. We call those six senses "gates" to the Dharma as well as "barriers" to the Dharma. They can get in the way if you're attached to them, yet they are also the way of entry into the Dharma.

Q: If we sat more zazen, would that cut down on how long the koan study would take?

A: Zazen makes a big difference. The heart of this practice is zazen, and if you did nothing else other than zazen, you would definitely clarify your life. You would definitely deepen your understanding of the self. Zazen is crucial. It's as important as the heartbeat is to life. There is a saturation point, though. When you get beyond a certain point in the amount of sitting, the sitting becomes lethargic. I think we've hit a nice balance at this Monastery. The way we interrupt the sitting with other aspects of training and *hosan* revitalizes it. It provides contrast.

Q: How does work practice inform your zazen and how does zazen inform your work practice? What's the connection?

A: You're sitting there in the zendo, and you're working with your breath. And every time a thought comes up, you acknowledge the thought, you let go of it, and you come back to the breath. In doing so, you empower yourself with the ability to put your mind where you want it, when you want it there. Now zazen is over and liturgy starts. You're chanting and you're bowing and a thought comes up, "It's a nice day today." You realize what you're doing, you let go of the thought, and you go back to the chant. You go into *oryoki*. You're sitting there eating, and you find yourself saying, "What the hell did the cook put in the food today?" You realize what you're doing, and you come back to just eating. The same with work. You're shoveling snow, your mind drifts off, you acknowledge it. You're cutting carrots, you let go of thoughts and come back to just cutting carrots. Just being present. Just working on the koan. What you were doing in zazen, you're now doing in every aspect of your life. Basically what that means is, you're simply being present. You are doing what you're doing while you're doing it.

Q: Why then does the koan have a greater ability to cut through conditioning?

A: Because the koan is going further than just awareness and just being present. What you're doing when you break through the koan is gaining insight into a whole other aspect of your life. Who are you? [*Holds up his glasses*] If you call this a pair of glasses, you're caught up in the words and ideas that describe it, and that's not it. You miss it. If you say it's not a pair of glasses, you miss it because you're denying their existence. What is it? They don't fall into either side. It's not "glasses." Nor is it not "not glasses." Nor is it "both glasses and not glasses." Nor is it "either glasses or not glasses." How do you transcend all of that? The koan is giving you insight into something other than just being present, being aware. Each koan cuts a little bit deeper and a little bit further. All the extra is trimmed away until there are just the bones, and that's trimmed until there is just the marrow. The great Master Bodhidharma said, "My successor Hui-k'o has the marrow of my teachings." It's been like that ever since, generation after generation, down to this time and this place. This incredible Dharma is now in our hands. What will we do with it? It's truly no small thing.

Lineage Relationships of Key Ancestors Appearing in the Text

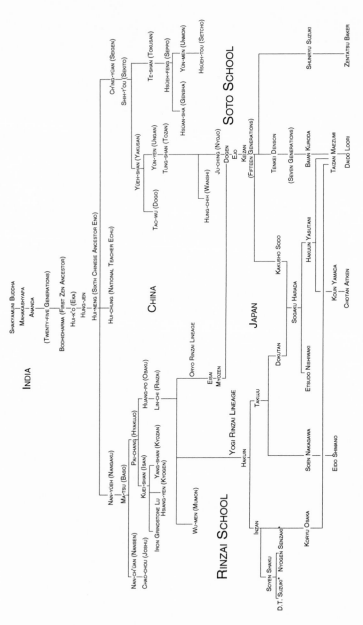

* Do not receive Dharma transmission

# GLOSSARY

Absolute/Relative: Perfectly interrelated, mutually arising aspects of reality; absolute is oneness, emptiness, the true nature of reality, while the relative is its phenomenal manifestation.

Anatman: No-self; the anatman doctrine is one of the essential teachings of Buddhism, stating that there is no permanent, enduring substance within any entity; self is an idea.

Ango: "Peaceful dwelling"; a three-month-long period of intensified spiritual training.

Anuttara-samyaksambodhi: Supreme perfect enlightenment of a complete Buddha.

Avalokiteshvara: The bodhisattva of compassion; "she

who hears the outcries of the world"; also Kannon or Kanzeon.

Blue Cliff Record: A collection of 100 koans compiled, with appreciatory verses, by Master Hsueh-tou Ch'ung-hsien, 980-1052 (Jap. Setcho Juken) and with commentaries by Master Yuan-wu K'o-Ch'in, 1063-1135 (Jap. Engo Kokugon); a key text in the Rinzai Zen School, it was studied by Master Dogen, who carried a handwritten copy back to Japan from China.

Bodhi Mind: Mind in which the aspiration for enlightenment has been awakened; the impulse that moves one towards self-realization.

Bodhisattva: One who practices the Buddha Way and compassionately postpones final enlightenment for the sake of others; the ideal of practice in Mahayana Buddhism.

Bodhi Tree: The fig tree under which the historical Buddha, Siddhartha Guatama, attained complete enlightenment.

Book of Equanimity: A collection of 100 koans gathered by Master Hung-chih Chen-chueh, and commented on by Master Wan-sung Hsing-hsiu, used primarily within the Soto lineage of Zen.

Buddha-dharma: Teachings of the Buddha based on his enlightenment experience; in Zen they are not to be conceptually understood but rather personally realized by each practitioner.

Buji Zen: Free-styled, non-conformist attitude toward Zen training that arises out of an intellectual misunderstanding of Zen practice and enlightenment.

Dana: Voluntary giving; considered in Buddhism as one of the most important virtues; one of the six paramitas, or perfections.

Dharani: A short sutra consisting of fundamental sounds that carry no extrinsic meaning.

Dharma: Universal truth or law; the Buddha's teachings; all phenomena that make up reality.

Dharma Combat: Unrehearsed dialogue in which two Zen practitioners test and sharpen their understanding of Zen truths.

Dharma Discourse: A formal talk on a koan or on significant aspects of Zen teachings; not an intellectual presentation or a philosophical explanation, but a direct expression of the spirit of Zen by the teacher.

Dharmakaya: One of the three kayas, or bodies, of the Buddha; the body of the great order, essential reality; the unity of the Buddha with the existing universe.

Dharma Name: Name given to a student by the teacher during *jukai*, the Precepts ceremony.

Diamond Net of Indra: A description of the universe presented in the Flower Garland Sutra; it clearly displays the interconnections and interdependence of all the facets of reality through time and space.

Diamond Sutra: Key part of the *Prajnaparamita* collection of Buddha's teachings; it repeatedly reiterates that phenomenal appearances are illusory projections of the mind, empty of the self.

Dokusan: Private interviews with the teacher during which students present and clarify their understanding of the Dharma.

Dragons and Snakes: Enlightened and deluded beings; in Zen writings dragons frequently represent true adepts while snakes denote people who hold and expound spurious views.

Duhkha: Suffering; the first of the Four Noble Truths and one of the three marks of existence.

Eightfold Path: The content of the Buddha's Fourth Noble Truth, the way out of suffering; it consists of right views, right determination, right speech, right action, right livelihood, right effort, right mindfulness, and right concentration; some translators replace "right" with "perfect" to avoid dualistic connotations.

Eight Gates of Training: Training system used at Zen Mountain Monastery for complete living and realization; it includes zazen, Zen study with the teacher, academic study, liturgy, Precepts practice, art practice, body practice, and work practice; it corresponds roughly to the aspects of the Buddha's Eightfold Path.

Enlightenment: The direct experience of one's true nature.

Five Ranks of Tung-shan: A system of understanding the interplay between existence's two components, the absolute and the relative, developed by the Chinese Zen Master Tung-shan Liang-chieh in the ninth century; it is also a formulation of different degrees of enlightenment.

Four Noble Truths: The first teaching of the historical Buddha; it addresses the nature of all suffering and points to the way of overcoming suffering; the Truths are: (1) life is suffering, (2) suffering has a cause, (3) there is an end to the cause of suffering, (4) the way to put an end to suffering is the Eightfold Path.

Four Vows: Vows taken by the bodhisattvas, expressing a commitment to postponing their own enlightenment until all beings are liberated from delusion; they are chanted at the end of each day at Zen monasteries.

Fusatsu: Renewal of vows; a ceremony and a service, conducted periodically at monasteries, during which practitioners atone for their deluded actions and resolve to continue on the path of self-realization.

Gassho: Gesture of bringing one's hands together, palm to palm, embodying the identity of all dualities.

Gatha: Short sutra that presents the Dharma teachings in terse, pithy wording; frequently chanted.

Genjo-koans: Koans that arise within one's life; the problems, questions, conflicts, and paradoxes that we encounter in our living and dying that are taken up as points of departure for self-study.

Genjokoan: The Way of Everyday Life: The first fascicle and the heart of Master Dogen's master-work, *Shobogenzo*.

Goi Koans: In Master Hakuin's classification, these koans take up the Five Ranks of Tung-shan, the various ways that the absolute and relative aspects of reality seamlessly interpenetrate.

Gonsen Koans: In Master Hakuin's classification, koans that deal with the use of words and phrases.

Hara: Physical and spiritual center of one's body/mind; area in the lower belly used in centering one's attention in meditation and any activity.

Hosshin Koans: In Master Hakuin's classification, koans that pertain to the experience of the absolute nature of reality; the dharmakaya koans.

Joriki: Power of concentration, developed through the practice of meditation, allowing people to place their focus of attention where they choose for extended periods of time.

Jukai: Acknowledgment of and the reception of the Buddhist Precepts; the ceremony of becoming a Buddhist.

Kalpa: A world cycle; an endlessly long period of time.

Karma: The universal law of cause and effect, linking an action's underlying intention to that action's consequences; it equates the actions of body, speech, and thought as potential sources of karmic consequences.

Kensho: "Seeing into one's own nature"; first experience of realization.

Kesa: Monastic's outer robe, worn across one shoulder.

Ki: Vital life-force present in and permeating all things; the energy that is the source of all creative activity.

Kikan Koans: In Master Hakuin's classification, koans that address the questions of differentiation; they are taken up after a student has experienced and clarified the absolute nature of reality.

Kinhin: Walking meditation; it provides a transitional stage for shifting the concentration developed in zazen into activity.

Koan: An apparently paradoxical statement or question used in Zen training to induce in the student an intense level of doubt, allowing them to cut through conventional and conditioned descriptions of reality and see directly into their true nature.

Koans of the Way of Reality: A collection of 108 Zen koans, together with prologue, capping verse, and footnotes, culled from ancient and modern sources that are particularly relevant to Zen practitioners today. It is part of koan study at Zen Mountain Monastery.

Kyosaku: "Wake-up stick"; a flattened stick used by the monitors in the zendo to strike acupressure points on a person's shoulders, relieving tension and promoting wakefulness.

Mahayana: "Great vehicle"; the northern school of Buddhism that expresses and aims at the intrinsic connection between an individual's realization and the simultaneous enlightenment of all beings.

Maitreya Buddha: The Buddha of the future; she is supposed to be the fifth and the last of the earthly Buddhas.

Mandala: A symbolic representation of cosmic forces in two- or three-dimensional form, understood as the synthesis of numerous distinctive elements in a unified scheme; through meditiation it can be recognized as the basic nature of existence.

Manjushri: The bodhisattva of wisdom.

Mondo: An informal, free-wheeling dialogue between the teacher and the students that centers on some relevant aspect of the teachings.

Mountains and Rivers Sutra: A chapter in the *Shobogenzo* depicting the interrelatedness of the absolute and the relative.

Mu: One of the first koans used in koan training; the first case in Master Wu-men's *Gateless Gate* collection of koans.

Mumonkan: The Gateless Gate: In Chinese, *Wu-men-kuan;* a koan collection compiled and published by Master Wu-men in 1229; it consists of forty-eight cases and includes as its first koan "Chao-chou's Mu."

Nanto Koans: In Master Hakuin's classification, these are the subtle cases that are difficult to penetrate.

Nirmanakaya: One of the three bodies of the Buddha; the earthly body and manifestation that a Buddha assumes to guide all sentient beings toward liberation.

Nirvana: Union with the absolute; in Zen it is essential to realize that samsara is nirvana, form is emptiness, that all beings are innately perfect from the outset.

Oryoki: "Containing just enough"; set of bowls and the ceremonial meal eaten in silence in Buddhist monasteries.

Paramitas: Perfections; virtues of attitude and behavior cultivated by bodhisattvas in the course of their development, necessary on the path of transcendence or realization; "reaching the other shore"; the six paramitas are generosity, discipline, patience, exertion, meditation, and wisdom.

Prajna: Wisdom; not that which is possessed but that which is directly and thoroughly experienced.

Precepts: Moral and ethical guidelines that, in Buddhism, are a description of the life of a Buddha, one who realizes the nature of existence and acts out of that realization.

Rakusu: The miniaturized version of the kesa, a bib-shaped garment worn by Zen Buddhist practitioners across their chests.

Rinzai School: School of Zen that originated with the great Chinese Zen Master Lin-chi I-hsuan in the ninth century and was reformed by Master Hakuin in Japan; it stresses koan practice.

Roshi: "Old venerable master"; title of Zen teachers.

Samadhi: State in which the mind is absorbed in intense concentration, free from distractions and goals; the essential nature of the self can be experienced directly within *samadhi*.

Sambhogakaya: One of the three bodies of the Buddha; "body of bliss" or reward body.

Samsara: Existence prior to liberation, conditioned by the three attitudes of greed, anger, and ignorance and marked by continuous rebirths.

Sangha: Community of practitioners; all sentient and insentient beings.

Satori: The experience of awakening; enlightenment.

Sesshin: "Gathering of the mind"; an extended period of intensive meditation practice lasting between five and ten days, centered on zazen but encompassing every aspect of the daily schedule.

Shakyamuni Buddha: Siddhartha Gautama, the historical Buddha and the founder of Buddhism; he was a prince of the Shakya clan, living in the northern India in the sixth century B.C.

Shikantaza: "Just sitting"; form of zazen in which one practices pure awareness.

Shobogenzo: "Treasury of the True Dharma Eye"; a collection of writings and discourses of the Japanese Master Eihei Dogen.

Shosan: Dharma combat.

Shunyata: Void. Central principle of Buddhism that recognizes the emptiness of all composite entities, without reifying nothingness. Resolution of all dualities.

Soto School: One of the existing schools of Zen Buddhism, founded by the Chinese Masters Tung-shan Liang-chieh and Ts'ao-shan Pen-chi in the ninth century; it was revitalized and brought to Japan by Eihei Dogen.

Sutra: Narrative text consisting chiefly of the discourses and teachings of the Buddha

Tao: The Way, truth, primary principle, universal reality, teaching; the nameless and the unnameable source of all things; key concept in Taoism and Zen.

Tathagatha: One of the titles of the Buddha, "thus-come one," referring to one who has attained perfect enlightenment.

Teisho: A Dharma discourse; presentation of Zen realization by a teacher.

Ten Directions: All-pervading space.

Ten Ox-Herding Pictures: An ancient Chinese descriptive device; a collection of drawings with accompanying comments and poems that presents the progress of a person on the path of self-realization.

Ten Stages: A schematic system delineating progressive phases of Zen training at Zen Mountain Monastery, based on the *Ten Ox-Herding Pictures* of Master K'uo-an.

Ten Thousand Things: The phenomenal universe of distinct entities.

Tenzo: The chief cook of the monastery; usually a senior monastic or roshi who uses the context of food preparation and serving as a skillful means for teaching those working with him or her.

Three-hundred Koan *Shobogenzo*: A collection of koans put together and used by Master Dogen in his writings and teachings.

Three Pillars of Practice: The essential components of the Zen path of realization—great doubt, great faith, and great perseverance.

Three Poisons: Greed, anger, and ignorance; characteristics of human existence that arise out of the deluded view of the universe.

Three Treasures: Buddha, Dharma, and Sangha; one who is awakened, the true teachings, and the group of people living in accord with the teachings; the Treasures are also known as the places of refuge for Buddhist practitioners.

Tokudo: Ceremony of ordination.

Transmission: Complete, mind-to-mind merging of the teacher and the student; the confirmation of a student's realization.

Transmission of Light: Collection of fifty-two koans compiled by Master Keizan in 1303, based on the enlightenment experiences of the ancestors beginning with Shakyamuni and concluding with Keizan's teacher Ejo.

Upaya: Skillful means; forms that the teachings take, reflecting their appropriateness to the circumstances in which they appear.

Vinaya: School of Buddhism that centers its practice on strict and precise observance of monastic rules and ethical precepts; collection of Buddhist Precepts.

Vulture Peak: Mount Gridhrakuta, site near the city of Rajagriha where Buddha offered many of his discourses and teachings.

Zafu: Round pillow used in sitting meditation.

Zendo: Meditation hall.

ABOUT ZEN MOUNTAIN MONASTERY

Zen Mountain Monastery is an American Zen Buddhist monastery and training center for monastics and lay practitioners. It is located on a 230-acre site on Tremper Mountain in New York's Catskill Mountains, surrounded by state forest wilderness and featuring an Environmental Studies Area.

The Monastery provides a year-round daily training program that includes Zen meditation, various forms of face-to-face teaching, academic studies, liturgy, work practice, body practice, art practice, and study of the Buddhist Precepts.

Each month a weekend introductory Zen training workshop, and a week-long silent Zen meditation retreat (*sesshin*) are offered. During the spring and fall quarters of each year, ninety-day intensive programs (*Angos*) are conducted. Throughout the year, the regular daily schedule is supplemented with seminars and workshops in the Zen arts, the martial arts, Buddhist studies, and other areas relevant to present-day Western practitioners. Students can train in either full-time or part-time residency or as non-residents whose "home practice" is fueled by periodic visits to the Monastery.

For further information, contact:
Registrar
Zen Mountain Monastery
P.O. Box 197
Mount Tremper, NY 12457
(914) 688-2228